FACING THE DEATH PENALTY

Essays on a Cruel and Unusual Punishment

Facing the Death Penalty

Essays on a Cruel and Unusual Punishment

Edited by
Michael L. Radelet

TEMPLE UNIVERSITY PRESS

PHILADELPHIA

Temple University Press, Philadelphia 19122
Copyright © 1989 by Temple University. All rights reserved
Published 1989
Printed in the United States of America

The paper used in this publication meets the minimum
requirements of American National Standard for Information
Sciences—Permanence of Paper for Printed Library Materials,
ANSI Z39.48-1984

Library of Congress Cataloging-in-Publication Data

Facing the death penalty.

Bibliography: p.
Includes index.
1. Death row—United States.   2. Prisoners—
United States. 3. Capital punishment—United States.
I. Radelet, Michael L.
HV8699.U5F33   1989   364.6'6   88-29602
ISBN 0-87722-611-3

For Craig S. Barnard
1949–1989

Therefore was one single man created first, Adam, to teach you that if anyone destroys a single soul from the children of man, Scripture charges him as though he had destroyed a whole universe—and whoever rescues a single soul from the children of man, Scripture credits him as if he had saved a whole universe.

Mishnah, Sanhedrin 4:5

Contents

Foreword

HENRY SCHWARZSCHILD

Speaking on the floor of the House of Commons in Ottawa in 1976 in support of a bill to abolish capital punishment in Canada, then–Prime Minister Pierre Trudeau reminded the members of the Commons: "It is not open to anyone among us to take refuge in the comforting illusion that we are debating nothing more than an abstract theory of criminal justice. . . . I want to make it very clear that if the majority of the Honourable Members vote against abolition, some people are going to be hanged. . . . [I]t is inevitable that the defeat of this bill would eventually place the hangman's noose around some person's neck. To make that quite clear: if this bill is defeated, some people will certainly hang" (press release, Office of the Prime Minister, 15 June 1976).

This book is melancholic testimony to Trudeau's angry but realistic wisdom. Canada did, then and there, abolish the death penalty, in the same year that the U.S. Supreme Court handed down a series of complex decisions on the constitutional issues that executions necessarily raise. These decisions in effect reopened the execution chambers of this country. As a result, we have since that time executed well over a hundred prisoners (by firing squad, in the electric chair, in the gas chamber, and by lethal injection), and we have a death row population easily in excess of 2,100. That condemned population grows larger by about two hundred persons per year.

Some thirty-seven states and two federal jurisdictions have death penalty laws on their books.

Gregg v. Georgia (428 U.S. 153 [1976]), its companion cases, and a seemingly endless series of subsequent decisions on capital punishment are dense and contradictory rationalizations of constitutional doctrine, statutory texts, social objectives, criminological analysis, moral theory, psychological assumptions, and political judgments. And the prevailing majority on the Court has become ever more impatient, even surly, at being compelled, by advertence to their own rules, to act (or to refuse explicitly to act) on each and every capital case that is otherwise at the point of exhaustion of legal remedies. The justices are acutely discomforted by such constant reminders that their decisions "place the hangman's noose around some person's neck."

The effort to abolish the death penalty is not new. It was begun in modern times in the Enlightenment (Cesare Beccaria, Benjamin Rush), but its antecedents go back at least to Talmudic times. In the 1840s, it came close to succeeding in this country, but was largely defeated in an upsurge of fundamentalist religious reaction. The Sacco and Vanzetti case of the 1920s revived abolitionist passions, but the death penalty reached its modern peak in the mid-1930s (199 executions in 1935), and did not significantly recede until the early 1960s. The civil rights revolution of the 1960s, seeking to undo the vestiges (and they were racist vestiges, indeed) of what remained of capital punishment in the United States, for the first time mounted a frontal challenge to the constitutionality of the death penalty. This attack sought to persuade the Supreme Court to declare capital punishment an inherent violation of the Eighth Amendment's prohibition of cruel and unusual punishment and, as actually applied, a violation of the equal protection clause of the Fourteenth Amendment and the due process clause of the Fifth Amendment. It was a brilliantly led and executed campaign, but it failed, perhaps by an accident of history: the tidal shift from the Warren court to the Burger court intervened. *Gregg* and its sequelae were the governing result, and the execution by a volunteer firing squad of Gary Mark Gilmore in Utah in 1977 marked the resumption of the executioner's deeds.

The abolition of capital punishment is not a preoccupation merely of isolated or marginal people. Every major religious denomination (the Roman Catholic bishops, the National Council of the Churches of Christ in the U.S.A. and its constituent Protestant elements [including the Episcopal church, the Presbyterians, the Methodists, the Baptists, the Lutherans, and the United Church of Christ], and the major Jewish religious groupings), the national minority-community organizations, the human rights and civil liberties agencies, international bodies (the United Nations, the Council of Europe, and others), all oppose the death penalty, as do thoughtful lawyers, physicians, writers, academics, artists, and community activists all over the country. But the majority of the public, as well as majorities in most state legislatures and on most courts of appeal, favor it. Abolition does not have the support of most governors or prosecutors or law enforcement officials. Our generation will not see the abolition of the death penalty.

This book will inform and remind people of what support for the death penalty means in real life and in real death; what it means to those who are objects of the premeditated, violent homicides called executions; what it means to the families of the condemned; what it means to those who work in prisons and minister to prisoners, especially prisoners on death row. It is a terribly sober book. By giving us a peek at the hangman's noose, it dispels the comforting illusion that the death penalty is an abstract theory of criminal justice. It does for the death penalty what *All Quiet on the Western Front*, *The Naked and the Dead*, and *Dispatches* did for war. It is not about the glory and the abstractions and the heroism and the slogans and the political and social theory. It is about human beings.

This book serves us well and makes us deeply uncomfortable. As well it might.

Case Cited

Gregg v. Georgia, 428 U.S. 153 (1976).

FACING THE DEATH PENALTY

Essays on a Cruel
and Unusual Punishment

1

Introduction and Overview

MICHAEL L. RADELET

Between 1930 and 1967 there were 3,859 executions carried out under state and civil authority in the United States (U.S. Department of Justice, 1986). The peak year, 1935, saw 199 executions, but not since 1951 has the annual figure surpassed 100. Between then and 1967 the pace of executions declined to the point where, in the decade of the 1960s, a total of 191 executions were carried out. After 1967, in fact, challenges to the constitutional validity of death penalty statutes led to a ten-year moratorium. Executions resumed in 1977 (with that of Gary Gilmore in Utah), and on 14 June 1988, Louisiana prisoner Edward Byrne became the hundredth inmate to be executed since the moratorium ended. By the end of 1988, another 2,182 men and women were living under a sentence of death (NAACP Legal Defense and Educational Fund, 1988). At the rate of one execution per week (that is, double the present execution rate), it would take 39 years, or until 2027, just to eliminate this backlog.

This situation raises a number of important questions. There are no comparable situations in which otherwise healthy men, women, and children are forced to spend years contemplating their intended demise. They do so with few resources, in a severely restricted physical environment and a less-than-supportive social atmosphere.

The scholars and practitioners contributing to this volume have studied the condemned population, handled their appeals, and/or assisted them in preparing for death. The authors include historians, attorneys, sociologists, anthropologists, criminologists, a minister, a philosopher, and three men sentenced to death. The chapters that follow, taken as a whole, present not only the struggles of the condemned and their families, but also those of a group of people who have dedicated themselves to working with the condemned or studying the death penalty and what it says about the society that uses it.

The primary goal of this book is not to debate the wisdom of capital punishment; several general overviews are already easily accessible (e.g., Bedau, 1982; Berns, 1979; Black, 1981; van den Haag and Conrad, 1983). Nor is it to generate sympathy for those convicted of horrible crimes. Our goal is instead to examine what life under a sentence of death is like for condemned inmates, how and why various professionals assist them in their struggles for life, and what these personal experiences with capital punishment tell us about the wisdom of this penal policy. Little support for capital punishment will be found in these pages. Few people close to the condemned count themselves as death penalty retentionists: even prison wardens have been known to call for universal abolition (Duffy, 1962; Lawes, 1932). The interdisciplinary perspectives in this book will not resolve the death penalty debate, but they offer important and unique insights to all readers who wish to study the full effects of the penalty.

Death Penalty Litigation

In the 1972 case of *Furman v. Georgia* (408 U.S. 238), a divided U.S. Supreme Court ruled that the death penalty was arbitrarily applied and hence in violation of the Eighth Amendment's protection against cruel and unusual punishment. The vote was five to four, and each Justice wrote a separate opinion. In effect, all inmates then living under a sentence of death (633 in 32 states) had their sentences commuted to life imprisonment by this decision (Meltsner, 1973:292). Many believed the abolition would be permanent.

Today, however, 37 states and the U.S. military have operational death penalty statutes, and 34 states have prisoners living under a sentence of death (NAACP Legal Defense and Educational Fund, 1988). The movement to reinstate the death penalty was led by Florida, where, five months after the *Furman* decision, a special session of the legislature was called for the purpose of enacting a new capital statute (Ehrhardt and Levinson, 1973). Florida's law is an example of a "guided discretion" statute; it lists specific aggravating and mitigating circumstances that are intended to guide the judge and jury in their sentencing decisions. This law was approved by the U.S. Supreme Court in 1976 (*Proffitt v. Florida*, 428 U.S. 242); at the same time the Court ruled that mandatory death penalty statutes were unconstitutional (*S. Roberts v. Louisiana*, 428 U.S. 325). In later years the Court also invalidated mandatory death penalties for the murder of a police officer (*H. Roberts v. Louisiana*, 431 U.S. 633 [1977]) and for murders committed by inmates while serving a previous sentence of life imprisonment without the possibility of parole (*Sumner v. Schuman*, 107 S.Ct. 2716 [1987]).

Of the 34 states that at the end of 1988 housed condemned prisoners, five had death row populations of over one hundred: Florida (296), Texas (284), California (238), Illinois (119), and Georgia (106) (NAACP Legal Defense and Educational Fund, 1988). The primary reason for Florida's lead is that its statute, like Indiana's and Alabama's, allows a judge to sentence a defendant to death even if the jury has recommended a sentence of life imprisonment. While this override provision has been used infrequently in both Indiana and Alabama, in Florida it has been used in 20 percent of the 572 cases in which the death penalty has been imposed since 1972 (Mello and Robson, 1985; Radelet, 1985). Two men, Ernest Dobbert and Beauford White, have been executed in Florida after their trial jury's recommendation of life imprisonment was rejected and overridden by the judge. White's jury had voted unanimously for life.

Of the first 100 executions in America after the ten-year moratorium ended in 1977, 11 were "consensual": the inmate dropped his appeals and demanded immediate execution. All but one of the remaining executions occurred in the states of the former Confederacy, so that executions today remain almost exclusively a southern phenomenon. By the end of 1988, Texas led the country with 29 "post-*Furman*" executions, followed by 19 in Florida and 18 in Louisiana. One woman has been executed (Velma Barfield in North Carolina), as have three men whose crimes predated their eighteenth birthdays. There are 31 others currently on death row for crimes committed when they were juveniles (NAACP Legal Defense and Educational Fund, 1988).

Public Opinion and the Death Penalty

The death penalty is one of the most controversial issues in American politics. In this section I will briefly outline some of the major issues in contemporary death penalty debates, referring readers to sources for additional information (for a comprehensive bibliography, see Radelet and Vandiver, 1988). To see why Americans support or oppose the death penalty, we can use the *Gallup Report* of January 1986. Although some would argue that even in a democracy the life or death of a citizen should not be subject to a simple majority vote, opinion polls can give us important insights into the factual, mythical, and philosophical foundations of current attitudes.

The United States and South Africa stand alone among Western countries today in their use of capital punishment (Amnesty International, 1979). But despite the worldwide rejection of the death penalty, there is no question that at least in theory (the death penalty as it is actually applied is another matter), the majority of American citizens support its use. When asked "Are you in favor of the death penalty for persons convicted of murder," 70 percent voice support, and 22 percent stand opposed. Supporters are more likely to be male (74 percent versus 66 percent), white (73 versus 50 percent), and Republican (83 versus 62 percent). These figures stand in marked contrast to those of two decades ago; in 1966 only 42 percent of the public supported executions (Gallup, 1986). Interestingly, support declines when respondents are asked if they would still favor death if life imprisonment with no possibility of parole was an option (as it is in most states); in this case 55 percent support the death penalty, while 35 percent favor life imprisonment (Gallup, 1986). No data are available that measure support for use of the death penalty for crimes other than homicide; all inmates on death row today were convicted of murder (with the exception of a Mississippi man convicted of the rape of a minor). The Supreme Court struck down the use of the death penalty for the rape of an adult in 1977 (*Coker v. Georgia*, 433 U.S. 584).

Many notable groups are on record as opposing the death penalty, among them almost all Christian and Jewish denominations (National Interreligious Task Force on Criminal Justice, n.d.). The fight against capital punishment in the United States is being led by such groups as the American Civil Liberties Union, the NAACP Legal Defense and Educational Fund, and Amnesty International (see, e.g., Amnesty International, 1987). Two Supreme Court Justices, Thurgood Marshall and William Brennan, stand opposed to its use in all cases. Popular opposition, however, is not (and never has been) represented on juries in capital trials, as prosecutors are permitted to exclude for cause from both the guilt and penalty phases of the trial all potential jurors who stand opposed to the death penalty (*Lockhart v. McCree*, 476 U.S. 162 [1986]).

The primary argument in support of the death penalty, and one not directly amenable to empirical research, is retribution. When a 1985 Gallup poll asked death penalty supporters to explain their position, 30 percent cited a desire for revenge and 18 percent said, "Murderers deserve punishment" (Gallup, 1985). Another 22 percent cited deterrence, 11 percent believed it was too costly to house prisoners for life, and 16 percent said it kept prisoners from killing again or removed a potential threat. Thirteen percent gave other responses; 2 percent had no opinion (multiple responses were allowed). Those who opposed the death penalty offered these reasons: it is wrong to take a life (40 percent); wrongful convictions occur (15 percent); punishment should be left to God (15 percent); it does not deter crime (5 percent); rehabilitation is possible (5 percent); it is unfairly applied (3 percent). Seven percent gave other reasons; 16 percent had no opinion (Gallup, 1986).

The deterrence question is quite controversial among the lay public. Whereas many politicians argue that the death penalty is a deterrent, virtually no criminologist agrees. The 1986 Gallup poll found that 61 percent of the public believed the death penalty to be a deterrent; support for executions would decline from 70 percent to 56 percent if new evidence proved that it was not. Those who believe that public support for the death penalty is strong and solid will be surprised to learn that only 43 percent of the public would favor the death penalty, given the option of life imprisonment, if it were proved not to be a deterrent to murder (Gallup, 1986).

The argument that the death penalty is superior to long imprisonment in its deterrent effect receives its strongest support from a study conducted by Isaac Ehrlich that purported to show that each execution between 1933 and 1967 prevented approximately eight homicides (Ehrlich, 1975). This study has been criticized at length by several scholars, including a panel appointed by the National Academy of Sciences and headed by the 1980 Nobel laureate in economics, Lawrence Klein. This panel concluded: "[I]t seems unthinkable to us to base decisions on the use of the death penalty on Ehrlich's findings" (Klein et al., 1978:358). Other studies have found that the homicide rate actually increases after executions (Bowers and Pierce, 1980). A fair conclusion from this body of research is that if the death penalty does have a deterrent effect, it is so minuscule that the vast majority of researchers have failed to find it.

To the degree that the death penalty is a more severe punishment than is life imprisonment, an assertion that some would challenge, retribution is a solid pro–death penalty argument. Whether retribution should be a proper goal of state policy is more controversial. Clearly there are limits to the degree of retribution that can be permitted; we can all think of punishments worse than death (e.g., torture), and everyone agrees that they would be improper. The death penalty is superior to life imprisonment in its ability to incapacitate, as some convicted murderers (and other prisoners) will kill in prison if they are not put to death. The number of repeated murders prevented by the death penalty is quite small, (Marquart and Sorensen, 1988; Wolfson, 1982), though some would argue that it would be worth executing dozens of murderers to incapacitate the one who would otherwise repeat his crime.

Also used to support the death penalty (though not probed in the Gallup surveys) is the argument that execution of the offender gives comfort and support to the family of the homicide victim. This argument is generally not foremost in the pro–death penalty position, however, since 98 percent of all homicide victims are not avenged with the death penalty, and the groups to which the victims' families most often turn for support—the churches—are also generally opposed to executions. By any measure, the needs of these families are not being met by the death penalty or any other public policy, and regardless of our positions on the death penalty, we can all probably agree that attention to their agony is desperately needed in both scholarship and public policy. Among the best sources for information about these families are the recent works by Danto (1982), Magee (1983), and Rynearson (1984); Margaret Vandiver's essay in this volume (Chapter 9) compares the misery of the families of homicide victims and the misery of the equally innocent families of death row inmates.

Cost, though cited by 11 percent of the death penalty supporters in the *Gallup Report*, is actually a strong argument against the death penalty (Garey, 1985; Nakell, 1978). Homicide trials are more expensive if the death penalty is being sought, as are the costs in the executive and especially the judicial branches of government as the case is being appealed. Some, of course, will argue that costs would drop if we further restricted the appellate process in capital cases, although the Constitution presents strong barriers to such restrictions. Thus, for now and the foreseeable future, it is clear: each execution costs millions, several times more than the cost of incarcerating an offender for his or her natural life. This raises a question of growing importance: could not the millions we spend on executing our prisoners be better spent on more effective solutions to violence and more concrete assistance for the families of homicide victims?

Anti–death penalty citizens point out (correctly) that the execution of the innocent is inevitable (Bedau and Radelet, 1987). Death penalty retentionists now agree. As Ernest van den Haag, one of our country's most accomplished death penalty proponents, puts it: "However rare, such miscarriages of justice are likely to occur" (van den Haag and Conrad, 1983:55). He argues, however, that the benefits of the death penalty outweigh this definite liability. Abolitionists are also correct in stating that the problem of racial bias in sentencing has not been eliminated (Baldus et al., 1986; Bowers, 1984; Gross, 1985; Gross and Mauro, 1984; Nakell and Hardy, 1987; Radelet and Pierce, 1985), although it is noteworthy that only 3 percent of the abolitionists polled offer this rationale to support their position. Pre-*Furman* racial bias in the administration of the death penalty was particularly evident in the punishment for rape; 89 percent (405 out of 455) of the prisoners executed for rape since 1930 were black men whose victims were white (Wolfgang and Riedel, 1976). Today, the allegations of racial bias center on the race of the victim, as almost all of those on death row were condemned for murdering whites. In fact, when other predictive factors are controlled, having a white victim increases the probability of a death sentence by a greater amount than smoking increases the probability of heart disease (Gross, 1985). The Supreme Court acknowledges the validity of these conclusions, though in 1987 it failed (by one vote) to find in the statistics the type of *intentional* discrimination that would warrant relief (*McCleskey v. Kemp*, 107 S.Ct. 1756).

The lives of those condemned to death have been described (Gettinger, 1979; Johnson, 1981; Magee, 1980; Radelet et al., 1983), but rarely by those close to them. The families of the condemned must work frantically to deal with the inmates' needs. Furthermore, for obvious reasons, the condemned and their families rarely welcome the media when last-minute legal issues are being litigated and preparations for death are being made. The essays collected for this volume attempt to fill this gap and help shed light on what the death penalty actually entails.

Contributors to This Collection

The contributors to this volume have had extensive contact with those on death row or have developed special expertise in this area. We begin with a historical perspective, with three essays that describe how executioners and inmates (both adults and children) approach execution dates. Chapter 2, by Michael Kroll, a California journalist who has written extensively about prisons and prisoners, results from interviews with some of the people who planned and carried out executions in San Quentin's gas chamber. Next is a paper by Watt Espy, this country's most widely recognized death penalty historian. Espy has spent the last 17 years, usually at his own expense, gathering information on every execution in American history. Thus far, he has documented nearly sixteen thousand cases. In Chapter 3 he presents several vignettes from his files to describe the various ways in which prisoners have approached their impending executions.

Victor Streib's essay (Chapter 4) nicely complements Espy's. Streib, an attorney and law professor, focuses on cases involving the execution of offenders for crimes committed when they were juveniles. He is the country's leading authority on the execution of juveniles, and regularly monitors relevant legislation and judicial decisions.

The three chapters that follow were also written by attorneys. Russell Canan describes the frantic days, hours, and minutes preceding the 1983 execution in Alabama of his client John Evans. In Chapter 5 Canan describes his fruitless attempts to persuade Governor George Wallace to commute the sentence, and then his last-minute effort to halt the execution when the electric chair malfunctioned.

Michael Mello follows with a description of the burdens of representing a death row inmate, especially when the legal efforts fail and the client is executed. Few are as well qualified to speak on this issue as Mello, who has spent the last five years, regularly working hundred-hour weeks, handling death penalty cases. Many of his clients have had their lives extended through his efforts. This chapter, however, was first drafted in the weeks after one of Mello's clients, Ronald Straight, was executed in Florida in 1986.

Given the stresses and financial difficulties of adequately representing death row inmates, it is little wonder that there is a severe shortage of attorneys willing to handle such cases. In Chapter 7 Laurin Wollan discusses this problem and the ethical dilemmas facing an attorney who is considering whether to represent a death row inmate in collateral proceedings (that is, after the initial appeal has failed). Wollan is one of the attorneys for Alvin Ford, who was the subject of an important ruling by the Supreme Court in 1986. In *Ford v. Wainwright* (106 S.Ct. 2595), the Court ruled that death row inmates have a constitutional right not to be executed if their mental status has deteriorated while on death row to the point where they are insane.

The next two chapters offer other perspectives on death row inmates and their families. Rev. Joseph Ingle, who has more than once shared the last hours of a condemned man's life, focuses in Chapter 8 on the events surrounding the execution of a Florida inmate in 1984. Ingle's work with death row inmates in the South was acknowledged in 1987 when five members of the Swedish parliament nominated him for a Nobel Peace Prize. Margaret Vandiver follows with an essay comparing families with a terminally ill relative, families of homicide victims, and families with a loved one on death row. Since 1979 she, like Ingle, has worked closely with several death row inmates in the days before their executions, helping them prepare for death and put their worldly affairs in order.

The next two chapters present anthropological perspectives on the death penalty. Florida State University anthropologists Elizabeth Purdum and J. Anthony Paredes compare contemporary executions in Florida with certain forms of human sacrifice practiced by the Aztecs in Mexico in the sixteenth century and find that both rituals serve similar functions. Chapter 11 offers an anthropological perspective on the death penalty by Colin Turnbull, based on his experiences with former and current death row inmates. In it he discusses such anthropological issues as objectivity versus subjectivity, comparison, holism, and cultural relativism as they relate to the study of the death penalty.

The final two contributions from the professional community

look at alternatives to executions and how such alternatives should be presented in arguments about the death penalty. Jonathan Sorensen and James Marquart's research (Chapter 12) challenges the prevailing stereotype that all death row prisoners are so dangerous that they need to be kept permanently confined in isolation cells. Their examination of Texas death row inmates who work in a prison industry program shows that such prisoners can indeed work peacefully with one another and make productive use of their time. The message here is clear: viable alternatives to conventional procedures are available. Given such alternatives, Hugo Adam Bedau outlines in Chapter 13 what he sees as the major parameters of modern death penalty debates. Few in the world are as qualified as Bedau to teach us how to argue about the death penalty, as he can comfortably claim to have written more on the subject than any other scholar in history.

The last three chapters of the book are by Joseph Giarratano, Michael Lambrix, and Willie Darden, written while their authors were living under a sentence of death and hence in a better position than any observers outside the prison walls to teach us about the experience of living on death row. Two of these men are still living under sentence of death; the third, Willie Jasper Darden, was executed in Florida shortly after his essay was completed. Only a few hours before his death, Darden expressed a wish to three of his co-authors (Ingle, Vandiver, and Radelet) that he would live to see this book in print.

It is hoped that this collection will offer readers a more personal glimpse of death row inmates and those who work with them, and some new ideas and perspectives that might enlighten contemporary death penalty debates. All of the essays, as I read them, support the argument that the death penalty as practiced today can only be considered a cruel, unusual, and unnecessary punishment. But it is hoped that even those readers who believe that the benefits of the death penalty outweigh these concerns will find some food for thought on what capital punishment does to the inmates, their families and attorneys, and our society as a whole.

References

Amnesty International. 1979. *The Death Penalty*. London: Amnesty International Publications.

————. 1987. *United States of America: The Death Penalty*. London: Amnesty International Publications.

Baldus, David C.; Charles A. Pulaski, Jr.; and George Woodworth. 1986. "Arbitrariness and Discrimination in the Administration of the Death Penalty: A Challenge to State Supreme Courts." *Stetson Law Review* 15:133–261.

Bedau, Hugo Adam. 1982. *The Death Penalty in America*. 3d ed. New York: Oxford University Press.

Bedau, Hugo Adam, and Michael L. Radelet. 1987. "Miscarriages of Justice in Potentially Capital Cases." *Stanford Law Review* 40:21–179.

Berns, Walter. 1979. *For Capital Punishment: Crime and the Morality of the Death Penalty*. New York: Basic Books.

Black, Charles L., Jr. 1981. *Capital Punishment: The Inevitability of Caprice and Mistake*. 2d ed. New York: W. W. Norton.

Bowers, William J. 1984. *Legal Homicide: Death as Punishment in America, 1864–1982*. Boston: Northeastern University Press.

Bowers, William J., and Glenn L. Pierce. 1980. "Deterrence or Brutalization: What Is the Effect of Executions?" *Crime and Delinquency* 26 (1980):453–84.

Danto, B. L. 1982. "Survivors of Homicide." Pp. 85–97 in *The Human Side of Homicide*, edited by B. L. Danto, John Bruhns, and A. H. Kutscher. New York: Columbia University Press.

Duffy, Clinton T., with Al Hirshberg. 1962. *Eighty-eight Men and Two Women*. Garden City, N.Y.: Doubleday.

Ehrhardt, Charles W., and L. Harold Levinson. 1973. "Florida's Legislative Response to *Furman*: An Exercise in Futility?" *Journal of Criminal Law and Criminology* 64:10–21.

Ehrlich, Isaac. 1975. "The Deterrent Effect of Capital Punishment: A Question of Life or Death." *American Economic Review* 65:397–417.

Gallup, George. 1985. "The Death Penalty." *Gallup Report* 232–33 (Jan.–Feb.):3–11.

————. 1986. "The Death Penalty." *Gallup Report* 244–45 (Jan.–Feb.):10–16.

Garey, Margot. 1985. "The Cost of Taking a Life: Dollars and Sense of the Death Penalty." *University of California–Davis Law Review* 18:1221–73.

Gettinger, Stephen H. 1979. *Sentenced to Die: The People, the Crimes, and the Controversy*. New York: Macmillan.

Gross, Samuel R. 1985. "Race and Death: The Judicial Evaluation of Evidence of Discrimination in Capital Sentencing." *University of California–Davis Law Review* 18:1275–325.

Gross, Samuel R., and Robert Mauro. 1984. "Patterns of Death: An Analysis of Racial Disparities in Capital Sentencing and Homicide Victimization." *Stanford Law Review* 37:27–153.

Johnson, Robert. 1981. *Condemned to Die: Life Under Sentence of Death*. New York: Elsevier.

Klein, Lawrence R.; Brian Forst; and Victor Filatov. 1978. "The Deterrent Effect of Capital Punishment: An Assessment of the Evidence." Pp. 336–60 in *Deterrence and Incapacitation: Estimating the Effects of Criminal Sanctions on Crime Rates*, edited by Alfred Blumstein, Jacqueline Cohen, and Daniel Nagin. Washington, D.C.: National Academy of Sciences.

Lawes, Lewis E. 1932. *Twenty Thousand Years in Sing Sing*. New York: Long and Smith.

Magee, Doug. 1980. *Slow Coming Dark: Interviews on Death Row*. New York: Pilgrim Press.

———. 1983. *What Murder Leaves Behind: The Victim's Family*. New York: Dodd, Mead.

Marquart, James W., and Jonathan R. Sorensen. 1988. "Institutional and Postrelease Behavior of *Furman*-Commuted Inmates in Texas." *Criminology* 26:677–93.

Mello, Michael, and Ruthann Robson. 1985. "Judge Over Jury: Florida's Practice of Imposing Death Over Life in Capital Cases." *Florida State University Law Review* 13:31–75.

Meltsner, Michael. 1973. *Cruel and Unusual: The Supreme Court and Capital Punishment*. New York: William Morrow.

NAACP Legal Defense and Educational Fund. 1988. "Death Row, U.S.A." Unpublished compilation, available from 99 Hudson St., New York, N.Y., 10013.

Nakell, Barry. 1978. "The Cost of the Death Penalty." *Criminal Law Bulletin* 14:69–80.

Nakell, Barry, and Kenneth A. Hardy. 1987. *The Arbitrariness of the Death Penalty*. Philadelphia: Temple University Press.

National Interreligious Task Force on Criminal Justice. N.d. *Capital Punishment: What the Religious Community Says*. New York: NITFCJ.

Radelet, Michael L. 1985. "Rejecting the Jury: The Imposition of the Death Penalty in Florida." *University of California–Davis Law Review* 18: 1409–31.

Radelet, Michael L., and Glenn L. Pierce. 1985. "Race and Prosecutorial Discretion in Homicide Cases." *Law and Society Review* 19:587–621.

Radelet, Michael L., and Margaret Vandiver. 1988. *Capital Punishment in America: An Annotated Bibliography*. New York: Garland Press.

Radelet, Michael L.; Margaret Vandiver; and Felix M. Berardo. 1983. "Families, Prisons, and Men with Death Sentences: The Human Impact of Structured Uncertainty." *Journal of Family Issues* 4:593–612.

Rynearson, E. K. 1984. "Bereavement After Homicide: A Descriptive Study." *American Journal of Psychiatry* 141:1452–54.

U.S. Department of Justice. 1986. *Capital Punishment, 1984.* Washington, D.C.: U.S. Government Printing Office.

van den Haag, Ernest, and John P. Conrad. 1983. *The Death Penalty: A Debate.* New York: Plenum.

Wolfgang, Marvin E., and Mark Riedel. 1976. "Rape, Racial Discrimination, and the Death Penalty." Pp. 99–121 in *Capital Punishment in the United States*, edited by Hugo Adam Bedau and Chester M. Pierce. New York: AMS Press.

Wolfson, Wendy Phillips. 1982. "The Deterrent Effect of the Death Penalty Upon Prison Murder." Pp. 159–73 in *The Death Penalty in America*, 3d ed., edited by Hugo Adam Bedau. New York: Oxford University Press.

Cases Cited

Coker v. Georgia, 433 U.S. 584 (1977).
Ford v. Wainwright, 106 S.Ct. 2595 (1986).
Furman v. Georgia, 408 U.S. 238 (1972).
Lockhart v. McCree, 476 U.S. 162 (1986).
McCleskey v. Kemp, 107 S.Ct. 1756 (1987).
Proffitt v. Florida, 428 U.S. 242 (1976).
H. Roberts v. Louisiana, 431 U.S. 633 (1977).
S. Roberts v. Louisiana, 428 U.S. 325 (1976).
Sumner v. Schuman, 107 S.Ct. 2716 (1987).

2

The Fraternity of Death

MICHAEL A. KROLL

In 1977 the California state legislature passed Senator George Deukmejian's bill establishing death as punishment for certain classes of first-degree murder. In 1978 California voters passed the Briggs initiative, which widened the scope of the death penalty's application.

From that time until 1 November 1987, 265 death sentences or resentences have been meted out, all for the crime of murder. One of the condemned, Chol Soo Lee, had his death sentence reversed and was later acquitted of the crime for which he was sent to prison. Four others committed suicide on death row. Of those cases remaining, 195 are currently pending appeal in the state supreme court, which has reversed 59 death sentences and affirmed 6: Clarence Ray Allen, Stevie Lamar Field, Oscar Gates, David Luther Ghent, Robert Alton Harris, and Earl Lloyd Jackson.

On 23 January 1984 the U.S. Supreme Court held in Robert Harris's case that states are not required by the Constitution to conduct proportionality review to ensure that, relative to the sentences of other persons convicted of murder, a death sentence is neither discriminatory nor arbitrary.

Harris returned to U.S. District Court in San Diego for a hear-

An earlier version of this paper was published in *California Living* (*Los Angeles Herald-Examiner*), 25 March 1984.

ing on his other claim that the death penalty is discriminatorily imposed against those whose victims were white. Whereas 42 percent of California's death row population is white and 37 percent is black, 72 percent of the victims of those on death row are white and only 8 percent are black. (Hispanics account for 17 percent of those condemned to death, and 14 percent of the victims.) The court ruled against Harris, and his appeal to a panel of the 9th Circuit Court of Appeals was denied. He has requested a rehearing before the full court.

It has been over two decades since California's last gassing. Today there are more people awaiting their rendezvous with California's gas chamber than have been executed in its 50-year history. The number of those condemned to die there grows by 25 to 35 people a year.

□   □   □

When the Supreme Court rejected the claim of Robert Alton Harris in 1984, there were many who hoped that executions in California would resume immediately. Los Angeles County District Attorney Robert H. Philibosian, no doubt expressing the sentiments of a majority of his constitutents, let it be known that he was looking forward to witnessing the grisly spectacle. Within two days, more than a hundred people had put in their bids for ringside seats at the next killing of a human being in the gas chamber at San Quentin Prison, just across the Golden Gate Bridge from San Francisco.

California Department of Corrections spokesperson Phil Guthrie, while promising to accommodate Philibosian's request, made it clear that he himself had no desire to watch. Unlike the district attorney and the other would-be spectators, Guthrie has already witnessed an execution—and for him, one was enough.

The first victim of official lethal gassing in California was a pig. It was in March 1938, only two weeks after San Quentin prisoners had unloaded the two-ton, eight-sided chamber from the barge that brought it across the Bay. According to Horace Jackson, whose Denver-based Eaton Metal Products Company built the chamber, a pig is the hardest thing to kill. And "if it works on a pig," he says, "it'll work on a man."

The animal was put into a wire cage that was then laid across the armrests of the two stainless steel chairs inside the chamber. When the gas reached its snout, the pig jumped to its feet and tried to turn around within the tiny space. Climbing up the side of the cage to the top, it tried to push its nose through the wire, outside the reach of the deadly fumes. Finally, it fell to the floor of the cage, drooling and snorting. And then it died.

Warden Court Smith, a tough prison administrator who had presided over many hangings—and who supported capital punishment—turned his back, unable to watch the pig's desperate attempts to breathe. He did not see "that little pig die, straining away from the choking fumes, dashing his head against unyielding steel, fighting with all the strength of his little body for those awful seconds," as *San Francisco Chronicle* reporter Willis O'Brien described it.

O'Brien wrote: "If the men and women whom the State throws into the maw of this devouring monster suffer as that little pig suffered, if the mercy of nepenthe comes as slowly for the human body as it did for the little porker, then there will be terrible things done to men's souls and their tortured brains. . . . It is the most hellish form of capital punishment since civilized courts sentenced men to be hanged, drawn and quartered."

Despite the promise of the early promoters of the gas chamber that the hydrocyanic acid gas fumes would bring quick, clean, and painless death in 15 seconds, nearly three minutes passed before the 25-pound pig died. Since that day in 1938, Californians have gassed 196 human beings—sometimes alone, sometimes two at a time, strapped side by side in Chair A and Chair B. And, as in the pig's final moments, the end has not always been particularly quick or painless for many who have faced their deaths at San Quentin.

□   □   □

The gas chamber squats like a green toadstool in the corner of a high-ceilinged room. There is an ineffable quality here that causes your stomach to shrink up. It smells like a tomb, and you feel a chill that cannot be explained by the absence of the sun. As Lieutenant Bill McMullen turns the huge brass key in the door to admit us, he shudders slightly. "This place is eerie," he says. "I always feel it when I come into this room, like it's haunted or something. So many people have died here."

The room itself is outside the main wall, as if banished by the living, but attached to the north cell block, which houses death row six floors above. The condemned enter from an inside door opposite the entrance to the chamber itself and only a few feet away from it.

Official witnesses enter through a door of heavy steel and then one of prison bars. No outward signs identify the deadly contents of the room except for a T-shaped exhaust pipe, high atop the building, that spews the poison into the Marin sky after it has done its deed.

Because of the time that has transpired since the last gassing, the staff at San Quentin is unfamiliar with the operation of the chamber, and preparing for the next execution will not be an easy task.

The official manual for operating and maintaining the gas chamber is nine pages long. It covers everything from the types of chemicals to use (such as sodium cyanide, manufactured by DuPont in one-ounce, pillow-shaped briquettes the size of pigeon eggs and marketed in one-pound cans) to instructions for removing the corpse ("It is recommended that the doctor and those removing the body wear hydrocyanic gas masks and rubber gloves and that he ruffle the hair of the prisoner to allow any gas to escape which may be trapped.")

But a written manual, no matter how complete, is no substitute for experience. So in 1984 San Quentin called on Joe Ferretti to break in the five-member team that will officiate at upcoming executions.

A short, affable man, Ferretti does not look his 79 years. When it comes to the gas chamber, there are few people, living or dead, with as much experience as he has. In his 29 years at San Quentin, Ferretti participated in 126 executions. "I called my job baby-sitting," he says, "but the official name was death watch officer."

Ferretti was the officer at the main gate before he got into this other line of work. He liked working outdoors and meeting the public. He remembers wondering how anyone could work in the gas chamber—until he was asked to do the job. "First I went home and asked my wife," he says. "She said it was all right with her if it was all right with me. So I tried it." He remained at the job for the next 27 years. "I still kept my regular job at the front gate," he says, "but they'd assign someone else to do it when I was on death watch."

"We earned $15 for death duty in the beginning," he says, chuckling. "The last one I got $75. The executioner was making a lot more—$500 I think. He's dead now. Pretty near everyone's dead now."

Of his more recent experience as teacher to the new crop of executioners, he says, "I showed them the regular routine—what we done when I was there. We did executions at ten in the morning on Friday. On Thursday, around four, we'd go upstairs and get the inmate and bring him downstairs to the death cell next to the gas chamber. Then we'd stay there, two of us, till about 9:45 the next morning. We'd change his clothes to fresh jeans and a white shirt without any pockets, and no underwear or shoes. I guess gas could accumulate in places like that, and when you went in to get him you could get a whiff of the stuff."

After strapping the condemned man into the chamber and sealing the great steel door of the tank, he waited. "When the doctor says he's dead," Ferretti continues, "we start the pumps to pump the gas into the air outside. In about fifteen minutes, we crack the door a bit and turn a valve that lets air in the bottom. You have to pump for about half an hour before you can get in. Then two of us go in with a garden sprayer filled with ammonia to spray around his pants and clothes. It kind of neutralizes the gas. We go in in a hurry and unbuckle the straps. One grabs one side and one the other, and we scoot him into a redwood box made by prisoners in the carpentry shop. It's waiting just outside the door. Then a truck picks it up and takes it to the prison hospital, where the family claims it."

Although the official manual recommends a minimum of ten minutes to kill a man, sometimes it takes longer. "I remember one colored guy that took about fifteen minutes," Ferretti says. Unable to remember the man's name, he consults one of the most prized of his many prison mementos—a small red-vinyl-covered notebook. It contains photographs of 117 people whom Ferretti helped dispatch, as well as brief descriptions of their crimes. "Of course, I helped in 126 executions," he explains, "but back in '57 they decided I shouldn't keep this book. So I had to stop after 117." On the inside back cover, he has written the number of people whose deaths he attended by year, beginning in 1943 and ending in 1957: "1945—13; 1949—11; 1954—9 . . ."

When anything unusual happened during an execution, Ferretti faithfully recorded it in his little red book. Under the name Leanderess Riley, Ferretti wrote: "Had to carry to gas chamber. He unstrapped himself."

Leanderess Riley went to death row in 1949 for killing a Sacramento laundry man. The gassing of the 33-year-old one-eyed, nearly deaf man was, according to Joe Ferretti, "the nastiest execution we ever had. We had to carry the little colored guy in hollering. You could hear him a block away. I never saw a guy so scared in all my life. His wrists were so damn small—he only weighed 80 pounds or so—he managed to get out of the straps three times."

Riley managed to undo his restraints just before the executioner lowered the cyanide into the vats of acid. He jumped up and frantically raced around inside the chamber, screaming in terror, beating wildly on the thick glass windows. "We had to stop the process, open the chamber and strap him in again," Ferretti recalls. "Then he did it again, but the third time they already gave him the gas. He kept right on screaming, though, right up until he got that first whiff."

Former warden Louis ("Big Red") Nelson also remembers Leanderess Riley. To get himself through the execution, the tough-talking administrator had to rely on rote. "The fact that the fellow is crying and baying like a dog . . . you just can't deal with it at that point. You've got to carry out the job at hand. A grown man afraid to go to his death—as all of us are, to some degree—makes you sad. You feel sympathy for him, but you have to put those feelings aside."

Nelson has no qualms about the death penalty. To him, our time on earth is like a tenant's relationship with a landlord. "If you mess up the place or don't pay the rent, you get evicted," says the man who is still remembered by convicts as a firm but fair administrator.

On 6 April 1956, Nelson presided over the most unusual gassing he had ever witnessed, one of the 22 double executions carried out in the gas chamber. The two men, both in their early twenties, had been convicted three years earlier for killing an Oakland cabdriver after robbing him of seven dollars and his wristwatch. Only seconds before Nelson gave the signal to begin, one of the prisoners, Robert Pierce, managed to cut his throat with a tiny sliver of mirror he had secreted in a book. Cutting deep enough to hit a vein, he bled profusely. Nelson remembers that "they wrapped the blue shirt he had just changed out of around his neck and led him into the chamber with blood all over his arm and shirt. He began cursing the witnesses and society in general. He nodded toward the prison officials and made sure they knew he didn't hold them responsible. It was the witnesses. He called them every filthy name in the book."

Then Pierce's partner, Smith Jordon, was brought in and strapped into Chair A. While Pierce screamed his curses, his new white shirt turning red, Jordon remained completely calm.

"Because his arm was slippery with blood," Nelson recalls, "he was able to get his right forearm free. He was trying to free the other arm when the gas hit. Everything just stopped. His arm fell, and his sentence ended in the middle of a curse." Pierce's invective was welcomed by the pro–death penalty warden. "That kind of behavior made it personally easier," Nelson says now. "You could tell yourself the SOB deserved it."

Max Brice also remembers. Tall and gaunt, Brice was the officer in charge of executions for 35 years until he retired to his Napa home in 1974. He says he was never really bothered by his job, never had bad dreams, hasn't thought about it much since. "If you're gonna have mental problems about it," he says, "it's better not to get on the detail to begin with."

As the officer in charge, Brice tested the machinery three days before an execution, as well as the morning before, to make sure the vacuum was intact. The day before, he filled each of the two cheesecloth bags with 16 cyanide tablets and attached them to the rocker arms below Chair A and Chair B. There the bags remained suspended until lowered into the vats of acid.

On the morning of the execution, Brice telephoned Western Union to make sure the gas chamber clock was accurate to the second. About ten minutes before the gassing, Brice poured a gallon and a half of distilled water into each of two mixing pots, connected by pipes to the wells under the chairs. To the water he added five pints of sulphuric acid. According to the official operating manual, ten minutes are required for the mixture to reach "an intimate mix and maximum temperature."

Usually at a minute past ten the warden nodded his head, and the ritual began. "Once the warden gave the signal," Brice says, "there was never a word spoken. Everybody knew his job, and we did our work."

Sometimes, of course, the procedure was interrupted by a last-minute reprieve. Caryl Chessman spent 12 years on death row before being executed in 1960 for a crime that did not involve the taking of a life. In that time, his execution was postponed numerous times. "He used to send me notes that said, 'Well, you didn't get me this time,'" says Brice.

Chessman, however, was the exception. "Most were real routine," Brice says. "They came downstairs pretty well resigned to their fate. They took it like men."

Even the women took it like men. Barbara Graham, the third

woman of the four who have been gassed in California, was executed on 3 June 1955. Convicted, along with Emmett Perkins and Jack Santo, of murdering a Los Angeles woman in her home in 1953, she denied her guilt until the very end. It was her execution that most got under the skin of Joe Ferretti.

"God, she was a beautiful woman," Ferretti remembers. "I was with her all night. We told jokes. What made it real bad was she got two stays right there, that morning. She was just walking into the chamber the first time when the phone rang, and she had to wait some more. Then it happened again. When she finally started in for the third time, she asked for a blindfold. She was the only one who ever did. I don't think she wanted to see anyone in the witness room."

Ferretti strapped Graham in, patted her knee and said, as he had to the hundred before her, "Now take a deep breath and it won't bother you." "How in the hell would you know?" she retorted. Ferretti backed quickly out of the chamber, pushed the great steel door closed, and spun the heavy wheel with its bright red handles, sealing the chamber tight.

Three hours later, after the chamber had been aired out, Perkins and Santo followed Graham to their deaths. "After I got home, I just felt real down," Ferretti remembers. "Even my wife asked me what the matter was."

For Byron Eshelman, chaplain at San Quentin for two decades, it is the last execution, in 1967, that is most haunting. The chaplain came to know Aaron Mitchell well, visiting the prisoner many times in his death row cell, where he had been placed in 1963 for shooting a Sacramento police officer. Eshelman came to regard Mitchell as "quiet, intelligent, and composed."

The warden at the time was Lawrence Wilson, an administrator who has never believed in the death penalty. "You never get used to seeing it," he says. "You get a sort of sinking, sick feeling. After all, there's a guy in front of you, and he struggles to stay alive, but his life support system fails him. He expires before your eyes."

There was much to be done in the week before Mitchell's gassing. The chamber had not been used in four years, and new gaskets needed to be installed. The exhaust fan also had to be replaced, since it was hitting against the housing, causing a terrible racket. "That banging sound would have done nothing to provide decorum at the execution," Wilson says.

Like Chaplain Eshelman, Wilson also remembers Aaron Mitchell. "I had become acquainted with him on my twice-monthly visits to the row," he said. "He wasn't a demanding guy, just a normal individual."

Normal until 11 April 1967, the day before the execution. "After Aaron saw his mother for the last time," Wilson recalls, "he went berserk in the yard; he acted like a crazy man would act." He was dragged, screaming, back to his cell, and the warden was called.

"I went up and found him lying there, yelling that he was Jesus Christ and knocking his head on the concrete floor and flailing his arms," the former warden remembers sadly. "I had seen him so normal just a short time before, but the scene was very believable."

The prison's chief psychiatrist, Dr. David Schmidt, was summoned. He arrived to find that Mitchell's condition had not changed. It was then about three in the afternoon, just an hour before Ferretti was to come up the elevator to take the 38-year-old man to the gas chamber's holding cell. Schmidt called Wilson a few minutes later to say he did not think that Mitchell was insane. The law in California forbids the execution of an individual who is insane, because the person being executed must be aware of what is happening to him, and why.

When the time came for Mitchell to be taken downstairs, he did not walk the length of the row, as the condemned usually do, saying goodbye to the only companions they have had, often, for years. Nor did he protest when his body was searched for weapons before he was given a change of clothes. He remained passive even as his wrists were bound with leather straps and he was taken downstairs in the tiny elevator.

When Eshelman saw him that evening in the holding cell, "he was a stranger I had never met. He stood there naked, his arms outstretched, like a man in a trance." Despite the precautions, Mitchell had cut his left arm with a piece of glass, and it oozed fresh blood. To Eshelman's growing horror, Mitchell wiped the blood with the palm of his right hand and said, "This is the blood of Jesus Christ."

Early the next morning, Dr. Schmidt called Wilson to reiterate that Mitchell was not crazy. The warden felt that he could not overrule his medical staff. The execution could proceed.

Eshelman arrived at eight to find the condemned man just as he had left him the night before, standing naked in the center of the cell. Mitchell had to be wrestled to the floor so that the harness with the stethescope attached could be fastened around his chest. And then, Eshelman remembers, just two minutes before Wilson gave the silent signal to begin, Mitchell suddenly "let out a sustained, blood-curdling shriek and fell back convulsively on the mattress."

In the witness room just beyond the gas chamber, 58 people stood talking quietly among themselves. Nearest to one of the chamber's seven windows was Howard Brodie, an artist and journalist. Like the others, he heard the scream, and it chilled him.

Brodie could not see the two death watch officers drag the barefoot Mitchell across the green rug that was rolled out from the death cell to the chamber. He could not hear Mitchell moaning as he passed Wilson, who stood looking at the clock. He could not see Eshelman trailing helplessly behind. What he did see was the death watch officers strap Mitchell into Chair B, the one on the left as you enter the chamber, the one closest to where Brodie was standing. He saw Ferretti attach the thin rubber tubing to the stethescope so that Dr. McNamara, the chief medical officer, could listen to the condemned man's heartbeat from outside the chamber. He watched as Mitchell was left alone in the chamber, and he heard the huge steel door clang shut. Suddenly Mitchell cried out, "I am Jesus Christ."

Max Brice performed his duties quickly now. He signaled the chemical operator to open the valves into the chamber. The wells under both chairs filled with a gurgle through openings in the bottom. As soon as the outside vats were empty and sealed, they were filled with water to prevent the acid from backing up into them. Brice then carried out the final test, checking his gauges to make sure the chamber was airtight.

The executioner took a cotter pin from the bright red handle of the green lever, making sure to restrain it with one hand. If he let go of it, the lever would lurch forward from the weight of the rocker arms, slam against the steel wall of the chamber, and startle the man inside and the witnesses beyond. So he released it slowly, submerging the two cheesecloth bags of cyanide into the acid.

Brice looked down through the slats in the venetian blinds that keep the witnesses and the condemned person from seeing the executioners. He saw the faint wisp of smoke rising up through the perforated metal seat of the chair in which Aaron Mitchell was strapped.

Howard Brodie was on the opposite side of the chamber. He describes what he saw: "As the gas hit him, his head immediately fell to his chest. Then his head came up and he looked directly into the window I was standing next to. For nearly seven minutes, he sat up that way, with his chest heaving, saliva bubbling between his lips. He tucked his thumbs into his fist, and, finally, his head fell again."

Warden Wilson recalls feeling sick. "It seemed to take ten years. He kept gasping for air."

It took 12 minutes by the clock for Aaron Mitchell's heart to stop for good. McNamara signaled to Wilson that it was all over. A guard told the witnesses that they could leave.

Outside, it was a beautiful, warm spring day. Five hundred people had gathered at the prison gates, some to protest, some to approve. Former governor Edmund G. ("Pat") Brown said he was there "to protest this barbarity. It's a terrible thing to snuff out a human life as you would a dog's." Perhaps he recalled a letter he had received from the man whose corpse now sagged against the straps in Chair B while the blowers evacuated the cyanide from the chamber. "There is so much good in the worst of us, and so much bad in the best of us," Mitchell had written. Curiously, as governor, Brown had refused to commute Mitchell's death sentence, leaving the decision to his successor, Governor Ronald Reagan, who in turn delegated the responsibility to his counsel, Edwin Meese.

George Lincoln Rockwell, leader of the American Nazi Party, was also there to lend his voice. It was Mitchell's color that had drawn Rockwell to San Quentin that morning. His placard read, "GAS—THE ONLY CURE FOR BLACK CRIME."

3

Facing the Death Penalty

WATT ESPY

Only one who has endured the experience can fully understand the thoughts and emotions of a person who has been condemned to die at the hands of the executioner. Such an individual is kept in close confinement, deprived of all the creature comforts of life, forced to contemplate a sudden and violent death by a means already ordained and known to him or her. It is a period during which the soul and spirit of any mortal is severely tested. In this chapter I will illustrate, by factual examples, the manner in which some of those who have been judicially executed have prepared themselves for and met their fates.

Twenty-year-old Crawford Goldsby killed his first man at the age of 14. During the ensuing six years, many others fell victim to the pistols of this desperado, who was known and feared throughout the Indian Territory as "Cherokee Bill." Even as a prisoner under sentence of death at Fort Smith, Arkansas, he managed to secure a gun and claim another victim in an aborted jailbreak.

On 17 March 1896, he stood on the gallows in the yard of U.S. District Judge Isaac Parker's court, prepared to expiate his crimes pursuant to the sentence of the man often referred to as the "Hanging Judge." His mother stood beside him on the gallows, stoic and dry-eyed, as her son was asked if he had anything to say. Cherokee Bill coldly stared at the executioner who was about to carry out the law's mandate and replied: "No. I came here to die, not to talk." He kissed his mother goodbye, the trap was sprung, and he fell to his death at the end of a rope (*New York Times*, 18 March 1896).

Goldsby, who had shown nothing but contempt for society, met his death in a calm and dignified manner, but Andrew Taylor, who was hanged at Loudon, Tennessee, on 23 November 1883, could not resist a final opportunity to show his hatred for the law and its enforcers.

Taylor and his brothers, John and Robert, had terrorized east Tennessee for years. When John was sentenced to ten years in the state prison for an unprovoked murder, Andy and Bob determined that he would never serve a day.

On 14 September 1882, as Sheriff W. T. Cate of Hamilton County and his deputy, J. J. Conway, were transporting John to prison, his brothers boarded the train in Loudon County and shot the two lawmen, killing both. The three brothers then fled to Missouri, where John and Robert were killed resisting arrest and Andrew was taken into custody.

When asked if he had any last words before his execution, Andrew replied, "Not a goddamned word," but he changed his mind after the noose had been adjusted and, looking at the sheriff who was about to spring the trap, exclaimed: "God damn you! I could drink your heart's blood!" That was Taylor's final act of defiance. The drop fell, and nine minutes later Andrew Taylor was pronounced dead of strangulation (Goodspeed, 1896:237–38; *News* [Galveston, Texas], 24 Nov. 1883).

Even advanced age and the advent of our modern industrial society did not dampen the spirit of James ("Mancos Jim") Stephens. Stephens had been raised among the Navajo Indians. In his early manhood he had been a range rider, but as age overtook him he settled down to the easier life of herding sheep. The wizened, toothless old man was considered a harmless relic of the past in Motezuma County, Colorado, when, on 9 October 1939, he shot and killed Town Marshall Lynn Deat at Mancos.

Appeals and respites delayed his execution until 20 June 1941, when Governor Ralph Carr announced that even though he was reluctant to allow the execution to proceed because of the man's advanced age, he had decided to interfere no further. Mancos Jim expressed some disappointment at the decision, but said that he was ready to go.

After his last meal of soft foods, fruit juice, and eggs, the 76-

year-old former cowboy had to be driven in an automobile the last half-mile up a hill to the execution chamber. As he entered, he muttered a few words in the Navajo language and then, after he had been strapped into the chair, he let out a Navajo war whoop that witnesses described as "a terrible sound."

Determined not to die strapped down like an animal, he waited until the gas was released and then held his breath while he freed one hand and then removed the blindfold and the other straps. After that he sat back calmly and breathed deeply (*Post* [Denver, Colorado], 21 June 1941).

The courage of Native Americans facing death at the hands of an executioner has never ceased to amaze me. The various Indian nations were at one time allowed to administer justice through their own courts in the Indian Territory. After a man had been tried and condemned to death, an execution date was set, usually after the harvesting season, so that the prisoner could bring in a crop for his family. He was allowed to go free until that time. I know of no instance where one failed to appear on the appointed day to meet his fate.

Indian tribal executions were generally carried out by shooting, but when the Indian faced the white man's justice, execution was in the manner provided for by the laws of the jurisdiction wherein the crime was committed. The Indians considered hanging to be particularly odious, but when executed in that manner, they invariably accepted their fate with a detachment that amazed spectators.

On 29 June 1827, three Indians were hanged at Milledgeville, Georgia, for the murder of two white men. A contemporary report states: "They bore their fate with uncommon fortitude. When one of them (the last one executed) was launched off, the rope by which he was suspended broke. He rose up and inquired whether they (the officers of justice) were done with him. Upon receiving an answer in the negative, he said with great non-chalance, "Try it again then" (*Southern Advocate* [Huntsville, Alabama], 10 Aug. 1827).

Indians were the victims of the greatest mass execution in American history. During the Civil War, the Sioux rose in revolt in Minnesota, and following their defeat by Union Army forces, 307 were tried and sentenced to death by hanging. President Lincoln, to the disappointment of most white Minnesotans, approved the death sentences of only 38 of the condemned leaders and braves.

The attitude of those about to die, ranging in age from youths in their teens to old men, was cogently summarized in the letter that one Rdainyanka dictated to his father-in-law, which ended: "My wife and children are dear to me. Let them not grieve for me. Let them remember that the brave should be prepared to meet death; and I will die as becomes a Dakota."

Early in the morning on 26 December 1862, the condemned men began chanting their death songs and painting their faces with war paint. They submitted peacefully to being bound, though they strenuously objected to having hoods placed over their heads, since they considered this to be a humiliation. They continued to chant as they mounted the huge gallows, which was built in the shape of a hollow square to accommodate all of them, and their death songs were silenced only when the drop fell. The only noise to be heard was "the prolonged cheer from the citizenry and soldiery" (Carley, 1976:68–75).

Jeroboam Beauchamp, a young Kentucky lawyer, was convicted in 1826 of having murdered former congressman and then–Attorney General Solomon Sharp, whom Beauchamp's wife had accused of seducing her. On the night before his execution, she was allowed to stay with him in his dungeon cell. Evidently she was not thoroughly searched. She had brought a dagger with her, and that night they attempted to carry out a suicide pact.

She was successful, but he failed. When the officers arrived the next morning to escort him to the gallows, they found him still living in spite of a gaping wound in his throat and a severe loss of blood. The arms of his wife, stiff from rigor mortis, were draped around his neck, and it was necessary to pry them loose before he could be carried to the gallows. He was so weak that he could hardly stand. After the execution on 7 July 1826, the Beauchamps were buried in a common grave (Johnson, 1972:44–57).

While it was not uncommon for a relative to attempt to aid one under sentence of death to cheat the law, few joined their loved one in death. Another such incident occurred in 1898. Benjamin R. Willis, the illegitimate son of a wealthy New York broker, had been sent by his father to the Wilton Academy, an exclusive school in Connecticut that was run by Professor David S. R. Lambert.

Even after he had graduated, young Willis retained a hatred for the elderly teacher because of punishment administered to him on one occasion. He solicited the help of Frederick M. Brockhaus, a professional burglar, and on the afternoon of 16 December 1897, Lambert caught them burglarizing the school. Willis shot and killed his former teacher. Both of the young men were subsequently caught, convicted, and sentenced to die. He was executed on 30 December 1898.

On the night before Willis's date with the executioner, his mother smuggled some poison to him, but alert guards discovered it and saved his life for the waiting hangman. The next day, after Willis's execution, his mother killed herself by taking some of the poison (Boswell and Thompson, 1962:39–52).

A public execution in a democratic society is unquestionably the most ignominious manner in which a person can die. Not only is he marked as a social misfit who does not deserve to live, but his family must live the remainder of their lives with the shame of a loved one's crimes and execution. Many persons whose guilt is obvious have gone to their deaths stoutly protesting their innocence— not to save their lives, I believe, because as they stand on the scaffold or sit strapped in the chair, they know that the state is determined to exact its pound of flesh. Nor do they entertain hope that their protestations of innocence will influence the feelings of the majority of the people about them. Instead, I believe, they do so because they feel that it will be a source of comfort to those who care for them —that their loved ones will believe them and take solace in their innocence.

Many people have met their deaths by legal execution without revealing their true names. They maintained that it was better that they should die alone and unmourned than that their families should know of the crimes which they committed and the dreadful penalty which they paid.

Such was the case of a man who was hanged at San Quentin under the name of Thomas Green on 13 April 1914. Green and his companion, Paul Case, unsuccessful in their attempts to become rodeo riders, had robbed the Palo Verde Bank at Blythe, and Green had shot and killed a cashier.

During their escape, one of Green's eyes was torn from its socket when he ran into a mesquite tree. He and his companion were captured three days later while sleeping in an El Centro hotel. Both confessed; Case was sentenced to life imprisonment, and Green, the actual triggerman, was condemned. From the gallows he stated that Green was not his correct name, explaining that his parents were

Christian people, respected in their community, and that he did not want them to know of his crime or his fate (*Enterprise* [Riverside, California], 3 Dec. 1913, 5 Dec. 1913, 3 April 1914).

Often the mere thought of being executed is more than a person can bear. When Albert Pitts was sentenced to die in Houston, Texas, in 1938 for a holdup-murder, he literally dropped dead in the courtroom (*Crime Detective*, 19 Oct. 1938, p. 10).

The shock of having his middle-aged bride arrested and charged with the murder of an elderly benefactor who had secured her release from prison (where she was serving a life sentence for a prior murder conviction) proved to be too much for Lee Judson, a California bank messenger. He leaped to his death from the thirteenth floor of an office building.

Mrs. Judson, who used the name Louise Peete, took the news philosophically, saying: "Our life together was so beautiful. He told me 'If you ever leave me, I'll take sleeping powders.'" She then proceeded to read Lin Yutang's *The Importance of Living* throughout her trial.

Mrs. Peete confidently expected a commutation of her sentence until the very end, saying just before she entered the gas chamber: "Governor Warren is a gentleman. No gentleman would send a lady to her death." When the chivalry of the future Chief Justice of the United States failed to materialize, she went to her death with quiet dignity (deFord, 1965:73–82).

Another condemned woman was described by Warden Clinton Duffy as "the coldest, hardest character, male or female, I have ever known." Her name was Eithel Leta Juanita Spinelli, and she was the leader of a gang of hoodlums that included, in addition to her lover, gangster Mike Simeone, her own children, and other young people of their acquaintance.

After one of the gang had killed the proprietor of a San Francisco barbecue stand who resisted a holdup, all of them fled to Sacramento and hid out in a cheap hotel. Mrs. Spinelli, known to her followers as "the Duchess," was worried that 19-year-old Robert Sherrard, whom she considered the weakest of the lot, might betray them. She slipped chloral hydrate into his drink and, when he was unconscious, ordered Simeone, her son-in-law, Gordon Hawkins, and another member of the gang to throw him into the Sacramento River, where he drowned.

Mrs. Spinelli, Simeone, and Hawkins were all sentenced to

die, while the other's life was spared when he turned state's evidence. Thirty prisoners signed a petition addressed to the governor requesting that one of them, selected by lot, be allowed to take the Duchess's place in the gas chamber. The petition was, of course, rejected, and on 21 November 1941 she was put to death.

Even though she had lived a life of callous indifference toward everyone, including her own children, whom she had raised in a criminal environment, her maternal instincts were evident in her last request. She asked that photographs of her three children and an infant grandchild be taped over her heart (Duffy, 1962:133–41).

Nineteen-year-old Francis ("Two-Gun") Crowley was depicted by the press as one of the most ruthless and heartless killers of all time. When he entered Sing Sing's death house, where he was to die for the murder of a policeman, he attempted to maintain his tough guy image and was so unruly that it was necessary to place him in an isolation cell.

After he succeeded in taming a sparrow that flew into his cell one day, a change came over Crowley. He developed an interest in drawing and woodworking, showing an unexpected sensitivity and ultimately gaining the respect and friendship of Warden Lewis Lawes. A few days before his execution, when Lawes was in his cell, they noticed a small waterbug crawling across the floor, and Crowley said: "See that? I was about to kill it. Several times I wanted to crush it. It's a dirty looking thing. But then I decided to give it a chance and let it live." On 21 January 1932, when he walked the last mile, he did so "calmly, without braggadocio, without swagger. 'Give my love to mother,' he called, just as the hood was placed over his head" (Lawes, 1932:313–22).

Two Gun Crowley showed to lesser creatures a compassion that he had not shown to his fellow man, but "Little Jim" Guild, a 12-year-old slave who was hanged at Flemington, New Jersey, on 28 November 1828 for the murder of his elderly mistress, did not. He captured 13 mice in his cell, used 12 of them as jurors, and, following a proper trial and condemnation by its peers, hanged the thirteenth.

Little Jim provided a bizarre gallows scene himself when he managed to shake the hood from his head and balance his toes on the edge of the drop just as the trap fell. The horrified sheriff rushed to the top of the scaffold and pushed the little boy's feet from the plank, allowing him to strangle to death (Snell, 1881:200–201).

James Dooley was only 16 when he raped and murdered his aunt and killed his cousin. Two years later, on 19 October 1894, as he stood on the gallows in the Iowa State Prison, he showed a knowledge of the technicalities of the law and a philosophical bent that belied his years when asked if he had anything to say. Dooley replied: "I have. You have violated the law. The law allows but 17 persons to witness an execution and there are 25 or more present now and more coming. A poor man cannot violate the law without he suffers the penalty. A rich man can do the same and he goes free. I hope God will forgive your sins as mine are" (*News* [Galveston, Texas], 20 Oct. 1894).

During the days of public executions, crowds loved them. I suppose many people still would. Those spectacles of death failed to deter at least one murderer. When Stephen Short was hanged on 19 January 1855 in Greenup County, Kentucky, he observed from the gallows: "I have been to a good many hanging scrapes myself, and thought it was great fun, but I never thought I'd be hung myself!" (*Daily Advertiser* [Mobile, Alabama], 4 Feb. 1885).

Dick Townsend, a black man who killed at least four men and possibly more, joked and laughed throughout his trial at Valdosta, Georgia. He was convicted of the murder of Sheriff Epperson of Bradford County, Florida, who had come to Georgia to arrest him for another murder. After his conviction and condemnation, he took great delight in making as much trouble as possible for his jailers. When he was hanged before three thousand witnesses on 16 July 1886, his request that he be allowed to speak for one hour was granted, but after only five minutes he could say no more, and the execution proceeded (*Atlanta Constitution*, 17 July 1886).

Ezelle Heard, who was hanged at Aberdeen, Mississippi, on 5 September 1914, did not even have the chance to speak for five minutes. On the preceding day, when he was informed that the governor had declined to interfere with the sentence of the court, Heard fainted and mercifully remained comatose. He had to be carried to the scaffold and supported by braces until the trap fell (*Atlanta Journal*, 6 Sept. 1914).

Another Mississippi murderer, Charles Calvert, who was hanged at West Point on 2 March 1898, waxed poetic before his death (*Leader* [West Point, Mississippi], 4 March 1898). After confessing to the huge crowd gathered to see him die that he had mur-

dered his wife with an axe and then burned their cabin in an effort
to conceal the crime, Calvert quipped:

> Hang me high and stretch me wide,
> So the world can see how free I died.

Willard Richardson, 29, electrocuted in Kentucky on 19 April
1912, was not sentimental, nor did he encourage the expression of
tender sentiments on his behalf. When his gray-haired father sobbed
during their last meeting, Richardson snarled to the old man: "Cut
out all of that confounded beefin'. What's it to you, anyway?" (*Florida
Times Union* [Jacksonville], 20 April 1912).

Walter O. Mirikle, a young Alabamian, killed Dr. C. J. Nunn, a
Mississippi dentist, while breaking a friend out of the Green County
jail. One of Mirikle's relatives attended the execution, which was
carried out at Leakesville in the state's portable electric chair. After
the youth had been pronounced dead, the sheriff asked the kinsman
what he wanted to do about funeral arrangements and received the
terse reply: "Not a damn thing. The State of Mississippi killed him.
Let the State of Mississippi bury him!" (*Official Detective*, April
1976, pp. 14–15).

Caspar Pastoni, an Italian musician, became infatuated with
Mrs. Elizabeth Witchell, who had befriended him and taught him
to speak English. When she rejected his love, he killed her and her
four-year-old daughter. As the hangman's noose was being adjusted
around his neck in Chicago's Cook County Jail on 15 June 1923, he
shrugged and said: "Oh well, what's the use of crying? They won't
let me go, and I'd rather die laughing" (*Arkansas Gazette*, 16 June
1923).

William West, a black farm laborer, was convicted in Washington County, Pennsylvania, of the murder of his former employers,
Mr. and Mrs. John Crouch, and their son Andrew, all of whom were
clubbed to death and robbed in their home near Bentleyville on the
night of 12 May 1860. West protested his innocence until the very
end and swore that he would not be hanged. First he used a rusty
nail, which he had somehow secreted in his cell, to slash his arms
and wrists. When this failed, he took poison that had been smuggled
in to him, and once again the doctors were called to save his life in
order that the penalty of the law might be carried out.

His last chance of suicide gone, West became unmanageable, and he was given enough chloroform and morphine to render him unconscious. He was then carried to the gallows strapped on a board. When the drop fell, the rope broke and its burden fell to the ground. "The murderer was carried back onto the gallows, and the rope tied again; and six minutes after the trap had been sprung the first time, William West paid the penalty for his crime" (Forrest, 1926:385–86).

After Frank Brenish used a butcher's knife to kill his estranged wife in Memphis, Tennessee, he turned the same weapon upon himself in a suicide attempt. Even though it was thought for some time that he would die, the skill of the hastily summoned surgeons saved him for trial and execution.

Brenish did not seem to mind dying. He slashed his wrists on the morning of 24 June 1890, the day of the execution, but once again the physicians did their duty. His main complaint about the proposed execution was that he was scheduled to share a common gallows with three black men who were hanged the same day. It was the segregated and racially bigoted South, so the sheriff granted his wish that he be spared this indignity. He was hanged only after the other three murderers had been pronounced dead.

As frequently happened during this period, Brenish was allowed all he wished to drink so that his nerves might be steadied for the ordeal that lay ahead. Consequently, he mounted the gallows in a drunken stupor, and his last words were: "They oughtn't to hang a man when he ain't in his right mind" (*Memphis Appeal*, 16 May 1890, 25 June 1890).

□   □   □

Regardless of whether persons who are executed exhibit cowardice or bravery during their last moments of life, death itself is probably a merciful release from the agony and torment that they have suffered during their long period of confinement. As I see it (though others will disagree), no murderer is so heartless and cruel as the society that executes him. No individual murderer confines the victim to restricted quarters over a sustained period of time, or arranges things so that the person who is to die knows the manner in which death will come and the time at which it will arrive, hoping against hope for the magical reprieve, stay, or commutation that might prolong his life.

These examples of the attitudes and behavior of people about to die a judicially decreed death, selected from over sixteen thousand legal executions in our nation's history, demonstrate that some have shown more consideration for the feelings of their loved ones at the moment of death than they ever showed before. Others were contemptuous of their relatives' grief and the heartbreak that they were causing even as they departed this life.

Imminent death brought out surprising compassion and gentleness in some who were considered depraved beyond belief, while others died without surrendering the reckless and deviant violence with which they had lived.

No glorification of these men and women, or the despicable acts for which they forfeited their lives, is intended. Instead, I have merely sought to illustrate with a few case histories the observation that although some have died as they lived, others faced the ultimate victor over all mankind with a dignity that any of us might envy.

References

Boswell, Charles, and Lewis Thompson. 1962. *Curriculum of Murder*. New York: Collier Books.

Carley, Kenneth. 1976. *The Sioux Uprising of 1862*. St. Paul: Minnesota Historical Society.

deFord, Miriam Allen. 1965. *Murderers, Sane and Mad*. New York: Avon Books.

Duffy, Clinton T., with Al Hirshberg. 1962. *Eighty-eight Men and Two Women*. Garden City, N.Y. Doubleday.

Forrest, Earle. 1926. *History of Washington County, Pennsylvania*, vol. 1. Chicago: Clark Publishing Co.

Goodspeed's History of Tennessee with a Sketch of Hamilton County. 1896. Nashville: Goodspeed Publishing Co.

Johnson, Lewis F. 1972. *Famous Kentucky Trials and Tragedies*. Lexington: Henry Clay Press.

Lawes, Lewis E. 1932. *Twenty Thousand Years in Sing Sing*. New York: Long and Smith.

Snell, James P. 1881. *History of Hunterdon and Somerset Counties, New Jersey*. Philadelphia: Everts and Peck.

4

Juveniles' Attitudes Toward Their Impending Executions

VICTOR L. STREIB

Over the last three and a half centuries, American jurisdictions have executed 281 people for crimes committed while they were under the age of 18 (see Streib, 1987:55–71). Their ages at execution ranged from 12 to 28. All were healthy young people with no reason to expect to die from natural causes in the foreseeable future. All came to contemplate their deaths from execution during waiting periods that lasted from a few weeks to over ten years. The focus of this chapter is on the attitudes and perceptions of these executed young persons as they face execution.

First consider the American experience with the death penalty for juvenile crimes. This topic is not merely a current concern of courts and legislatures but has deep historical roots in our society. Most American death penalty jurisdictions have executed juvenile offenders in the past and many still have a few on their death rows awaiting execution.

This chapter is based largely upon the author's recently published book (Streib, 1987), and in particular chapter 8, "Juveniles' Attitudes Toward Impending Execution," pp. 155–64.

History of the Juvenile Death Penalty

The American history of the juvenile death penalty began in Plymouth Colony in 1642 with the execution of Thomas Graunger (16 at the time of his crime and execution). The most recent execution for a juvenile offense occurred on 15 May 1986, when Jay Kelly Pinkerton (17 at the time of his crime, and 24 at the time of his execution) was put to death in Texas (Streib, 1987:73, 127–29). Offenders as young as 10 at the time of crime have been executed; several youths aged 13 or 14 have been executed in this century. Ten of the 281 have been females, the last female juvenile execution having occurred over three-quarters of a century ago (Streib, 1987: 58–59).

Most (69 percent) of these executed juvenile offenders were black, and almost all (89 percent) of their victims were white. Their crimes include arson, bestiality, and theft, but 81 percent were convicted of murder, and 15 percent of rape. Although two-thirds of these juvenile executions have been carried out in the South, 36 jurisdictions have had at least one such execution. Georgia is by far the leader with 41 juvenile executions—more than double the number of its nearest competitor. Next in line, with 18 or 19 each, are the southern states of North Carolina, Texas, and Virginia, and the northern industrial states of New York and Ohio (Streib, 1987: 63–70).

The heaviest concentrations of juvenile executions have been in the older, more populous states east of the Mississippi River, particularly along the eastern seaboard. The Deep South states, except for Louisiana, are consistently heavy, but so are such northeastern states as Massachusetts, New York, and Ohio. Several central and western states, ranging from North Dakota down to Oklahoma and over to Idaho, have never executed any juveniles. The only western state with significant juvenile executions is California, and its six juvenile executions (1864–1923) still constitute only 1 percent of its total of approximately five hundred executions in the past century.

Juvenile executions were rare before the Civil War, with only a few being carried out each decade. The number jumped to 12 in the 1860s, rose steadily to 27 in the 1920s, and then jumped again to a peak of 53 in the 1940s. This rate then plummeted to 16 in the 1950s and to 3 in the 1960s (Streib, 1987:55–56). The only executions for juvenile crimes since 1970 have been those of Charles F. Rumbaugh in Texas on 11 September 1985, James Terry Roach in South Carolina on 10 January 1986, and Jay Kelly Pinkerton in Texas on 15 May 1986.

Recent Juvenile Death Sentences

The willingness of judges and juries to sentence people to death for crimes committed while they were under the age of 18 is slackening markedly. Eleven such sentences were imposed in 1982; 9 in 1983; 6 in 1984; 5 in 1985; 7 in 1986; 2 in 1987; and three during the first nine months of 1988 (Streib, 1988). These are years for which the death-sentencing rate for adults has been about 280 per year. Thus, for the last seven years, juvenile death sentences have usually constituted only about 1 to 2 percent of the total death sentences meted out each year.

These 43 juvenile death sentences have been imposed in 17 states, ranging from New Jersey to Florida and from North Carolina to Nevada. The leading state is Texas, with 6 juvenile death sentences, followed by Florida with 5 and Maryland with 4. Georgia, Indiana, North Carolina, and Pennsylvania have each condemned 3 defendants to death for crimes committed as juveniles.

Twenty-eight (65 percent) of the 43 have been imposed on offenders who were 17 years old at the time of their crimes. Another 9 (21 percent) were 16, and 6 (14 percent) were 15. Most (26, or 60 percent) are black, and almost all (41, or 95 percent) are male. Only 22 of the 43 remain on death row as of 1 October 1988 (Streib, 1988: 14–22).

These 22, plus 6 others sentenced before 1982, make up the 28 people now on American death rows for crimes committed as juveniles (Streib, 1988:14–22). They constitute only 1.5 percent of the total number of 2,182 persons on death row (NAACP Legal Defense and Educational Fund, 1988). Moreover, this 1988 juvenile total represents a low point: it is the smallest figure for persons on death row for juvenile crimes since systematic record keeping began in 1981 (Streib, 1983–88; Streib, 1987:167–83).

All 28 juvenile offenders now on death rows were convicted and sentenced to death for murder; all but three were convicted of murder in combination with some other crime, such as robbery or rape.

Twenty (71 percent) of them were aged 17 at the time of their crimes; 6 (21 percent) were 16; and 2 (7 percent) were 15. They continue to be predominantly black (54 percent) and male (93 percent).

The opposite racial and sex pattern applies to the 32 victims of these 28 offenders. Of the 31 victims for whom race is known, 26 (84 percent) were white. Twenty (61 percent) of the victims were female, often elderly. Thus, the typical juvenile death sentence case involves a 17-year-old black male who robs or rapes and kills an older white female.

These 28 juvenile offenders are on death row in 12 states. The leading states are Texas with six, and Florida and Georgia with four each.

Those on death row today for juvenile crimes range in age from 17 to 30. At one extreme is Troy Dugar, a 15-year-old black male convicted of the robbery and murder of a white male in Louisiana. Dugar was sentenced to death on his sixteenth birthday, 1 May 1987. Now 17, he is the youngest person on death row as of 1 October 1988. The opposite extreme is represented by Jose High, a black male 17 years old when he was convicted of the kidnap and murder of an 11-year-old white male in Georgia. Under a death sentence for almost 10 years, High is now 27 years old and still facing execution for a crime committed at 17.

Paula Cooper is a rarity now or at any time in our history: a juvenile female on death row. Cooper, now past her nineteenth birthday, was only 15 when she robbed and murdered an elderly white woman in Indiana. Her case has received worldwide attention from the media and from such august moral leaders as Pope John Paul II (*Newsweek*, 21 Sept. 1987, p. 37; *New York Times*, 27 Sept. 1987).

Also on death row at the start of 1988 was William Wayne Thompson, then under a death sentence in Oklahoma for murdering a white male when Thompson was only 15 years old. Aged 21 as of this writing, Thompson has just had his death sentence reversed by the U.S. Supreme Court in *Thompson v. Oklahoma*, a decision that in effect establishes a minimum age at crime of 16 before the death penalty may be imposed (*Thompson v. Oklahoma*, 108 S.Ct. 2687 [1988]; see also Reidinger, 1987).

Juveniles' Attitudes

Any attempt to present information about the attitudes toward impending execution of juvenile offenders for all 281 cases in American history would be doomed to failure, since in most cases this information either has never been recorded or, if recorded, is lost to contemporary researchers. The cases selected for description herein are those for which adequate information exists.

In a recent book on the juvenile death penalty (Streib, 1987), I present detailed case studies of 79 of the 281 people executed for crimes committed while they were under age 18. This paper focuses on 34 of these 79 cases in order to examine the much narrower issue of attitude toward impending execution. While not necessarily a representative sample of the universe of 281 cases, the cases presented here involve different time periods, offenders of varying ages, and a wide range of orientations toward their impending doom.

Some rough categorizing may help us to examine the attitudes and perceptions of these juveniles without obscuring the uniqueness of each case or erroneously implying that members of a category behave in an identical manner. Members of the categories express similar sentiments and manifest similar attitudes at a particular time. (It is of course quite common for a prisoner to show several attitudes during the time spent awaiting the executioner.) In this spirit the categories have been inductively formulated and cases have been selected for illustrative purposes. The six categories are (1) lack of concern or indifference; (2) resignation and weariness with waiting; (3) fear, a sense of abandonment, and a wish to be rescued; (4) pride, defiance, boastfulness and joking; (5) penitence, acceptance, a desire to serve as an example to others; and (6) religious conversion.

Indifference

Some condemned juveniles are expressionless and without apparent concern over their impending execution, particularly during the trial and early posttrial periods of their cases. Their attitudes sometimes change dramatically as execution grows more imminent. This lack of concern or indifference may stem from an unrealistic perception of death or from stoicism, but it is manifested in a fairly consistent manner.

Hannah Ocuish, a 12-year-old retarded American Indian girl,

was executed by Connecticut in 1786.[1] At her trial for the murder of a 6-year-old white girl, Ocuish seemed unconcerned and reasonably contented. In contrast, the presiding judge could barely speak, and spectators wept openly as Ocuish was sentenced to death.

James Guild was executed, also at the age of 12, in 1828 in New Jersey.[2] This young black slave murdered a white grandmother from a prominent family. Awaiting execution for 14 months, he seemed not to fully comprehend his situation. To pass the time, Guild enacted a bizarre mock trial with mice captured in his cell. This trial, complete with twelve mouse jurors, resulted in the ceremonial hanging of the mouse defendant, all to the indifferent amusement of the young boy.

Another example of indifference is George Stinney, a 14-year-old black youth executed in South Carolina in 1944 for the murder of two young white girls.[3] As Stinney entered the death chamber and was strapped into the electric chair, he "appeared far more at ease than some of those who came to watch him die" (*Columbia* [S.C.] *Record*, 16 June 1944). As the guards fumbled with an electrocution apparatus designed for full-grown adults, they were relieved that Stinney was calm and cooperative (Stout, 1982).

In 1947 Mississippi executed James Lewis, aged 15, and Charles Trudell, aged 16, black youths who had murdered their white employer.[4] During the 16 months they awaited execution and endured the ups and downs of the appellate and clemency processes, they seemed unconcerned about their fate, reading their comic books and plunking their guitars to pass the time in the local jail.

Charles Rumbaugh, executed in Texas in 1985 for a robbery-murder committed over ten years earlier, exhibited all of the attitudes listed above before finally meeting his death.[5] Yet his perception of the death penalty and its deterrent effect in his case seem to fit best in this category: "I was 17 years old when I committed the offense for which I was sentenced to die, and I didn't even start thinking and caring about my life until I was at least 20" (*National Catholic Reporter*, 8 Nov. 1985, p. 16).

A final example is Terry Roach, executed in South Carolina in 1986.[6] A retarded 17-year-old when he raped and murdered, he deteriorated mentally from Huntington's chorea during his eight years on death row and had the mental age of a 12-year-old when executed. Supreme Court Justice Thurgood Marshall observed that Roach's mental condition "raises substantial doubts as to whether Roach has any understanding that he is scheduled to die tomorrow" (*Roach v. Aiken*, 106 S.Ct. 647 [1986]). Early the next morning, Roach seemed "calm and resigned as he shuffled into the death chamber" (*Time*, 20 Jan. 1986, p. 22).

All but seven of these youths manifested a lack of understanding and concern about the death penalty both before committing their crimes and after being sentenced to death. For the younger and more retarded ones, this may simply have stemmed from ignorance and immaturity. For the older ones, it may be illustrative of adolescents' endemic lack of understanding of the nature of death.

Resignation and Weariness

Some condemned juveniles conclude that they would rather die than spend their lives in prison. (When life expectancy is taken into account, a sentence of life imprisonment is in fact harsher for younger than for older defendants.) For some, resignation comes quickly, stemming from a desire to be free of confinement. For others it reaches full cognition only after many years in prison.

An example of the former category is Joseph Nuana, executed in Washington Territory in 1874.[7] He had murdered a prominent farmer and the farmer's pregnant wife. Nuana spent less than four months awaiting execution, but he was in a jail far away from his home. Prior to his trial he had seemed carefree and unconcerned, but he concluded rather quickly that an American jail was no place for a Hawaiian-Indian boy from San Juan Island (Washington Territory) to spend the rest of his life. As Nuana walked briskly up the steps of the scaffold, he announced to the large assembled crowd: "I would sooner be dead than live in jail here" (Paterson, 1976:49). He made this life and death decision at the age of 17.

James ("Sleepy") Coleman was executed in Ohio in 1928 for murdering a police officer.[8] His crime was committed along with an older man, who had given Coleman the gun and signaled when to shoot the officer. Both Coleman and his partner were convicted and sentenced to death. Coleman's co-defendant appealed repeatedly and vigorously sought clemency from the governor, but to no avail. Coleman, in contrast, admitted his guilt and refused to seek either appellate review or executive clemency. The two murderers, one who fought fate and one who accepted it, died only minutes apart in Ohio's electric chair.

Charles Rumbaugh, at first, as we have seen, unconcerned with death, spent almost ten years on death row (1976–1985), more than any other executed juvenile in American history. During that decade of waiting for death, Rumbaugh became so weary of the vigil that he volunteered for execution and fought against any further appeals on his behalf. This weariness began early, as illustrated by a 1978 letter:

> You know, D. J., if they were to come to my cell and tell me I was going to be executed tomorrow, I would feel relieved, in a way. The waiting would be over. I would know what to expect. To me, the dying part is easy; its [sic] the waiting and not knowing that's hard. (Stubben, 1980:215)

By 1982 Rumbaugh had instructed his attorneys not to appeal his case further. He even fought against a court petition filed by his parents. Rumbaugh's frustration even led to a plan to commit suicide. At a 1983 court hearing, he brandished a smuggled knife and pointed it at a marshall, imploring the marshall to shoot (*National Catholic Reporter*, 8 Nov. 1985, pp. 11, 18). The marshall did, hitting Rumbaugh in the heart and lungs, but Rumbaugh recovered to face another two and a half years of waiting. By January 1984 he had sunk deeper into clinically diagnosed depression and psychosis:

> I feel like I have been traveling down a long, dark and winding tunnel for the past nine years—the length of time I have been on death row—and now I can see no end to the tunnel, no light at the end of it, just more long years of the same. I have reached the point where I no longer really care. . . .
>
> I'm so damn tired and disgusted with sitting here and watching my friends take that final trip to the execution chamber, one after another, while I continue to wait and speculate about when my time will come. They're killing me a little bit each day. (*National Catholic Reporter*, 8 Nov. 1985, p. 26)

The three cases in this category suggest a rejection of long-term confinement more than a desire to die. If the option of release from prison had been available, or, in Rumbaugh's case, if treatment for his spiraling depression and psychosis had been provided, death might not have been seen as the preferable alternative. These cases do not illustrate a desire to commit suicide by committing a capital crime and getting executed for it. Instead, they suggest that those convicted and sentenced to death perceive a lack of reasonable options.

Fear and Abandonment

Younger juveniles, as well as most of the nine executed girls, have exhibited what can best be described as mortal fear and a feeling of being lost and abandoned. These feelings are manifested by uncontrollable crying and severe emotional depression as well as childlike pleas for rescue to a parent or authoritative adult.

Consider as an example 12-year-old Hannah Ocuish, who experienced her trial with indifference. As her execution grew imminent, her attitude changed. When a visitor explained to Ocuish exactly what was going to happen to her, she wept uncontrollably for most of the day. Then the execution date arrived: "At the place of execution she said very little—appeared greatly afraid, and seemed to want somebody to help her" (Sanders, 1970:323).

Fourteen years old and black, Brad Beard had experienced the lynching of his older brother for eloping with a white girl, a relationship forbidden in 1897 in Alabama.[9] When Beard was legally sentenced to death only a few months later for the rape of a young white girl, he barely avoided being lynched himself. He was terrified as he was moved from jail to jail to befuddle the lynch mobs. Finally hanged in 1897, the legal ceremony was calm and peaceful for everyone except Beard. He remained terrified until the end.

Charles Oxnam was executed by California in 1916 for murdering his burglary victim.[10] He was described as a feeble-minded imbecile with a mental age of eight. Although the debate raged to the end about his sanity at the time of his crime, the governor allowed the execution to occur. At the age of 18, Oxnam "went to the scaffold at San Quentin penitentiary quivering and weeping. He sobbed until the drop fell" (*Los Angeles Daily Times*, 4 Mar. 1916).

Ignatius (Sam) Pupera, a robber, died in Ohio's electric chair in 1922.[11] Only 16 years old when the robbery-murder occurred, he turned 17 before the police could arrest him. His concern upon being arrested was manifested in his plaintive question to the police: "They'd never send a boy of seventeen to the chair in Ohio, would they?" (*Cleveland Plain Dealer*, 26 Mar. 1921). After being convicted and sentenced to death, he spent a year fighting for his life through court appeals and petitions to the governor. He lost his battle but won one small point. He was not sent to the chair in Ohio as a boy of 17. He celebrated his eighteenth birthday on death row, two and a half months before being executed.

One of three Chinese persons executed for juvenile crimes was Pang Young, electrocuted in Ohio in 1939.[12] Variously described as "a childlike oriental" and a "sobbing Chinese," he seemed to have no friends or family. His intense fear and remorse are indicated by his attempt at suicide soon after the crime. Aged 17 at his crime and 18 at his execution, Young was described by seasoned observers as "one of the loneliest figures who ever waited out the hours in the death row of Ohio Penitentiary" (*Cleveland Press*, 13 July 1939).

Edward Haight expressed loneliness and a sense of abandonment more than fear.[13] After eight months of waiting, he was executed by New York in 1943 for the kidnap-murder of two young girls. The day before he died, he seemed anxious but philosophical: "I guess this is my last day and I am only seventeen. I wish somebody would come and visit me. I'd like some company."[14] Unfortunately for Haight, no one came.

George Stinney, executed in South Carolina in 1944, began his death row experience with an apparent lack of concern. After the 14-year-old boy received the sentence of death and came to understand what he faced, his attitude changed. A few weeks before he died, he wrote to his mother, claiming innocence and begging her to help him. It was to no avail: "All she knew how to do was pray" (Stout, 1982).

A final illustration of this category is Terry Roach, the retarded and mentally deteriorating boy executed in South Carolina in 1986. Because of his brutal crimes, he was characterized by the state as mean and cruel (*New York Times*, 11 Jan. 1986). But a reporter who interviewed Roach shortly before his execution saw him as "a terrified, cornered human being. He personified fear, not evil" (McCarthy, 1986).

The eight cases used to illustrate this category suggest a wide range of attitudes. Most of these juveniles were simply in mortal fear of the unknown and unknowable dimensions of death. Some seemed devastated by the indifference and impotence of their family and friends. A few, such as Hannah Ocuish and Pang Young, were truly alone in a hostile world and seemed crushed by that aloneness.

Pride, Defiance, Boastfulness, and Joking

Defiance in the face of execution seems consistent with the attitudes of many adolescent males. Prisoners in this category refuse to admit fear or error, even joking and playing games with the people intent upon executing them. The examples for this category all involve older males.

The first case is not an obvious example and is atypical in many respects. David Dodd was hanged in Little Rock in 1864 for being a Confederate spy.[15] He had been gathering information about the Union Army behind their lines and was caught, convicted, and sentenced to death. When given the chance to save his life by identifying other spies who had assisted him, Dodd adamantly refused and recalled a lesson from his earlier days as a cadet in a private military school: ". . . and like Nathan Hale, my only regret is that I have but one life to give to my country" (Parham, 1908:533). Dodd gave his one life at age 17 and is remembered to this day in Arkansas as a war hero.

Edward Deacons, executed at age 16 by New York in 1888, was a boastful tough guy when he died.[16] He seemed to enjoy devising complicated lies to befuddle those around him and cheerfully declared in open court that all witnesses against him were liars. Just days before his execution, the governor refused to intervene, evoking a defiant laugh from Deacons. Atop the scaffold, Deacons remained defiant to the end: "Friends, the law is about to take the life of an innocent man. That is all I have to say" (Galveston Daily News, 11 July 1888).

Joseph Murphy and his older brother James were executed by Ohio in 1933 for a murder during a bank robbery.[17] They might never have been identified and arrested had they not boasted about their crime to anyone who would listen. They recanted these boasts once arrested. They were highly critical of the criminal justice process that brought them to Ohio's electric chair and went to their deaths defiant and denying their guilt.

A New Yorker with a similar attitude was William Byers, executed there in 1956 at the age of 19.[18] He and his much younger girlfriend had murdered her mother two years earlier. Awaiting trial, Byers wrote to his girlfriend ridiculing his fate: "If I do get the electric chair, I hope that they do not burn me too badly. Maybe medium rare, or well done, but not to a crisp" (Lipsig, 1962:154). Although he made an effort at trial to avoid the death penalty, when unsuccessful he reverted to his former demeanor: "He went to his death at a slow, indifferent trot, chewing bubble gum" (Lipsig, 1962:158).

Charles Rumbaugh, executed in 1985, had aspired to become a notorious criminal. Before depression descended upon him, he gave boastful accounts of his exploits and intentions. An appellate court later described him as "engaged in boasting and in making himself out to be a fearsome desperado in the eyes of his companions and in the face of peace officers" (*Rumbaugh v. State*, 589 S.W.2d 419 [1979]). When first arrested for the crime that led to his execution, he boasted to the police: "I ain't going nowhere but the electric chair" (Cox, 1979:80). The essence of his boast was to be fulfilled, if not exactly in the manner he had predicted. By the time his execution date arrived ten years later, Texas was using lethal injection to kill its prisoners. Rumbaugh went to the hospital gurney, not the electric chair (*New York Times*, 12 Sept. 1985).

These five young males, executed over a 101-year period, personify the familiar "tough young punk." All tried their best to camouflage any feelings of self-doubt or fear that they experienced, and they did so with varying degrees of success.

Penitence and Acceptance

Many condemned juveniles approach death with a desire to be forgiven by family and friends and by the surviving victims of their crimes. They politely thank the prison guards for kindnesses to them while awaiting their execution dates. They issue messages to other juveniles to learn from their fate. At least some of their words and actions are prompted by the various counselors who hover around them near the end, but some apparently arise from within, the fruits of childhood lessons.

An early example is William Batton, aged 17 when executed by the Commonwealth of Pennsylvania in 1722.[19] He had set fire to his master's house, killing three young children asleep within. Although he was mentally dull, ignorant, and illiterate, his last statement, read for him at the gallows, included an elaborate admonition: "I greatly desire all youth may take example by me, and have a care how they disobey their parents, which if I had not done, I should not have been here this day, and brought to this untimely end" (*American Weekly Mercury* [Philadelphia], 16–23 Aug. 1722, p. 2). The statement was obviously written and probably even composed by someone else, but Batton signed it with his mark.

Manuel Hernandez was executed in Arizona's gas chamber in 1934, sitting next to and holding the hand of his older brother.[20] They had been convicted and sentenced to death for killing an old prospector when Hernandez was only 17 years old. The night before their joint execution, Hernandez tried to save his older brother's life by claiming that his brother had nothing to do with the murder, but this desperate ploy was unsuccessful.

The 14-year-old boy whom South Carolina executed in 1944, George Stinney, finally came to seek forgiveness. Minutes before his execution, Stinney clutched his Bible tightly and told the sheriff that he was sorry he had committed the crime and hoped God and his parents would forgive him. He seemed to be at peace with himself, if nonetheless afraid of what was about to happen to him.

One of the loneliest juveniles ever executed, Frank Loveless, also sought at the end to win forgiveness and acceptance from his family.[21] Loveless had escaped from an Indiana reformatory and had killed a constable in Nevada, over two thousand miles from his Indiana family. He was executed by Nevada in 1944 at the age of 17 after over two years on death row. He spent the day before his execution crying. On the day of his execution he wrote long apologetic letters to his father, grandmother, and brother back in Indiana. His last request to the prison warden was: "Send some roses to my grandmother" (*Elko* [Nev.] *Daily Press*, 29 Sept. 1944).

James Echols was the last juvenile to die for rape, executed in Texas in 1964.[22] Echols was black and went along with his older black friends in the kidnap and rape of a white woman. Seventeen years old at sentencing, 19 at the time of his execution, he maintained to the end that he had not raped the victim. Nevertheless, he came to accept his fate. As he entered the death chamber, he expressed these thoughts: "I have no hard feelings against anyone and I want to thank everyone for what they have done for me" (*Houston Post*, 7 May 1964). The last thing they did for him was to execute him.

Charles Rumbaugh's careening path from boastfulness to indifference to weariness ended in a conciliatory gesture. After ten years of waiting for the state of Texas to take his life, his last words were:

About all I can say is goodbye. For the rest of you, even though you don't forgive me my transgressions, I forgive you for yours against me. That's all I wish to say. I'm ready to begin my journey. (*New York Times*, 12 Sept. 1985)

Terry Roach spent the night before his execution trying to gain the approval of those around him and to understand what was about to happen to him. He listened with rapt attention to letters read to him by his attorney, not unlike a young child listening to a bedtime story. His last statement included a message to those he had injured: "To the families of the victims, my heart is still with you in your sorrow. May you forgive me just as I know the Lord has done" (*New York Times*, 11 Jan. 1986).

The most recently executed juvenile, Jay Pinkerton, uttered perhaps the most touching last words of any.[23] Having waited six and a half years, he was finally ushered into the death chamber and strapped onto the hospital gurney, where he endured the minor sting of having intravenous tubes inserted into his arms. He encouraged the witnesses at his execution, saying: "Be strong with me. I want you to know that I'm at peace with myself and my God." Pinkerton's father, in the death chamber with his condemned son, said, "Bye, Jay." Jay Pinkerton's last words, private and personal, were overheard by all who came to see him die: "I love you, Dad" (*New York Times*, 16 May 1986).

In all seven of these cases, condemned youths made some last effort to set things right with others. They asked for forgiveness, understanding, acceptance, or even love while offering the same or more to those who would listen. The prisoners were neither defiant nor frightened but simply wanted to leave this world with their personal accounts in order.

Religious Conversion

Probably the most common theme seen in the 281 cases is the last-minute conversion to an orthodox religion and a final prayer to God for salvation. Some conversions are apparently reaffirmations of childhood religious experiences. Others seem to have no foundation. One should keep in mind that unless the prisoner adamantly refuses, prison chaplains routinely counsel death row inmates and stay with them up to the moment of execution. If the condemned juvenile wants to discuss religion, he or she usually has someone right there with whom to do so.

Some executed juveniles seem simply to have accepted a prayer suggested by their religious counselor. A classic example is that of William Batton, the illiterate boy executed by Pennsylvania in 1722.

His last statement, signed by him with his mark, closed with this
eloquent sentence:

> I yield my body to this shameful and ignominious death this
> 15th day of August, 1722, being about seventeen years of age,
> hoping God will have mercy upon my poor soul. Lord Jesus, re-
> ceive my spirit. (*American Weekly Mercury*, 16–23 Aug. 1722,
> p. 2)

Irving Hanchett, barely 15 years of age, was executed by Florida in 1910.[24] Only three months elapsed between his crime (the murder of a teenaged girl who had rejected his advances) and his execution. Hanchett had just moved to Florida from Connecticut and had
no friends or family in the area. While he was awaiting execution,
a priest baptized him into the Catholic faith, and Hanchett seemed
to be buoyed by the hope of salvation. As the 15-year-old mounted
the scaffold, he said: "Mercy, my Jesus, my Jesus, mercy. Goodbye
everyone" (*Florida Times Union* [Jacksonville], 7 May 1910).

Harley Beard was a slow-witted orphan executed in Ohio in
1914 for murdering the three people with whom he lived and for
whom he worked.[25] He made a full confession of his crime and died
less than seven months after it had occurred. His well-publicized last
words were: "I think it is awful to send me to my Father this way"
(*Portsmouth* [Ohio] *Daily Times*, 4 Dec. 1914).

Willie Whitfield was executed in 1938 by Alabama for a robbery and murder.[26] He seemed defiant until near the end of the
11-month period between crime and execution. Then he began to
consult regularly with the prison minister. His final words were part
prayer, part confession, and part complaint:

> I'm goin' on home . . . tell 'em I'm going on home to rest
> with Jesus. Preacher, all you all, goodbye. I'm ready to go. I've
> made up with the Good Master. If I hadn't did what I did I
> wouldn't be ready to go. . . . don't pull those straps so tight.
> (*Montgomery Advertiser*, 19 Aug. 1938)

Willie Francis, a black youth from Louisiana, killed a prominent white man, the brother of a police chief.[27] Francis holds the
distinction of having been electrocuted twice on dates over a year
apart. His first electrocution failed when a wire burned out in the
electric chair. Francis saw this as divine intervention: "The Lord

was with me." When he was electrocuted again in 1947, 13 months after the first attempt, the chair worked, and Francis was not spared. Francis remembered that when strapped into the chair the first time, he was thinking about going to heaven and wondering what hell was like (*Weekly Messenger* [St. Martinsville, La.], 10 May 1946). His thoughts upon being electrocuted the second time will never be known.

James Echols, the Texas youth executed in 1964 for raping a white woman, was baptized as a Catholic by the prison chaplain only weeks before he died: a religious persuasion that is unusual for a young black man in Houston. On the day before he died, Echols reflected upon his newly embraced religion: "No one wants to die, but I would rather die knowing God than not knowing Him" (*Houston Post*, 7 May 1964).

The guilelessness and simplicity of the retarded and mentally deteriorating Terry Roach reveals the essence of the cases in this category. Although confused and afraid, he nonetheless spent a considerable amount of time going over various prayer options with the prison chaplain. His admitted reason was perhaps the same as that of other, less candid condemned juveniles. He kept asking the chaplain which prayers were most likely to work—most likely to get him into heaven (Bruck, 1986).

The conversion of so many of these condemned juveniles to an orthodox religion, typically Catholicism, may be explained in several ways. Perhaps belief in what they saw as a powerful religion helped resign them to death. Perhaps they were simply covering all bases, not certain about religion, but thinking it could not hurt to embrace it, just in case what was said about heaven and hell was true. Or perhaps these last-minute conversions to religion came about because the only counselors they had near the end were chaplains. When asked what the condemned youths should do about the frightening approach of death, the chaplains may have offered one answer: turn to God. If lay counselors had been equally available, the results might have been different.

Conclusions

This anecdotal but revealing collection of facts about the attitudes of juveniles facing execution can only serve to stimulate curiosity about their true, deeper feelings. For the more recent cases, particularly those of Rumbaugh and Roach, fairly extensive and reliable information exists. As for the others, we are typically left to infer their attitudes from their last words.

As with most research, the above sketch leaves us with more questions than answers. What did these boys and girls think and feel as they contemplated the government's taking their lives? Were attitudes and perceptions different for younger and older youths? Were they different for brighter, better-educated youths? Did most of the youths progress, as at least some did, from indifference to fear to penitence to religion? And how do their attitudes about and perceptions of their impending deaths compare with those of terminally ill youths? If governments continue to execute children, we may be able to provide more answers to these questions.

Notes

1. *Connecticut Gazette and the Universal Intelligencer* (New London), 28 July 1786, 13 Oct. 1786, 20 Oct. 1786; Bolles, 1865:12; Caulkins, 1895: 576; Channing, 1786; McDade, 1961:720; Nash, 1973:418; Nash, 1980: 312; Sanders, 1970:320; Teeters and Hedblom, 1967:16–17; interview with Elizabeth B. Knox, secretary and curator of the New London County Historical Society, New London, Conn., 15 Aug. 1985.
2. *State v. Guild*, 10 N.J.L. Rep. 163 (1828); Bag, 1901:681; Lequear, 1957: 75; Snell, 1881:200; Teeters and Hedblom, 1967:15.
3. Electrocution Record of George Stinney, Jr., South Carolina Penitentiary, 16 June 1944; *Columbia* (S.C.) *Record*, 30 March 1944, 13 June 1944, 15 June 1944, 16 June 1944; *Manning* (S.C.) *Times*, 25 March 1944, 27 March 1944, 29 March 1944, 26 April 1944, 21 June 1944; *News and Courier* (Charleston, S.C.), 26 March 1944, 28 March 1944, 30 March 1944, 16 June 1944, 17 June 1944 (article and editorial), 31 Dec. 1944; *The State* (Columbia, S.C.), 26 March 1944, 30 March 1944, 8 June 1944, 9 June 1944, 10 June 1944, 11 June 1944, 12 June 1944, 13 June 1944, 14 June 1944, 17 June 1944; Bowers, 1984:500; Bruck, 1984; Bruck, 1985; Stout, 1982; Teeters and Hedblom, 1967:13.
4. *Lewis v. Mississippi* and *Trudell v. Mississippi*, 331 U.S. 785 (1947); *Lewis v. State*, 28 So.2d 122 (1946); *Trudell v. State*, 28 So.2d 124 (1946); *Catholic Action* (Natchez, Miss.), 31 July 1947; *Clarion* (Miss.) *Ledger*, 5 Jan. 1947; *Jackson* (Miss.) *Daily News*, 10 Dec. 1946, 15 Jan. 1947, 9 June 1947, 14 June 1947; *The Tribune* (Berkeley, Calif.), 4 Jan. 1947; *Woodville* (Miss.) *Republican*, 15 Nov. 1946, 17 Jan. 1947, 21 March 1947, 6 June 1947, 25 July 1947.

5. *Rumbaugh v. McCotter,* 105 S.Ct. 3544 (1985); *Rumbaugh v. Procunier,* 753 F.2d 395 (1985); *Rumbaugh v. State,* 589 S.W.2d 414 (1979); *Rumbaugh v. State,* 629 S.W.2d 747 (1982); *National Catholic Reporter,* 8 Nov. 1985, pp. 11–12, 13 (editorial), 16, 18; *New York Times,* 5 Sept. 1985, 10 Sept. 1985, 11 Sept. 1985, 12 Sept. 1985, 15 Sept. 1985 (editorial); *Plain Dealer* (Cleveland), 12 Sept. 1985; Brashfield, 1985; Cox, 1979:37; Drinan, 1985; Stubben, 1980.

6. *In re Brooks,* 267 S.E.2d 74 (1980); *Roach v. Aiken,* 106 S.Ct. 645 (1986); *Roach v. South Carolina,* 444 U.S. 1026 (1980); *Roach v. Martin,* 757 F.2d 1463 (1985); *State v. Shaw,* 255 S.E.2d 799 (S.Car., 1979); *American Bar Association Journal,* 26 March 1986, p. 26; *Newsweek,* 13 Jan. 1986, p. 74; *New York Times,* 9 Jan. 1986, 10 Jan. 1986, 11 Jan. 1986; *Time,* 20 Jan. 1986, p. 22; Bruck, 1986.

7. *Olympia Transcript* (Washington), 14 March 1874; Herberg, 1974; Paterson, 1976; Richardson, 1971:159.

8. *Cleveland* (Ohio) *Press,* 6 July 1928; *Portsmouth* (Ohio) *Daily Times,* 7 Feb. 1928, 5 July 1928, 6 July 1928; Bowers, 1984:483.

9. *Birmingham News,* 5 Nov. 1897, 10 Dec. 1897, 18 Dec. 1897, 22 Dec. 1897; Teeters and Hedblom, 1967:18; letter from Madge D. Barefield, executive secretary, Birmingham Historical Society, Birmingham, Ala., to Victor L. Streib (3 Aug. 1985).

10. *People v. Oxnam,* 149 P. 165 (1915); Bowers, 1984:411; *Los Angeles Daily Times,* 3 March 1916, 4 March 1916.

11. *Cleveland Plain Dealer,* 1 Jan. 1921, 17 March 1921, 26 March 1921, 28 March 1921, 2 May 1921, 8 May 1921, 16 May 1921, 17 May 1921, 18 May 1921, 19 May 1921, 20 May 1921, 10 May 1922; Bowers, 1984:481.

12. *Cleveland* (Ohio) *Press,* 13 July 1939; *The Enquirer* (Cincinnati), 13 July 1939; Bowers 1984:484.

13. *People v. Haight,* 50 N.E. 2d 237 (1943); *Katonah* (N.Y.) *Record,* 17 Sept. 1942, 19 Nov. 1942, 29 July 1943; *North Westchester* (N.Y.) *Times,* 24 Sept. 1942, 22 Oct. 1942, 29 Oct. 1942, 5 Nov. 1942, 12 Nov. 1942, 19 Nov. 1942; Bowers, 1984:469; Deutsch, 1950:200; letter from Thomas McDade to Watt Espy (27 June 1978).

14. Letter from McDade to Espy.

15. *Columbus* (Ga.) *Enquirer,* 16 March 1864; Parham, 1908:531; Wright, 1984:127.

16. *People v. Deacons,* 16 N.E. 676 (1888); *Galveston* (Tex.) *Daily News,* 11 July 1888; *Union and Advertiser* (Rochester, N.Y.), 10 July 1888.

17. *Cleveland* (Ohio) *Plain Dealer,* 15 Aug. 1933; *Cleveland* (Ohio) *Press,* 15 Aug. 1933; *The Enquirer* (Cincinnati), 15 July 1933; 15 Aug. 1933; Bowers, 1984:483.

18. *People v. Byers,* 131 N.E.2d 580 (1955); Bowers, 1984:471; Lipsig, 1962:147; *New York Times,* 13 Jan. 1956.

19. *American Weekly Mercury* (Philadelphia), 16–23 Aug. 1722, p. 2; Teeters and Hedblom, 1967:84.
20. *Hernandez v. State*, 32 P.2d 18 (1934); *Los Angeles Times*, 17 May 1933; *New Orleans Times-Picayune*, 7 July 1934; Bowers, 1984:402.
21. *State v. Loveless*, 36 P.2d 236 (1943); *State v. Loveless*, 150 P.2d 1015 (1944); *Elko* (Nev.) *Daily Press*, 20 Aug. 1942, 21 Aug. 1942, 24 Aug. 1942, 26 Sept. 1944, 29 Sept. 1944, 2 Oct. 1944; Bowers, 1984:452.
22. *Echols v. State*, 370 S.W.2d 892 (1963); *Houston Post*, 7 April 1964, 27 April 1964, 7 May 1964; Bowers, 1984:512.
23. *Pinkerton v. McCotter*, 106 S.Ct. 16 (1985); *Pinkerton v. McCotter*, 106 S.Ct. 400 (1985); *Pinkerton v. State*, 660 S.W.2d 58 (1983); *New York Times*, 15 Aug. 1985, 16 Aug. 1985, 26 Nov. 1985, 15 May 1986, 16 May 1986; Cox, 1981.
24. Transcript of Record of Proceedings in the Circuit Court of Volusia County, Florida, *State v. Hanchett* (6–11 April 1910); Death Warrant for Irving Hanchett, signed on 22 April 1910 and executed on 6 May 1910; *Atlanta Journal*, 7 May 1910; *Florida Times Union* (Jacksonville), 7 May 1910.
25. *Cleveland* (Ohio) *Plain Dealer*, 16 May 1914, 14 Dec. 1914; *Portsmouth* (Ohio) *Daily Times*, 4 Dec. 1914; Bowers, 1984:481.
26. *Whitfield v. State*, 182 So. 42 (1938); *Alabama* (Montgomery) *Journal*, 17 Sept. 1937, 18 Sept. 1937, 20 Sept. 1937; *Birmingham* (Ala.) *News*, 19 Aug. 1938; *Montgomery* (Ala.) *Advertiser*, 19 Aug. 1938; Bowers, 1984:400.
27. *State ex rel. Francis v. Resweber*, 31 So.2d 697 (1947); *Pittsburgh Courier*, 17 May 1947; *Weekly Messenger* (St. Martinsville, La.), 10 Nov. 1944, 17 Nov. 1944, 10 Aug. 1945, 14 Sept. 1945, 10 May 1946, 14 June 1946, 17 Jan. 1947, 11 April 1947, 18 April 1947, 25 April 1947, 2 May 1947, 9 May 1947; Miller and Bowman, 1982; Prettyman, 1961:83.

References

Bag, Green. 1901. "A Tragic New Jersey Case." *New Jersey Law Journal* 24:681–82.

Bolles, John A. 1865. *Genealogy of the Bolles Family in America*. Boston: H. W. Dutton and Son.

Bowers, William J. 1984. *Legal Homicide: Death as Punishment in America, 1864–1982*. Boston: Northeastern University Press.

Brasfield, Phillip. 1985. "'I Had Wanted to Tell Charles Rumbaugh Goodbye.'" *National Catholic Reporter*, 8 Nov., p. 12.

Bruck, David. 1984. "Executing Juveniles for Crime." *New York Times*, 16 June.

———. 1985. "Executing Teen Killers Again." *Washington Post*, 15 Sept.

———. 1986. Statement Concerning the Execution of Americans for Crimes Committed While Under the Age of Eighteen, 5 June 1986. Testimony Before the Subcommittee on Criminal Justice, Committee on the Judiciary, U.S. House of Representatives, 99th Cong., 2d sess.

Caulkins, Francis M. 1895. *History of New London, Connecticut.* New London: H. D. Utley.

Channing, Henry. 1786. "God Admonishing His People of Their Duty, as Parents and Masters: A Sermon, Preached at New London, December 20, 1786, Occasioned by the Execution of Hannah Ocuish, a Mulatto Girl, Aged 12 Years and 9 Months, for the Murder of Eunice Bolles, Aged 6 years and 6 months." Pamphlet. New London, Conn.: T. Green.

Cox, Bill G. 1979. "Crime Rampage of the Trigger-Happy Texas Killer." *True Detective,* Jan., pp. 37–39, 78–81.

Cox, Nina. 1981. "The Most Hideous Murder in Texas History." *True Detective,* Dec., pp. 30–33, 56–58.

Deutsch, Andrew. 1950. *Our Rejected Children.* Boston: Little, Brown.

Drinan, Robert. 1985. "Too Young to Die, Even by Execution." *National Catholic Reporter,* 8 Nov., p. 13.

Herberg, Ruth M. 1974. "Kanaka Joe." *Frontier Times* 48 (July–Aug.): 32–35, 41–42.

Lequear, James. 1957. *Traditions of Hunterdon.* Flemington, N.J.: D. H. Moreau.

Lipsig, Francis. 1962. *Murder—Family Style.* New York: Collier Books.

McCarthy, Colman. 1986. "A Last Talk with a Condemned Man." *Washington Post,* 13 Jan.

McDade, Thomas. 1980. *The Annals of Murder.* Norman: University of Oklahoma Press.

Miller, Arthur S., and Jeffrey H. Bowman. 1982. "Slow Dance on the Killing Grounds: The Willie Francis Case Revisited." *DePaul Law Review* 32:1–75.

NAACP Legal Defense and Educational Fund. 1988. "Death Row, U.S.A." Unpublished compilation. Available from 99 Hudson St., New York, N.Y. 10013.

Nash, Jay. 1973. *Blood Letters and Bad Men: A Narrative Encyclopedia of American Criminals from the Pilgrims to the Present.* Philadelphia: Lippincott.

―――. 1980. *Murder, America: Homicide in the United States from the Revolution to the Present.* New York: Simon and Schuster.

Parham, W. C. 1908. "David O. Dodd: The Nathan Hale of Arkansas." Pp. 531–35 in *Collection of Papers by Arkansas Historical Association,* vol. 2, edited by J. Reynolds. Fayetteville: Arkansas Historical Collection. (First published in the *Benton* [Ark.] *Times Courier,* 18 Jan. 1906.)

Paterson, T. W. 1976. "Did They Get the San Juan Killer?" *Western Frontier,* March, pp. 26–29, 49.

Prettyman, Barrett, Jr. 1961. *Death and the Supreme Court*. New York: Harcourt, Brace and World.

Reidinger, Paul. 1987. "Fate of the Teenage Killers." *American Bar Association Journal*, 1 Oct., pp. 88–92.

Richardson, David B. 1971. *Pig War Islands*. Eastsound, Wash.: Orcas Publishing Co.

Sanders, Wiley (ed.). 1970. *Juvenile Offenders for a Thousand Years*. Chapel Hill: University of North Carolina Press.

Snell, James P. 1881. *History of Hunterdon and Somerset Counties, New Jersey*. Philadelphia: Everts and Peck.

Stout, David. 1982. "A Life for a Life, Even at Age 14." *Sunday Record* (Bergen, Passaic, and Hudson counties, N.J.), 28 March.

Streib, Victor L. 1983–88. "Persons on Death Row for Crimes Committed While Under Age Eighteen." Unpublished report issued quarterly by the author.

———. 1987. *Death Penalty for Juveniles*. Bloomington: Indiana University Press.

———. 1988. "Decline and Fall of Juvenile Capital Punishment: The Beginning of the End of a Scandalous American Practice?" Paper presented at the 1988 mid-year conference of the American Psychology-Law Society, Division 41, American Psychological Association, Miami Beach, 12 March.

———. 1988. "Imposition of Death Sentences for Juvenile Offenses, January 1, 1982, Through August 1, 1988." Unpublished report.

Stubben, Dorothy. 1980. *Number 555 Death Row*. Amarillo: Coltharp Printing and Publishing (Budget Books).

Teeters, Negley, and Jack Hedblom. 1967. *Hang by the Neck: The Legal Use of Scaffold and Noose, Gibbet, Stake, and Firing Squad from Colonial Times to the Present*. Springfield, Ill.: Charles C. Thomas.

Wright, Buster W. 1984. *Burials and Deaths Reported in the Columbus (Ga.) Enquirer, 1832–1872*. Columbus, Ga.: Columbus Enquirer.

Cases Cited

In re Brooks, 267 S.E.2d 74 (1980).
Echols v. State, 370 S.W.2d 892 (1963).
Hernandez v. State, 32 P.2d 18 (1934).
Lewis v. Mississippi, 331 U.S. 785 (1947).
Lewis v. State, 28 So.2d 122 (1946).
People v. Byers, 131 N.E.2d 580 (1955).
People v. Deacons, 16 N.E. 676 (1888).
People v. Haight, 50 N.E.2d 237 (1943).
People v. Oxnam, 149 P. 165 (1915).

Pinkerton v. McCotter, 106 S.Ct 16 (1985).
Pinkerton v. McCotter, 106 S.Ct. 400 (1985).
Pinkerton v. State, 660 S.W.2d 58 (1983).
Roach v. Aiken, 106 S.Ct. 645 (1986).
Roach v. Martin, 757 F.2d 1463 (1985).
Roach v. South Carolina, 444 U.S. 1026 (1980).
Rumbaugh v. McCotter, 105 S.Ct. 3544 (1985).
Rumbaugh v. Procunier, 753 F.2d 395 (1985).
Rumbaugh v. State, 589 S.W.2d 414 (1979).
Rumbaugh v. State, 629 S.W.2d 747 (1982).
State ex rel. Francis v. Resweber, 31 So.2d 697 (1947).
State v. Guild, 10 N.J.L. Rep. 163 (1828).
State v. Hanchett (Transcript of Record of Proceedings in the Circuit Court
  of Volusia County, Florida, 6–11 April 1910).
State v. Loveless, 36 P.2d 236 (1943).
State v. Loveless, 150 P.2d 1015 (1944).
State v. Shaw, 255 S.E.2d 799 (S.Car., 1979).
Thompson v. Oklahoma, 108 S.Ct. 2687 (1988).
Trudell v. Mississippi, 331 U.S. 785 (1947).
Trudell v. State, 28 So.2d 124 (1946).
Whitfield v. State, 182 So. 42 (1938).

5

Burning at the Wire

The Execution of John Evans

RUSSELL F. CANAN

I stared at my client, John Evans, sitting on Alabama's electric chair. They call the chair "Yellow Mama." John's head was shaved; he had declined the State's offer to let him wear his own clothes and was wearing prison garb. His hands and legs were strapped to the chair. The witnesses were now in place in the observation room, separated by a glass partition from the execution chamber. John was sitting no more than fifteen feet away. The warden was about to begin the ritual of the execution.

My mind flashed to a conversation I had had with attorney Millard Farmer in Atlanta several days before. Millard has been on the front lines of the death penalty fight longer than just about anyone. Mentor and friend to all death penalty lawyers, he often speaks with great wisdom on matters far beyond the legal strategy of a case. John Evans's appeal had seemed hopeless, and there was some talk that perhaps it would be futile to go to Alabama and make a last-ditch fight. Millard said that we must never make it easy for them to kill our clients and that we should go. He also said, "Be careful, don't get dirty at no damn killing."

The State was seconds away from killing John Evans. John was

to die a long and terrifying death. The State would have blood on its
hands. Those chosen to bear witness would indeed get dirty.

□   □   □

John Evans killed Edwin Nassar during a pawn shop robbery.
Although it was clear that the shooting was not planned and that
it was done when Evans felt that Mr. Nassar was going to grab a
weapon and fire upon him, it was unquestioned that John Evans shot
and killed Mr. Nassar. John never denied his role in the crime and
in fact told the jury that he had done so.

John Evans was born into a steady middle-class family in Texas.
He had loving and concerned parents as well as fine brothers and
sisters. For reasons that could never be fully explained or understood, John had drifted from the family and entered a life of crime.
Starting with minor, juvenile-delinquent offenses, he moved his way
up to armed robbery. He lost contact with his family and ended up
in prison. Shortly after his release, he and another former prisoner
ended up in Mobile, Alabama, where they committed the capital
offense.

The legal battle to save his life was hard and complex. John
insisted on representing himself at critical times during the proceedings. At one point in 1979, the extremely harsh and cruel conditions
on death row drove him to waive his appeals and even volunteer for
execution. His attorney throughout these proceedings, John Carroll
of the Southern Poverty Law Center, had been brilliant in keeping
John alive. His family, and especially his mother, Betty, had rallied
around John's life and given him a reason to live.

By 1983 John Evans had decided to represent himself. The
conditions on death row had so depressed him that he felt that his
only choice was between immediate execution and a commutation to
life imprisonment by Governor George Wallace. When an execution
date had been set for 22 April 1983, his family prevailed upon him
to contact the Southern Prisoners' Defense Committee in Atlanta to
seek legal advice.

The Southern Prisoners' Defense Committee is a small, non-
profit project that represents death row prisoners and challenges
unconstitutional prison and jail conditions throughout the South.
Despite its rather powerful name, in 1983 the Committee consisted
of only four lawyers: Steve Bright, Bob Morin, Christy Freeman,

and myself. We often found ourselves traveling from state to state to handle last-minute crises.

At that time, only six men had been executed in the United States since the Supreme Court had upheld the death penalty. Four of those men—Gary Gilmore of Utah, Jesse Bishop of Nevada, Steven Judy of Indiana, and Frank Coppola of Virginia—had withdrawn their appeals and had volunteered for execution. John Spenkelink of Florida and Charles Brooks of Texas were unsuccessful in challenging their convictions and sentences and were put to death against their will.

Alabama had not executed a prisoner in over eighteen years. Public opinion and the media clamored for a killing in Alabama. The Attorney General of the State, Charles Graddick, was particularly in high gear. He had been the local county prosecutor who had brought the case against John and had exploited the prosecution for all it was worth in his later run for statewide office. Graddick now had his eye on the Governor's mansion and was pounding the drums in the media that if there was to be respect for law and order in the State, John Evans had to be executed, and executed now.

John was ready to give up the fight. Years on death row had worn him down. Life in the death house is the most dehumanizing and spiritually devastating form of existence that our society has chosen to inflict on its prisoners. Physically, the conditions of confinement are severe and harsh. The prisoner is locked in a small cell for 23 and a half hours a day. Imagine being locked up in your bathroom all day, year after year, John would say.

The prisoner is allowed a half-hour a day of solitary recreation in an isolated outside cage where he can do no more than walk in circles. And a death row inmate is always manacled in chains, hand and foot, whenever he is let out of his cell. John compared the recreation to a guard walking his dog. He often refused the walk as too demeaning. He'd rather exercise in his cell and try to maintain his dignity. For life on death row was a constant and never-ending battle for integrity. The barrenness, cruelty, and boredom of life on the row was designed to break down a man's will. John, I think, could have endured the physical deprivation. But like so many others, the despair of life on the row, the life of the "living dead," as they all called it, seeped into his very soul. For John was a proud man and life on death row was intended to reduce him to an animal state. He rebelled against this attempt to crush his spirit.

He did not have any faith in the legal system, and he knew the political reality all too well. He did not expect freedom, though he craved it. He knew that his crime deserved punishment and that by his actions he had surrendered his liberty. He only sought an inner peace with the hope of redemption. He had come to terms with his crime; his remorse for the death of Edwin Nassar was genuine and deeply felt. He knew that his actions had senselessly taken away a husband and father. He prayed that the Nassar family would someday forgive him.

Father Kevin was John's best friend and supporter. John's mother, Betty, had written to Father Kevin and asked him to look in on her son. Father Kevin, a boisterous and good-humored Irishman, was pastor of a small Catholic parish near the prison. He never thought that he would minister to a man on death row, and he very personally took John in as his son. John had always been cynical about the Catholic religion, but his relationship with Father Kevin gave him faith and a new-found sense of maturity.

And yet John was still a character. He had a ready grin and a sarcastic sense of humor. He made a show for his friends of his strength and would fight fear with a certain brashness. He liked me but made it quite clear that he would make the decisions on his legal case. It was, after all, his life, and he wanted to make his own statement.

Further legal appeals appeared hopeless. If Governor Wallace would grant him clemency, then he would accept a lifetime in prison. At least he would be off the "row," and he could study and participate in programs. The freedom to walk outside a cell without handcuffs on his wrists and chains on his legs meant everything to him.

I thought that John was rolling loaded dice by placing all his faith in the compassion of George Wallace. I could not believe that Wallace would commit political suicide and grant clemency. There were no established procedures for a commutation hearing, but it was clear that those who sought John's death were determined to bring public pressure to bear on George Wallace.

Attorney General Graddick set the tone with a press release issued four days before the execution, calling on Governor Wallace to deny clemency. In typically overblown language Graddick stated that "if you commute his sentence to life imprisonment your action will probably result in the de facto abolition of the death penalty in this State. . . . It is important that capital punishment exist and that it be applied in this case. Capital punishment reaffirms the moral sanctity of innocent life and it is a legitimate weapon in society's arsenal against crime."

Not content with challenging the Governor to be tough on crime, Graddick then took on the Alabama Parole Board, warning that "if you commute his sentence all that will stand between Evans and the law-abiding citizens of this State is the Parole Board and past experience has shown that the Parole Board is quite capable of and willing to release any criminal, no matter how dangerous he is." As for John Evans's character, Graddick said: "You take a gun out of his hands and he's a gutless wonder."

Graddick had certainly pushed all the right buttons, and he was only too happy to parade before the media and take credit for bringing John Evans to the electric chair. In April 1983 there was talk of little else in Alabama; letters to the editor, radio call-in shows, man-in-the-street television interviews, were all joining in the debate. Should John Louis Evans live or die?

Many people supported John. Family, friends, religious leaders, and numerous others all over the state and indeed the country wrote compassionate and pleading letters for Wallace's consideration.

John himself wrote to the Governor. His letter was a direct and sensitive plea for his life:

> There hasn't been a day since Edwin Nassar's death that I haven't thought about him, his wife, and his two little girls. Only God can know the extent of the hurt and shame that I feel.
>
> Because of my relationship with God, He has taught me how to love and care about others and He has blessed me with a fantastic desire to do something constructive and productive with my life. . . . I believe with all my heart that God wouldn't have reached so far down to lift me up and change my whole life around from being something ugly to being something worthwhile. I am a living example of the unlimited Love and Mercy of God and that fact never ceases to amaze me. . . .
>
> I've read several things that you have had to say about your physical tragedy and one thing is obvious—because of your faith in God, you were touched with a sense of mercy and the capacity for forgiveness. None of us can go through the

things we do in life without at some time needing God's Mercy but we in turn have to be able to show mercy. . . .

I pray that after reviewing all that I have said, you will find it in your heart to commute my death sentence.

May God Bless and keep you.

John Louis Evans III

The buildup for the meeting with the Governor was intense. Betty, Mark (John's brother), Father Kevin, and I drove up to the Capitol in Montgomery and used a side entrance in the hope of avoiding the media. We were unsuccessful. TV cameras, sound props, pushing and shoving, and general chaos followed us until we got inside the Capitol. The Governor's press aide ushered us into Wallace's office. John's life was in the balance.

The clemency hearing was a farce. Wallace was sitting somewhat imperiously behind a large desk. His legal aide and a PR person sat beside him on either side. Two security types stood erect in the back of the room.

Wallace greeted Betty and Mark warmly. He commented on Mark's military uniform and made small talk about place and duty of station. Father Kevin and the Governor talked briefly about common friends and seemed at ease with each other. The Governor shook my hand and nodded.

"Speak from your heart," he said. And Betty, Mark, and Father Kevin did just that. He looked at us intently with a kindly and paternal face. His presence was commanding, and he showed warmth. He really did. Betty talked about John and how he had grown and matured, and about how he had returned to the family after such a long absence. Mark said he had never known his older brother until John got locked up and they wrote to and confided in each other. Father Kevin talked about John's life in prison and how he learned to truly know Christ and how a young and angry man had learned to love others and care for those around him.

It was odd, but I felt that Wallace was moved and concerned. You could see it on his face, in his expression, and in his voice. And yet, as I sat there and watched him, I felt taken in. The guy's a great politician, he has charm, sincerity, and the right moves.

Perhaps in some way he was for real. Who knows with these guys? How could anyone not see the grief and agony of this wonder-

ful family? The sickness and the evil of the death penalty is never
more apparent than when another mother is reduced to tears in a
futile attempt to save a son.

Wallace saw those tears. He heard their pleas. He pulled out a
copy of the Bible. "This is a matter that weighs heavily with me. I'm
going to pray over John. Ma'am, you have a wonderful family and I
thank you for coming to see me."

After leaving Wallace's office, we were ushered into the office
of the Governor's press spokesman. While he was talking to the
family, another aide, a young lawyer, motioned for me to come into
the hallway.

"I just thought that you should know that although nothing is
official, the Governor's position is that he does not feel that it is appropriate to interfere in this case at this time. The Governor thought
that you as counsel would like to know that as soon as possible."
He looked at me somewhat sheepishly. Show time was over. The
execution would go forward as scheduled.

□   □   □

I waited until we were in the car before I told them the news.
We drove in silence to John Carroll's office in Montgomery. All hope
was lost and tears were shed. The execution was scheduled for Friday
morning at 12:01 A.M.

That night John Evans and I talked in the visitors' room. We
still had some legal options left, but John did not want to talk about
them. "I'll let you know. I know that Mom wants me to fight but I'm
so tired. Even if we win a new trial, Charley Graddick will never let
me alone. He needs me dead.

"Russ, I do have one request. But I want you to know that
you can say no and I'll understand completely. I've asked a friend
of mine, Rick Dent, to witness my execution. He's a young kid and
wants to write. I'm glad that he'll be there. I want to know if you
could go with him. He might need some help.

"I know that this is asking a lot, and please believe me, I will
understand. This is not part of your job. Do it, if you can, as my
friend."

I told John that I would be with him and that I would go as his
friend.

□   □   □

Albert Camus wrote in "Reflections on the Guillotine" that "[t]he man who enjoys his coffee while reading that justice has been done would spit it out at the least detail." This country has never used the guillotine but has tried almost every method of killing known to the Middle Ages. Burning at the stake, decapitation with the axe, gibbeting (a man is hung in a cage with the body exposed until decomposition), breaking at the wheel, hanging, and the firing squad are part of our history.

Daniel Frank of Jamestown, Virginia, was probably the first man executed in this country. He was hanged in 1622 for stealing a hog and a cow. In March 1988, Willie Darden was electrocuted by the State of Florida. Watt Espy, a historian living in Alabama, has so far documented and confirmed over sixteen thousand executions in the United States and expects the final tally to exceed 22,000 when his work is completed.

The electric chair was authorized by the New York State legislature in 1888. It was considered then to be the state-of-the-art technology for humane and practical executions. It was promoted by its supporters for its certainty in producing an instantaneous death.

Under the law, any method of execution that causes unnecessary pain, violence, or mutilation to the body is supposed to be barred by the Constitution. The "mere extinguishment of life" is acceptable; torture or a lingering death is not.

In 1890 William Kemmler became the first person to die in the electric chair. He was killed in Auburn Prison in New York State. By all accounts, it was a gruesome death. The generator was supplied by the Westinghouse Electric Company and used alternating current. George Westinghouse, the company's president, is reported to have said that he "thought that the job could have been done better with an axe." The *New York Press* stated that the "age of burning at the stake is past; the age of burning at the wire will pass also."

But it did not pass. Instead, electrocution became the most popular mode of slaying in the twentieth century in this country. The reports of numerous witnesses to these executions have much in common. The electrodes that make contact with the shaved human head and leg reach temperatures over 1,900 degrees Fahrenheit and can melt copper. The awesome power of 2,000 volts of electricity shoots through a human being and makes his body leap and cringe. The condemned's eyeballs can literally pop out of the sockets. The face, as well as the fingers, legs, and toes, become hideously contorted and disfigured.

It is not unusual for the prisoner to defecate and urinate during the surge of current. The vomiting of blood and saliva is common. The prisoner actually smolders under the force of the current, and the temperature of the brain approaches the boiling point of water. Doctors who have performed autopsies on electrocuted men report that the liver is so hot that it cannot be touched by a human hand.

Nicola Tesla reported after studying the effects of electrocution: "The current flows along a restricted path. . . . in the meantime the vital organs may be preserved; and pain, too great for us to imagine, is induced. . . . For the sufferer, time stands still; and this excruciating torture seems to last for an eternity."

This pain is often prolonged and repeated. In many cases it is necessary to refasten the power lines to the chair after the first surge of electricity sears the flesh but does not kill the prisoner. In May of 1946, Willie Francis of Louisiana, a 17-year-old teenager, survived two separate jolts of current. Sheriff Harold Resweber described the attempt to execute Willie Francis: "Then the electrocutioner turned on the switch and when he did Willie Francis' lips puffed out and he groaned and jumped so that the chair came off the floor. Apparently the switch was turned on twice and then the condemned man yelled, 'Take it off. Let me breathe.' "

The Sheriff finally unstrapped Mr. Francis, and the execution was halted. The State was unrelenting in its attempt to kill Mr. Francis. His attorneys argued before the Supreme Court that to subject a man to such an electrocution two separate times constituted cruel and unusual punishment. The Court rejected the plea. In a decision split by a 5–4 vote, the Court asserted that although the first attempt on Willie Francis's life caused "mental anguish and physical pain," it was "an unforeseeable accident" and not deliberate. That being the case, the Constitution was not offended.

In his dissent, Justice Burton called the Francis execution "a form of torture [that] would rival that of burning at the stake." A short time thereafter, Willie Francis was again strapped into Louisiana's electric chair. This time it worked and he was killed.

□   □   □

On the morning of 21 April 1983, I drove from Atmore to the federal courthouse in Mobile. The execution was set for 12:01 A.M.

on the twenty-second. Executions are often set at that time on the theory that if there are no stays of execution in effect, the killing should proceed at once. A midnight execution prevents the legal team from having another 24 hours to go to another court and try to stop it.

We were waiting for the Supreme Court to rule on our petition to stay the execution. We were ready to act as soon as the Court turned us down. Because the case was in a complex and unusual legal posture, we had the right to file another motion to stay the execution along with a writ of habeas corpus in the lower federal court. Steve Bright and I had drawn up the legal papers the past weekend. Although we had raised some new and substantial issues in our court papers—issues that, if given serious and reflective consideration, would have merited a reversal of John's death sentence —the timing was not right. John had tied his case in legal knots and had frustrated the system for too long. Besides, his case had become a *cause célèbre*. The public clearly wanted an execution, and legal delays were not going to save the day this time.

A Mobile attorney, Arthur Madsen, had graciously let me use his office to wait and take phone calls. Bright was in Atlanta, ready to file pleadings in the Eleventh Circuit Court of Appeals if necessary. Two other attorneys, Jerry Fisher and Brad Stetler, were in Washington, D.C., monitoring the Supreme Court. The waiting was on. The local federal magistrate had found out that I was in Mobile and called to ask my intentions. I had to put him off. I didn't really know at that time. It depended on the Supreme Court.

Word had filtered through that the Governor was open to seeing us again in less formal circumstances. Our source was a member of the press who had gotten to know John and wanted to do all that was possible to save him. He apparently had open lines to Wallace's staff. The execution was weighing on Wallace's conscience. The Governor might ask to see us again. There might be an opening. The Governor's aide would get back to us.

John's sister Susan called around noon. She was excited. The Governor wanted to see us. Could we be there by 4:00 P.M.? Was it really possible? A private plane could pick us up at Atmore at 1:00 P.M. and take us to Montgomery. We could be there by 3:00 P.M. I got on the phone to Betty and we talked it over. She wanted to be near John this day. Susan and I would take the plane.

I rushed to the Atmore airport. George Kendall of the ACLU

hurried from Atlanta to Mobile in case the pleadings had to be filed while I was in Montgomery. I met Susan and we were in the air. I don't mind flying, but small, private planes I can do without. I think Susan felt the same. We talked about John and how much he had grown over the past few years. About how he had come back to the family, and that no matter what, the family had been brought back together. She had feelings of guilt that she had let her brother down and that's why he had gone the way he did. Indeed, the whole family felt that way.

We started talking about my family. I also had a brother who somehow had gotten lost. Committing petty crimes, dropping out of high school, running around with juvenile delinquent types. My parents finally enlisted him in the army with a guaranteed posting in Western Europe. Vietnam heated up and he volunteered for duty there and was killed in action.

And so we talked of families and guilt and responsibility. I think Susan was grateful for the opportunity to plead for her brother's life. We arrived in Montgomery and went straight to the Governor's mansion.

Governor George Wallace sat in his wheelchair in his upstairs bedroom. He was dressed informally in casual slacks and a sport shirt. Next to him was his legal aide. Susan was next to me; she was all strength and grace. She was there to plead for her brother's life, but she would retain her dignity.

We were sitting in a small circle, all of us leaning forward as if sharing secrets. Wallace has impaired hearing, and one has to talk very, very loudly in order to be understood. The effect was strange; the four of us were sharing something very intense, the power of life and death in the balance, huddling together and almost shouting to be heard. The execution was seven hours away. This was our second meeting with the Governor. We had been through the formal clemency hearing, such as it was. John's mother, Betty, had been eloquent in her plea for her son. Why were we going through this again? To what point?

The Governor looked at Susan. "I heard that you all wanted to talk again, and I am always willing to talk to you folks so please talk from your heart."

Susan's hand slowly clenched. "Governor, you heard my mother the other day. You heard that John is really a different person today than he was years ago. That he has found the Lord and that he gives the family so much. We love him so much and need him so much.

"My mother has been through so much, this will just hurt her and grieve her so. After all this time John has come back to the family and we all need him.

"I know that you believe that people can change. I have heard so much that you have changed and that your feelings towards blacks have changed, you even said so in your inauguration speech. So John has changed and has become a good person. . . . Just like you he has seen the light, and we need him and love him so much. Please spare his life, Governor. Only you can do that now."

Wallace seemed a little startled. The reference to blacks and his well-publicized inauguration speech clearly surprised him. "I do believe that people can change. But you may have misunderstood some of the things about my feelings about black people. I grew up among black folk. In fact, black folks raised me. I love black people and always have. What I said recently is that we lived in a different time back then when things were done differently and the way of life was different. Times have changed for the better, and I wanted everyone to know that I for one am glad that times have changed. But I have always loved the black people. Always.

"I'm glad to know that John has found Christ. I have found him too and I pray for him and have prayed over him every day. I was deeply moved with what your mother said and with what you have said today about John. I am glad that he has found peace."

This all sounded like a canned speech to me. What were we doing here, wasting our time and listening to a politician give a speech? And yet something about the Governor was truly sincere. He did appear to be troubled about the execution. I certainly did not know the man, but my sense was that he was listening.

Wallace was in bad health. He had been in and out of hospitals the last few months. He looked terrible. His speech was slow and exaggerated, his face puffy. He seemed heavily medicated. It was clear that he had run for his last election. His political career was over. There was even talk that he might resign from office because of his health. Maybe he really didn't care about public opinion. I knew that such hope was perhaps naive, but we had no choice. George Wallace and George Wallace alone could save John Evans's life. If there was any chance to persuade him, it had to be now.

I had gone through a number of clemency pleas and had even

secured the minutes of appeals that had been made years ago. Those words didn't seem to fit. But I had also heard that Wallace had once defended a death row inmate many years ago.

"Governor, I heard that years ago when you were a young lawyer, you sat in my chair before another governor and that you saved a man's life. And now, years later, I am trying to search for those very same words that you used when you pled for clemency, the same feelings and thoughts that crossed your mind and came from within when you reached out and found that common bond of mercy that is within us all.

"You already know John's fine family. Betty told you about John's upbringing in Texas and how he got away from the family; of how he was lost at an early age. And you know the change in him, the real change that has been attested to by so many people, by his mother, sister, and brother. By Father Kevin, who has been with John for all these years on death row. And by John himself, you have read his words and I know taken them to heart. This a human being worth saving—and only you can save him, Governor. This a fine, good, decent family worth protecting—and only you can protect them from the pain and grief that is sure to follow."

Wallace sat there with his eyes locked into mine. He leaned back. "I remember that case very, very well," he said in a soft voice. "It was a case where a young colored fellow was as stubborn as he could be. Well, he just about cut his girlfriend's head off in a fight. Before the trial the State offered him a life sentence, and this fella was as stubborn as he could be and so he refused. The jury gave him the chair.

"I told the Governor two things, as I recall." He said this with just a slight smile, as every trial lawyer does when recounting a well-played move. "I told him that we shouldn't give this fella the chair just because he was stubborn and that the State didn't really want to see the man die."

Wallace then paused, thought something over for a few seconds, and then went on. "I also told him that in the county where the killing took place, there had never been an execution for a colored man who killed his girlfriend over a fight. It had never been done and I didn't think it fair that this fella should have been the first, just because he was stubborn—especially when the State was going to let him off with a life sentence.

"You know, in my other terms as Governor I never had to go

this far. I was always glad when the term ended and I didn't have to
make the decision." He gently tapped his Bible and said he would
pray some more. He then looked at Susan. "The Lord came to me
late in life, and I'm glad that John has found him too. When I was
young and vigorous I didn't really think of such things. But now . . .

"John has found some peace and he has a fine, fine family. If
the Lord takes him tonight, then he will be home."

□   □   □

John spent the day saying goodbye to his family and friends.
He saw Kathy Ansheles and Jenny Johnston of the Alabama Prison
Project. Kathy and Jenny had supported John through his many years
on death row and were very close to him. Their efforts for John and
other prisoners in seeking to make the conditions on death row more
humane were remarkable. Outside on the prison grounds, other supporters maintained a vigil in protest against John's execution.

Betty and Mark had their last few minutes with John. The loss
of a loved one is hard enough; that the State will deliberately kill a
son and brother in the name of justice is much too hard to bear.

Later that night, Mark drove me to the prison. He would wait
for me while I went in to see John. It was around 8:30 P.M.—three
and a half hours before the execution. I stopped in to see Warden
J. D. White. The Warden had been courteous and considerate to the
entire family. There was none of the harassment of the condemned
that seems to be part of the killing ritual. The guards had been re-
spectful of John's situation and had not taunted him. Some were even
sympathetic.

One guard in particular, Joe, was friendly with John and had
been asking me what I thought of his chances. He seemed very
nervous. "Russ, I'm damned glad that I'm not part of the execution
squad. I've grown to think that John's all right. I never wanted this
part of the job. Never really thought we'd have this back, if you want
to know the truth."

Joe let me in to see Warden White. The Warden let me know
the details. He talked about the last meal, steak and shrimp. No beer
allowed—it was against regulations. John's head would be shaved
an hour before the execution. Father Kevin would be allowed to
administer the last rites. At 11:30 P.M. the witnesses would assemble
at a guard station and would be escorted into the witness room.

Later, the prison chaplain, Martin Weber, would be allowed to see John. I didn't like Weber at all. He was all too much the company man. After all the years John had spent on death row, he hardly knew Weber. Now, with John's death hours away, Weber all of a sudden had a deep reverence for his soul. Weber also owned and operated the only motel in town, where we were all staying. He had made a deal with John that in exchange for free lodging for the family, John would make a video for Weber's church group on lessons for youth. After the execution, Weber hawked the video to the highest bidder in Hollywood, where it was used in a docudrama. Weber later had to plead guilty in criminal court to conflict-of-interest charges for profiting from his state employment.

The execution squad had practiced their roles every day for the past seven days. Under Alabama law, the Warden is the one who pulls the switch. No blank bullets in the rifle here. Everyone was a professional. The Yellow Mama had been tested every day for the past week, and she was all set.

"John seems ready. He seems at peace. In some way I think that he's relieved. Joe will bring you to John's cell. I hope you understand that regulations require stricter security, and he'll have to strip-search you. I appreciate your professional attitude through all this."

I thanked him too. I thanked him for his professional attitude and his courtesy. I thanked him for making it easier for John and his family. We shook hands.

I had to wonder at our roles. We were professionals. He was the executioner and I was the defense lawyer. Here we were thanking each other for being so professional. One pro to another. For doing what? Making a hard job more bearable? For helping reduce tensions all around? For making it go down easier?

Damn, I thought. This man is going to kill John in about three hours. He is going to pull the switch and shoot electricity through John's head and fry his brains out. That's exactly what he's going to do.

And here I am thanking him for being a pro. What was I doing in all this? Another pro. A respectable cog in this grotesque machinery of butchery. My job was to help provide a clean execution. I should be screaming and shouting. I should make them drag me out of there—create a scene. I should make it as hard and tough and as sick and inhumane as it was. I should be making my voice heard in this ritual of cruelty. I should make these bastards hear my voice and know what the hell they are doing.

And yet my rage gave way to thinking about John and his suffering. I had to serve him. And serving him meant taking my role as set out in the rites of the execution.

I tried to focus on the ceremony. Byron Eshelman, a former death row chaplain at San Quentin Prison, once wrote:

> Only the ritual of an execution makes it possible to endure. Without it the condemned could not give the expected measure of cooperation to the etiquette of dying. Without it, we who must preside at their deaths could not face the morning of each new execution day.
>
> Nor could you.
>
> No matter how you think you feel about capital punishment, no matter how you imagine you would face the legal giving or taking of life, you would meet the reality of it by holding tightly to the crutch of ritual.

I had to be strong for John. If it was easier for him to accept his death and make peace within himself, then I would do all I could do to help him.

Joe escorted me to a side office, where I was to be strip-searched. Joe was apologetic and I told him that I understood and that it didn't matter. I then took off all my clothes and, spread-eagled against the wall, was completely searched.

Joe told me that he thought John was holding up. I told him that if I didn't get the chance later on, I appreciated all he had done. I thought that his eyes were tearing up, although I'm not sure.

I walked past the execution chamber. I didn't look at the chair. I had seen it before. John's cell was next to the chair. A number of officers were assigned to watch him. According to prison regulations, he had been observed 24 hours a day for the past three days. John would not be allowed to commit suicide. The sentence of the court had to be fulfilled.

His TV was on for the guards to watch. I remember that it was loud and that "Hill Street Blues" was on. Frank and Joyce in bed or something.

They would not allow me into John's cell, but we embraced

through the bars. He was being strong for me. I told him that the Eleventh Circuit Court of Appeals was still considering his case and that there was hope. He knew this sounded false and he smiled. I forced a smile too. Even if we got the court in Atlanta to go our way, the Supreme Court would have their shot, and we both knew what that meant.

"Russ, if we get the stay tonight, I want to be alone to wait out the Supreme Court. I don't want to have to say goodbye all over again. It's just too hard on my mom and the family. They shouldn't have to go through it all over. They really love me . . ." He paused and got a little choked up. He paused and waited. We held hands. "And I really love them.

"Don't feel bad. You did all you could do. Thank all the people that I don't even know, in Atlanta and D.C. and those folks out there in the vigil. You know it's a great feeling to have all those people behind you. It makes it so much easier."

I looked at him and felt some trembling. "John, I really admire you. I wish that we could have done more. I . . ."

He interrupted me. "Hey, buddy, please. You guys were great. You really were. Have a Bud on me. I'll see you later. Thanks again."

We embraced one more time and I left.

□   □   □

Later that night the Eleventh Circuit Court of Appeals in Atlanta granted a stay of execution. Back at the motel there was confusion. Some of John's friends were ecstatic and joyous. The family was more restrained. I had told them that the fight was not over and that the State would undoubtedly take an emergency appeal to the Supreme Court.

The State did so the first thing in the morning. We filed our legal opposition shortly thereafter. Under Alabama law, the warrant to carry out the execution expired at 11:59 P.M. that night. If the Court failed to rule on the State's appeal by midnight, we might make it. Word was out from the prison that if the Court lifted the stay, the execution would go forward promptly. I was told by Warden White to be available by phone all day. If the authorities could not locate me, the execution would go on as planned.

We waited in the motel all day. Outside, more and more people joined the vigil. We walked from room to room in fearful anticipation. Betty, Susan, and Mark told warm stories of family life in Texas.

We all played with Jenny Johnston's two-year-old daughter, Sarah, who laughed and giggled at every chance. We created a game with Sarah's giant beachball as she ran up and down the hallway kicking and punching it all over.

Rick Dent and I talked briefly about our fear and wondered if we should actually watch the execution after they put the hood on John's head. We had no idea what to do.

Around 7:00 P.M. Steve Bright called from Atlanta. I could tell from the tone of his voice that it was all over. The Supreme Court had dissolved the stay. There was nothing left to do.

As soon as I hung up, Warden J. D. White was on the phone. He was very formal this time. I was informed that a state police car would pick us up at the motel in 45 minutes.

I went to tell Betty but she already knew. The news had flashed on the radio. There was confusion and fear. Jenny was hysterical. Rick and I looked at each other in desperation. I excused myself for a few minutes and called Dorothy in Atlanta. We talked about going to the country on Sunday. I asked her to call my parents and tell them that I was all right.

I sat down and wrote out a statement for the press. A last appeal to George Wallace.

We all gathered in Betty's room. We stood in a circle and held hands as Father Kevin said a prayer. Betty hugged Rick and me as we went to the motel lobby.

I went in front of the cameras and read my plea to Governor Wallace. "The legal process is at an end. There are no more appeals to take. Yesterday we had a personal conference with Governor Wallace asking clemency for John. The Governor said he would keep an open mind and would pray on the matter.

"We are now attempting to call the Governor to ask for mercy. John Evans' life is now in Governor Wallace's hands. We ask him to save it." The state police car was waiting for us outside.

It was pouring rain with thunderstorms and lightning. We could barely see the countryside in the storm. The flashes of lightning brightened the land every so often and made it all the more surreal. There were two state troopers in the front, Rick and I in the back seat. Nobody said a word.

We arrived at the prison in a few minutes. Drenched by the gusts of wind and rain, we were directed to a small guard outpost. Inside were three reporters. The five of us stood there waiting. Mark

Harris, from United Press International, was shaking his head. He had just found out that day that his wife was pregnant, and now he was doing this job. The wind and the rain pounded the shed.

A guard came in and patted us down. We then followed him outside to the rear entrance to the prison. It was a short walk to the witness room.

As soon as I walked in, I saw John sitting on the electric chair. Our eyes locked immediately, and he nodded to me. I nodded back and kept eye contact with him. His head was shaved and he was strapped around his legs, chest, and arms into the chair. There was a slit cut open on the left leg of his pants where an electrode was attached.

Inside were two doctors, Chaplain Weber, and Commissioner Fred Smith. Weber was operating a closed-circuit video camera, which was to show the execution to the rest of the press somewhere inside the prison. Smith was on an open telephone line to Governor Wallace and his aides. Warden White entered the witness room and announced that the civilian witnesses were now in place. Smith communicated that information to Wallace and asked if there were any stays of execution now in effect. He announced to Warden White that there were not and that the sentence of the Court could now be executed.

We were separated from the execution chamber by a glass window. We were about fifteen feet away from John. Warden White went into the chamber and read the formal death warrant. It was supposed to take only a few minutes but it seemed much longer. Two other uniformed guards were next to the chair.

John was calm. He kept staring at Rick and me. John was then allowed his final statement. He said, "I have no malice for anyone, no hatred for anyone."

Warden White then left the chamber and went to a room behind the chair, where he would pull the switch. John looked at us one more time. The guards attached an electrode-filled headpiece to his shaved head. They put a black hood over his face.

The guard then took a three-foot-long stick that looked like a lollipop with the word "Ready" on it and raised it to the back window of the chamber as a signal to Warden White.

At 8:30 P.M. the first jolt of 1,900 volts of electricity shot through John's body. It lasted 30 seconds. Sparks and flames erupted from the electrode tied to his leg. John's body slammed against the straps holding him in the chair, and his fists clenched. The electrode burst from the strap holding it in place and caught on fire. A large puff of grayish smoke and sparks poured out from under the hood that covered his face. John's body straightened out and quivered. An overpowering stench of burnt flesh and clothing began pervading the witness room. When the current stopped, he fell back into the chair.

The two doctors went into the chamber to pronounce him dead. One doctor put the stethoscope on his heart. He turned and nodded to us, the usual sign that a person is dead. But he meant the opposite, that he had found a heartbeat. The other doctor examined John and confirmed it.

The doctors left the execution chamber. The guard reattached the electrode to John's leg and fixed the strap. He set up the power lines again.

John's chest rose evenly as he continued breathing. A gush of saliva oozed from his face and out from the black hood onto his white prison clothes. John's breathing was slow and regular.

Mark Harris, the reporter, said out loud, "He's survived."

At 8:34 the second jolt of 1,900 volts of current was sent into John's body. The stench of burning flesh was nauseating. More smoke came from his head and leg. John's hands gripped the arms of the chair. Again, the doctors examined John. Again, they reported that he was still alive.

It was all out of control. Commissioner Smith did not know what he was doing. Warden White was walking from the generator to the execution chamber.

I called out to Smith: "Commissioner, I ask for clemency. This is cruel and unusual punishment. Communicate that to the Governor."

Smith ignored me. Again, I made my plea.

"I'm his lawyer. I ask for clemency."

Smith's eyes appeared to be tearing. This time he spoke into the phone and informed Wallace of my request. Meanwhile, they prepared the chair for the third attempt. Warden White opened the door to the witness room, and Smith said: "Hold everything. They're asking for clemency."

Minutes later Smith announced: "The Governor will not interfere. Proceed."

They were ready for the third jolt. Once again another charge of electricity was sent through John's body. Once again, his head and leg boiled. There was more smoke and sparks. Rick and I held hands in horror. This jolt lasted 30 seconds.

At 8:44 the doctors pronounced him dead. His body was charred and smoldering. The execution of John Evans took 14 minutes.

As Warden White escorted us out of the institution, a prisoner blew "Taps" on a trumpet. Outside the rain and thunder kept pounding.

Later that night Betty issued a statement for the press. It read: "I am proud of my son. He left this life as a true Christian."

□   □   □

John's barbaric death was just another part of the ritual of killing. He had been burned alive and his body mutilated. The cruelty and suffering that John endured shocked many people around the country and the world. The *Times* of London called John's death "grotesque." The *Oakland Tribune* said that the "torture execution of John Louis Evans lifts the veil on official murder. . . . It is the law of the jungle brought indoors, carrying with it, inevitably, jungle sights and sounds."

□   □   □

Several weeks later ten-year-old Stan Cox, a schoolboy in Valdosta, Georgia, decided to build a model electric chair as a school project. The press reported that he wanted to make the chair as realistic as possible. A photograph of young Stan and his electric chair made the papers. It did indeed look very realistic.

The boy got the idea following John Evans's execution in Alabama. According to Stan's teacher, the chair couldn't kill anyone, but you couldn't tell by looking at it. When you flip the switch, the chair lights up.

Stan got some help in building his electric chair from his Uncle Jack. The leg cuffs were made from an old belt. The headpiece was made from a baseball cap.

6

Another Attorney for Life

MICHAEL MELLO

As the number of condemned prisoners in the United States grows, so does the problem of finding competent attorneys to handle death penalty cases when the execution date draws near (Mello, 1988). In this essay, I would like to reflect on the motivations, rewards, and frustrations connected with this type of work, based on my five years of defending those who live under a sentence of death in Florida.

"Why do you represent people who are sentenced to death? Isn't it depressing?" I have been asked such questions so often, by so many people with different degrees of seriousness, that I have tried to find some pat answers, or at least one pat answer suitable for wineglass repartee. My attempts have been unsuccessful. This is not because I am ashamed of what I do or because I am unwilling to debate the merits of the death penalty. It is because I have been unable to find a way to express succinctly the intensity, the emotional highs and lows, of working for people who are litigating for their lives. I lack the words to describe how rewarding, as well as how frightening and stressful, this work can be.

This essay presents the same problem. I spend most of my working days (and a few nights) writing legal briefs, petitions, and

Acknowledgement: I would like to thank Ruthann Robson, without whom this essay would never have been written. It was first drafted when the author was a staff attorney with the Office of the Capital Collateral Representative in Tallahassee, Florida.

81

memoranda in capital cases. Yet this reflective essay is the most difficult death penalty writing assignment I have ever undertaken. I wonder if questions of motives would be so difficult were I a construction worker, a secretary, or a nuclear physicist. Jobs can have several different rewards, including money, prestige, education, and variety. Such reasons have only limited relevance in explaining why attorneys would ever want to handle death penalty cases.

Yet there are few other paying jobs that would permit me to spend all of my working time and energy fighting the system of government-sponsored homicide. I believe this system is an unambiguous disgrace to civilized humanity. My cases involve not so much debates about the wisdom of the death penalty in theory—its abstract morality or immorality—but rather case-by-case technical attacks upon a legal system that selects which citizens have lost their entitlement to live. As Charles Black demonstrated more than a decade ago in *Capital Punishment: The Inevitability of Caprice and Mistake* (2d ed., 1981), the probability of mistake and the omnipresence of arbitrariness in the imposition of the death penalty pervade this system. My experience supports Black's thesis that the death penalty can never be administered in a fair and evenhanded way. A clear sense of the system's basic unfairness is an important motivating factor for my work.

A second motivation is the belief that effective advocacy can reveal latent injustices and therefore force the system to work as it should, even in the most apparently hopeless and seemingly clear-cut cases. For example, Theodore Bundy, infamous as Tallahassee's Chi Omega killer, has been consistently portrayed by the national media as the essence of evil itself. Death penalty supporters cite Bundy as the ultimate justification for the death penalty. I have heard some people who generally oppose capital punishment say that they would make an exception for Theodore Bundy. Such death penalty opponents take care to distance themselves from Bundy's case, carefully pointing out that most capital cases are not nearly so heinous.

Yet Bundy's present attorneys, who are representing him without fee, have pieced together a picture of the case quite different from the media's portrayal of the former law student turned mass murderer. Bundy has never been charged with, much less convicted of, most of the crimes attributed to him. He has been convicted of, and sentenced to death for, two crimes. He might well be innocent of at least one; the prosecution's case at trial depended on hypnotically created and unreliable testimony. Concerning the other crime, the sentencing jury (culled of all death penalty opponents and drawn from a community that had been saturated for months with prejudicial pretrial publicity) initially split six to six on whether Bundy should receive the death penalty. The jury had never been told that a tie vote on penalty was permissible (and would be treated as a recommendation of life imprisonment), so they continued to deliberate. One juror finally switched sides, making the vote seven to five for death. In both cases, the state had been willing to accept pleas of guilty in exchange for sentences of life imprisonment, but Bundy refused to plea-bargain. There is a good argument that his decision was itself the product of mental illness and incapacity.

Posttrial investigation almost always discloses important factual information not discovered by trial attorneys, who often work with extremely limited resources (Goodpaster, 1983). Sometimes new evidence of innocence is found (Bedau and Radelet, 1987). Sometimes the crime may be explained, at least in part, by factors beyond the inmate's control, such as mental illness or a childhood of extreme abuse or neglect. Sometimes evidence of a defendant's positive qualities is found, making it less simple to reduce him or her to a subhuman object who has no right to live.

A major problem I regularly encounter is that the courts may be unwilling to revisit the case in light of such newly discovered evidence. However discouraging it may be when courts reject such legal claims, the litigation is still making a record for the future. Taken as a whole, these cases form a historical record of whom the state is killing and under what circumstances. The cases document that the "modern" death penalty is just as unfair as ever, that the new procedures are merely cosmetic, and that fundamental flaws in the system still exist (Amnesty International, 1987). I sometimes take the view that I am litigating for the historians, the sociologists, and the anthropologists, in addition to litigating for the courts.

Questions about my motives are most difficult to answer when they come from someone I represent. Our relationship will be greatly influenced by how far along in the legal process the inmate's case is when we first meet. All have already been sentenced to death. At the early stages, when we can expect that the execution will not happen for several years—if it happens at all—our relationship evolves at its own speed. It is, of course, impossible to generalize, as every case is unique. Sometimes we become close; in other cases we do not.

Some inmates are intensely interested in every legal development; others want to know, but they want the attorney to bring the subject up and pursue it; still others want to talk only about their families, their lives on death row, or the state of the world in general. Many inmates are mentally ill in one form or another, ranging from gentle neurosis to flamboyant psychoses, severe retardation, and neurological impairment (Lewis et al., 1986). Early in the legal process, the death penalty does not eclipse all else, although it provides the subtext for much of our conversation. We can be expansive and talk about a wide range of subjects, including my reasons for being there.

In most cases, however, the client and I have not had the luxury of getting to know each other through a slowly developing relationship. The scarcity of death row attorneys in Florida and the frequency with which execution dates have been scheduled by its governors have meant that I often meet the inmate for the first time when the execution date has been set for the forthcoming month. I must get to know the inmate fast and gain his trust so that he will rely on my judgment and, more important, share information with my colleagues and me. The first step in most postconviction efforts is to compile a complete life history of the inmate. Often the information needed is of the most intimate sort and may require the inmate to confront and share painful feelings and long-buried memories. The urgency of an impending execution date means that the legal team must develop, and sometimes force, trust and closeness at an accelerated pace.

The cases that are most difficult are those in which the inmate is running out of legal possibilities for relief. Such cases have been through the entire legal process in both state and federal courts at least once, and are therefore called "successors." When an execution date is set in a case requiring successive litigation, both the inmate and the lawyer know that the chances of obtaining a stay of the execution are slim. We must strike a balance between ephemeral hope and hard reality.

The improbability of securing a stay of execution, which is linked to the increasing hostility of the courts to successors, presents lawyers with intractable dilemmas. Should scarce legal resources be expended on cases in which we will probably not succeed in preventing the execution? The effort requires an enormous investment of time, work, and emotional energy. For me, one important component of this decision is the impact on the inmate of a last-ditch effort: does the litigation effort, which inevitably raises the inmate's hopes that he will escape his imminent execution date, impede his ability to work through the (uncertain) fact of impending death? Does such litigation—such literally last-minute litigation—foster denial of the reality of the possibility of death?

Perhaps the most chilling questions involve what a lawyer should do if the inmate decides not to pursue further attempts to ward off the executioner. I can appreciate that a person could conclude that death is preferable to the uncertainty of death row and even to life imprisonment in a maximum-security prison (Bluestone and McGahee, 1962; Gallemore and Panton, 1972; R. Johnson, 1981; Radelet et al., 1983). Assuming that the inmate is mentally competent and that the decision is an informed one, should the attorney give effect to his client's wishes? If so, then is the lawyer respecting the inmate's human dignity and his right to make the most personal and intimate life choice, one of the few such choices permitted to death row inmates (K. Johnson, 1981)? Or is the lawyer simply acquiescing in the inmate's suicide and, thus, making it easier for the state to execute others who do not want to die (Strafer, 1983; White, 1987)? How does one balance the choices and desires of one's client with the interests of other death row inmates in resisting executions?

I am thankful that I have not yet encountered a client who did not want to fight in the courts until the end, since Florida inmates have thus far refused to be volunteers for execution. From my perspective, legal resources must be spent in all cases, even in those where there is small likelihood of even temporary success. This is so because the legal system that decides who lives and who dies operates in no small measure on the basis of chance, luck, and arbitrariness. From time to time, albeit rarely, courts do grant stays in successors. The stakes, not the odds, are what is important. Even when the stays are temporary and even when they do not result in eventual victory—a life sentence or a new trial—this sort of litigation can buy the inmate time, sometimes as little as five hours and sometimes as much as years. This may not be what lawyers usually mean when they talk of "winning." But redefinition of the notion of winning is an important way of coping with a system that is often indifferent and increasingly hostile. To win time is to win. During that time, new evidence beneficial to the condemned person's case may come to light. Also during that time, the condemned, like the rest of us, feel joy and sorrow, have hopes and dreams, grow and change. In short, they live their lives.

Living one's life, even in the close confines of death row, is always much more than a legal matter. This is particularly so in the weeks and months prior to a scheduled execution date. It is essential that the human, extralegal needs of the inmates are recognized and, where necessary, advocated; often the attorneys challenging the inmate's underlying conviction and sentence are not the best ones to fulfill this role. In Florida, death row inmates are fortunate to have a few people who assist them and their families in coping with the psychological and spiritual process of preparing for possible death. This nonlegal counseling and support help turn death from an abstract principle to concrete reality, and also help the inmate take care of the unfinished business of this lifetime. This places the legal struggle in perspective. We fight not only death, but also despair. My goals are to ensure that the inmate knows that all hope is not lost —that the battle continues and that he will not be abandoned—but also that the outlook is grim and that he should be preparing himself to die.

Nevertheless, because of the nature of crisis advocacy, this perspective has only limited utility to me as a lawyer. To be a forceful advocate, one can never view the impending execution as inevitable. While a realistic appraisal of the legal situation is essential to effective lawyering, the zealous presentation of the case before the courts requires a belief in victory. The litigation at this stage is uniquely rough and tumble, with many of the trappings of judicial decorum suspended. Often, virtually all of the other actors in the system, from prosecutors to judges to courtroom personnel to prison officials, expect the execution to go forward and resent the interference by the inmate and his lawyer. Stopping that momentum requires a belief that the scheduled execution will not occur.

This belief has retarded my own process of dealing with the death of my clients. This was brought home to me forcefully in the case of Ronald Straight, who was executed in May 1986 following a round of successive litigation. I had become especially close to Mr. Straight and his mother in the last month of his life, and I strongly believed that his execution would offend the constitutional rights that protect us all. The Supreme Court ultimately denied a stay of execution (by a vote of five to four) less than five minutes before the scheduled time of execution. There was no time to assimilate the reality (of losing by only one vote) and the finality (of there being nothing left that lawyers could do to switch the one vote needed to save Ronnie Straight's life). Straight was being strapped into the electric chair. I will never forget the waves of helpless rage that washed over me as the clerk of the Supreme Court read me the orders denying the stay. It would have been easy—too easy—to blame the Court as an institution, the five Justices who voted to deny the stay, or the one Justice who could have changed his or her mind. Instead, I found that the real target of my rage was myself: a participant in the system of legal homicide. I am a participant who advocates for the condemned, but a participant nonetheless. Was I serving to legitimate the system by helping to provide sanitized executions, executions with the aura of legalism and therefore the appearance of fairness?

As a lawyer, I am constrained by the rules of the game I have chosen to play. Although a skilled manipulator of these rules can meet with success, to be "effective," a lawyer must understand and accept, at least tacitly, the system and its principles. On a personal level, the most frustrating principle to accept is one of the most fundamental: *stare decisis*, the doctrine of precedents. In the minds of a majority of the Justices on the Supreme Court, the constitutionality of the death penalty itself is no longer a serious question. The system of capital punishment still requires fine tuning, but the fundamental issues have been resolved by the Court in favor of the constitutionality of the death penalty. The cases upholding it have been affirmed repeatedly over the past decade, indicating that capital punishment is here to stay, at least for the foreseeable future. While it is certainly untrue to say that precedents are eternal, given the present political climate and the current personnel on the Supreme Court, there is little likelihood of the Court's redefining the death penalty as unconstitutional.

To be sure, important legal issues remain to be resolved in individual cases. Such issues, however, are different from the basic, systemic issues that once typified death penalty litigation. Prior issues revolved around such questions as whether retribution is a legitimate goal of the penal system, whether the death penalty is arbitrary, whether the imposition of capital punishment is racist, and whether capital punishment deters crime more effectively than lengthy imprisonment. This narrowing of issues from the systemic to the individual is exemplified by the present state of litigation surrounding deterrence. It is no longer viable to litigate that the evolving social scientific evidence demonstrates that the death penalty does not deter. Instead, advocacy concerns the right of an individual defendant to present social scientific evidence at his or her own trial. The goal is to save the individual defendant rather than to attack the core assumptions or constitutionality of the death penalty itself. In fact, to the extent that specific cases present issues of broader application, I often try to deemphasize the larger questions. The question I most dread at oral argument is, "Counsel, if we rule your way, won't we also have to grant relief in a lot of other cases that present the same claim?"

I do not mean to suggest that there is a clear line between "systemic" defects in capital punishment and "individual" defects in specific cases. The unfairness of a particular death sentence is often symptomatic of more general flaws in the death penalty system itself. There has, however, been a shift in the ways that courts and litigants understand and confront these problems. The courts are no longer interested in broad-based attacks on the death penalty. Thus, the fight is for one life at a time. The irony is the need to convince the courts that granting relief in a particular case will not "open the floodgates" to granting relief in many other cases.

The precedents that define the landscape of present litigation on the death penalty form the world within which the zealous advocate must operate. It is a world within which killing is accepted as legally permissible. Resistance to executions therefore becomes paradoxical. The system is attacked, but this attack becomes institutionalized and thus, to some extent, domesticated.

Yet the ironies inherent in the system of capital punishment are not confined to death row inmates and their advocates. For example, in 1985 the Florida legislature created and funded the Office of the Capital Collateral Representative (CCR) to represent those Florida death row inmates who did not otherwise have lawyers. The legislature did so at the behest of State Attorney General Jim Smith, who argued forcefully that giving inmates lawyers would make the system work more smoothly and would speed up executions. The legislative debates on CCR are extraordinary, as the following exchange illustrates:

Attorney General Smith: . . . [The federal courts have] made it clear they are going to exhaustively review every death case and if the people of Florida want to continue to have capital punishment, and I think they do, this is something we're going to have to do. . . .

Senator Crawford: . . . What you're saying basically is if you support the death penalty [and if you think the] State has a right to utilize that in a timely manner, that we should support this legislation?

Attorney General Smith: Yes, sir. (Elvin, 1986; Florida Senate, 1985)

However, once CCR became operational and succeeded in preventing a string of executions, some legislators grumbled that the office had violated the legislative intent behind its creation. It was apparently not foreseen that the attorneys and other personnel employed by CCR would be effective advocates who could win stays of execution for their clients.

The shifting of the battleground from the broad issue to the individual case, and the increasing impatience with capital cases generally, must be understood in terms of a burgeoning death row. There are presently over two thousand men and women under sentence of death in the United States, spread over 34 states. There are nearly three hundred in Florida alone. State and federal courts in the southeastern United States, where the concentration of condemned inmates is the greatest, have in the past decade been swamped by the sheer number and complexity of the appeals and collateral proceedings that reach them. Judges, being human, may begin to tire of these cases. It is easy to become numbed by the volume. I fear that our society's desire to make executions easier has made us forget that we are dealing with people's lives. The taking of life becomes routine.

Given the number and the emotional power of these cases, death row attorneys have been attacked as unethical and unprofessional by opposing attorneys representing the state. What is more disturbing is that some of this almost prosecutorial rhetoric is finding its way into the utterances of judicial officers. The most common charges include the intentional thwarting of justice by raising frivolous claims and the use of all available procedures to obtain a stay.

In particular, it is becoming common to hear accusations that legal papers are intentionally filed so close to the scheduled execution date that courts must grant stays simply to consider the claims raised —which usually turn out to lack merit anyway.

The American adversarial system of justice is based on the notion that lawyers on each side will use every legitimate means to win on behalf of their clients. In the words of the Code of Professional Responsibility, an attorney should represent a client zealously within the bounds of the law. More fundamentally, I do not see how an attorney could do otherwise, especially when a client's very life is at stake. Certainly a commercial or corporate litigator trying to prevent one company from acquiring another company would be expected —and indeed professionally required—to employ all available legal procedures for the client's benefit. Timing of actions, much criticized in death penalty defense work, is equally important in the realm of corporate acquisition practice, where the "life or death" of a company is often at stake. It seems to me that human life can be considered no less valuable. Those who criticize death penalty lawyers for using what they label "dilatory tactics" would see the issue quite differently if the case involved their client or their loved one.

Human life cannot be assigned a value, because it can never be replaced. I believe that the criminal justice system decides life and death on the basis of chance, racism, and financial resources and therefore has no business deciding who lives and who dies. I believe that the death penalty is anathema to civilization. I believe that basic morality negates any justification of homicide, whether institutionalized or not. And if I cannot and do not say these things in casual conversation, it is because they are not casual.

References

Amnesty International. 1987. *United States of America: The Death Penalty*. London: Amnesty International Publications.

Bedau, Hugo Adam, and Michael L. Radelet. 1987. "Miscarriages of Justice in Potentially Capital Cases." *Stanford Law Review* 40:21–179.

Black, Charles. 1981. *Capital Punishment: The Inevitability of Caprice and Mistake*. 2d ed. New York: W. W. Norton.

Bluestone, Harvey, and Carl L. McGahee. 1962. "Reaction to Extreme Stress: Impending Death by Execution." *American Journal of Psychiatry* 119:393–96.

Elvin, Jan. 1986. "Florida Death Penalty Appeals Office Opens." *National Prison Project Journal* 7 (Spring):1–9.

Florida Senate. 1985. Unofficial transcript of proceedings before Florida Senate Judiciary Committee (Criminal Commission) on Senate Bill 616, 24 April.

Gallemore, Johnnie L., Jr., and James H. Panton. 1972. "Inmate Responses to Lengthy Death Row Confinement." *American Journal of Psychiatry* 129:167–71.

Goodpaster, Gary. 1983. "The Trial for Life: Effective Assistance of Counsel in Death Penalty Cases." *New York University Law Review* 58:299–362.

Johnson, Kathleen L. 1981. "The Death Row Right to Die: Suicide or Intimate Decision?" *Southern California Law Review* 54:575–631.

Johnson, Robert. 1981. *Condemned to Die: Life Under Sentence of Death.* New York: Elsevier.

Lewis, Dorothy Otnow; Jonathan H. Pincus; Marilyn Feldman; Lori Jackson; and Barbara Bard. 1986. "Psychiatric, Neurological, and Psychoeducational Characteristics of 15 Death Row Inmates in the United States." *American Journal of Psychiatry* 143:838–45.

Mello, Michael. 1988. "Facing Death Alone: The Post-Conviction Attorney Crisis on Death Row." *American University Law Review* 37:513–607.

Radelet, Michael L.; Margaret Vandiver; and Felix M. Berardo. 1983. "Families, Prisons, and Men with Death Sentences: The Human Impact of Structured Uncertainty." *Journal of Family Issues* 4:593–612.

Strafer, G. Richard. 1983. "Volunteering for Execution: Competence, Voluntariness and Propriety of Third Party Intervention." *Journal of Criminal Law and Criminology* 74:860–912.

White, Welsh S. 1987. "Defendants Who Elect Execution." *University of Pittsburgh Law Review* 48:853–77.

7

Representing the Death Row Inmate

The Ethics of Advocacy, Collateral Style

LAURIN A. WOLLAN, JR.

Representing an inmate on death row in collateral proceedings, which occur after the trial and initial appeal have run their course, is an unusual undertaking for volunteer lawyers. But it can be one of the most important, and even one of the most rewarding, experiences in a legal career.

Handling capital cases in their collateral phase is unusual partly because there are relatively few lawyers who do it; hence the experience is reserved to a small but privileged minority. It is also unusual because it presents—or may present—special and difficult problems of advocacy, some of which are ethical and the subject of this essay.

The author has represented an inmate on Florida's death row since 1981. Lead counsel in the case since federal litigation began has been Richard H. Burr III, now of the NAACP Legal Defense Fund. To him, and to Michael D. Bayles, Steven G. Gey, Steven M. Goldstein, Kent S. Miller, Charles E. Miner, Jr., and Larry H. Spalding, I am grateful for encouragement and suggestions, while reserving to myself the usual responsibility for any shortcomings in this essay.

Capital collateral advocacy is of the utmost importance in several ways. It is probably the only time an ordinary lawyer will have the very life of a client resting on his or her advocacy. Liberty sometimes, property often, but life hardly ever depends on effective lawyering. Thus, the stakes are the highest they can ever be. In addition, each such case yields one or more appellate opinions, hence in some way helping explicitly to define important areas of constitutional law. Moreover, the so-called super due process of capital punishment law cannot but have significant effects in other areas of criminal process as time goes on and those areas come to be elaborated and refined.

The experience can be rewarding to the volunteer. The capital collateral lawyer will have a sense of participation in an important cause (even, paradoxically, if he or she is not ideologically opposed to the death penalty), of association with some of the most dedicated people he or she will ever know, of contribution to something of profound significance, even if the case—and client—is ultimately lost.

Taking the Case

To take—or not to take—a capital collateral case is a decision fraught with ethical dilemmas. And such a case, once taken, may confront the advocate with several more.

This essay attempts to identify ethical problems: some that have occurred, a few of them with regularity, and a handful that might occur. There is little attempt here to resolve these problems; instead, this exercise is largely exploratory. Reference to several bodies or codes of ethical rules, some of which are not in force, is meant to be suggestive, not dispositive, of the various issues identified here.[1]

Is the Duty Personal?

A threshold difficulty is presented by the combination of the very first of the so-called ethical considerations of Canons 1 and 2 of the Code of Professional Responsibility. The former states: "A basic tenet of the professional responsibility of lawyers is that every person in our society should have ready access to the independent professional services of a lawyer of integrity and competence" (EC 1-1). Canon 1 goes on: "The need for [sic] members of the public for legal services is met only if they recognize their legal problems, appreciate the importance of seeking assistance, and are able to obtain the services of acceptable legal counsel" (EC 2-1) (West, 1981:441–42). That consideration forms the foundation of Canon 2: "A lawyer should assist the legal profession in fulfilling its duty to make legal counsel available" (West, 1981:442). It was not so very long ago, in the history of the Constitution, that defendants in capital cases were not entitled to representation by counsel at all. Today there is a constitutional right to representation by counsel in capital cases up through the state appellate system, but not beyond it to the Supreme Court on certiorari, let alone into the subsequent collateral phases. Yet the death row inmate's need for representation by counsel is urgent and crucial. The rules are complicated, the process moves quickly (at the later stages), and the stakes are high. Do the Canons mean that one should urge the profession to make counsel available (as in letters to the board of governors), inspire the profession to do so (as in Law Day speeches), or guide the profession to do so (as in developing a plan)? Or does it mean, for the lawyer, putting oneself forward as counsel in cases that call for legal services? In other words, when the bar itself has not met that obligation, does the individual lawyer then have a duty to step into the breach and take a case in fulfillment of what the Canon calls for?

The Duty to Represent

The decision to take or not to take a capital collateral case involving a death row inmate who has been tried, adjudicated guilty, and sentenced, whose case has been carried to the state supreme court on appeal and to the U.S. Supreme Court on petition for writ of certiorari—unsuccessfully at each and every step—is a decision easily made at one ethical level, but not so easily at another. The easy answer to the prospective advocate's question whether or not to take the case is simply that neither constitution (U.S. or state) nor statute (federal or state) nor rule of court (federal or state) nor code of ethics *requires* it. The American lawyer, unlike his or her British counterpart, is free to take or not to take any case that comes along. Thus, no lawyer need take such a case however much a judge or a bar association or a private death penalty organization (like Florida's Clearinghouse for Criminal Justice) may implore, plead, cajole, or otherwise try to recruit the volunteer.

Most lawyers will happily let the cup pass without the slightest twinge of conscience. But for a few there may be second or third thoughts on the matter, inasmuch as ethical obligations are seldom fully resolved by rules of constitution, statute, court, or bar association. For such lawyers the decision to turn down a case is not so easy. The American Bar Association's oath of admission, urged upon the states and adopted by most, phrases the brand-new lawyer's commitment in these words: "I will never reject, from any consideration personal to myself, the cause of the defenseless or oppressed" (West, 1987:727). And that oath has continuing significance for some, beyond the solemn and portentous occasion of its administration.

Among the formal injunctions to undertake such cases is the Code of Trial Conduct of the American College of Trial Lawyers: "even though a lawyer is not bound to accept particular employment, requests for services in criminal cases should not lightly be declined or refused merely on the basis of the lawyer's personal desires, his or public opinion concerning the guilt of the accused, or his repugnance to the crime charged or to the accused" (Morgan and Rotunda, 1983: 432). Such rules contemplate representation from the beginning of a criminal case, but their spirit would seem to call for representation toward the end of a case as well.

Other statements suggest that a lawyer's duty goes beyond the letter of the formal rules. For instance, University of Chicago law students for many years have recited the pledge composed by Karl Llewellyn at the luncheon preceding their commencement. It contains these lines:

> In accepting the honor and responsibility of life in the profession of law, I engage, as best I can . . . to be at all times, even at personal sacrifice, a champion of fairness and due process, in court or out, and for all, whether the powerful or envied or my neighbors or the helpless or the hated or the oppressed. (Association of American Law Schools, 1962:546)

That statement echoed in at least one Chicago lawyer's ears, nearly twenty years after he first heard those words, when Scharlette

Holdman (Florida's "Mistress of Delay") first suggested to him that he might undertake the representation of an inmate on Florida's death row. That lawyer is this author.

Regard for Public and Professional Opinion

One source of hesitation for the lawyer who might volunteer for a capital collateral case arises from the very preamble to the Code of Professional Responsibility. It says: "Each lawyer must find within his own conscience the touchstone against which to test the extent to which his actions should rise above minimum standards." It notes "the dignity of the individual" as the basis of the rule of law and the role of lawyers "as guardians of the law." It goes on, however, to say this: "But in the last analysis it is the desire for the respect and confidence of the members of his profession and of the society which he serves that should provide to a lawyer the incentive for the highest possible degree of ethical conduct" (West, 1981:440).

But the respect and confidence of the public, or even of the bench and bar, is not often won by capital collateral work. Lawyers have been honored by bar associations for it, but clearly many lawyers and judges take a dim view of what must seem to be, at best, prolonging the inevitable or, at worst, obstructing the course of justice. Their reason may be found in the disciplinary rules for Canon 1, "a lawyer should assist in maintaining the integrity and competence of the legal profession," which concludes with DR 1-102(A)(5): "A lawyer shall not . . . engage in conduct that is prejudicial to the administration of justice" (West, 1981:442). Some of the bench and bar and much of the public deem death penalty defense work highly prejudicial to the administration of justice. How much weight ought a lawyer to attach to such community and professional sentiment, especially the latter? The Rules of Professional Conduct make this concern explicit in the preamble: "A lawyer is also guided by personal conscience and the approbation of professional peers" (West, 1987:599).

Representing the Unpopular Client

Representing an inmate on death row is analogous to representing the accused before and during trial, although the reasons for doing so are less compelling. Such a case, nevertheless, brings into play several ethical considerations relating to the acceptance of employment in the cause of the so-called unpopular client.

The ethical problem of "the guilty client" has been resolved by the supposed uncertainty of whether such a client is guilty or not, usually with reference to Dr. Johnson's homily:

> Sir, you do not know it to be good or bad till the judge determines it. . . . An argument which does not convince yourself may convince the judge to whom you urge it; and if it does convince him, why then, Sir, you are wrong and he is right. It is his business to judge, and you are not to be confident in your own opinion that a cause is bad, but to say all you can for your client, and then hear the judge's opinion. (Association of American Law Schools, 1962:186)

When that basis for resolution is no longer available—that is to say, when guilt beyond a reasonable doubt has been established, or more important, when adjudication of that guilt has already been reviewed and affirmed—then Dr. Johnson's teaching or some variation of it is no longer determinative. Moreover, whatever resistance a lawyer or a bar association may have to representing an unpopular client must deepen as the "acceptability" of the client declines and the client's case diverges from the kind of case a lawyer loves: that of a popular, innocent, unconvicted client. Few lawyers would resist such a case under any circumstances. But the death row inmate's case is not that one. The defendant is *un*popular (for good reason), no longer legally innocent, and above all, convicted.

Not only has this defendant been convicted, which usually resolves the issue of guilt, but the conviction and sentence have been reviewed at least once by the state's appellate judiciary. Beyond this, they have in all likelihood been reviewed (however cursorily) by the Supreme Court (or its clerks) in the certiorari stage. The willingness of a lawyer to undertake such a case understandably declines as the case descends that scale of acceptability from popular to unpopular, from innocent to guilty, from unconvicted to convicted, and from unreviewed to reviewed. When all that remain are issues of procedure and penalty, the cause is less compelling.

Is Competent Representation Possible?

At the threshold of acceptance of a capital collateral case is yet another difficulty of ethical dimension. Canons 1 and 2 both rest on the assumption that legal representation will be competent. Ethical consideration EC 2-30 makes it explicit: "Employment should not be accepted by a lawyer when he is unable to render competent service . . ." (West, 1981:446).

Canon 6, "a lawyer should represent a client competently," rests upon ethical consideration EC 6-1: "Because of his vital role in the legal process, a lawyer should act with competence and proper care in representing clients. He should strive to become and remain proficient in his practice and should accept employment only in matters which he is or intends to become competent to handle" (West, 1981:459). Capital collateral practice is extremely complex. Death penalty law is an area that few lawyers learn in law school; indeed, it has existed for only a decade or so. Thus, older lawyers have never encountered it. It deepens and changes direction quickly. It calls for knowledge that even the latest decisions will not supply. Indeed, capital collateral lawyers have watched other collateral lawyers in oral argument on one day in order to argue better the very next day. There is no other area of legal practice in which difficulty and the need for knowledge combine with such urgency.

Thus, no lawyer should take such a case until he or she has developed the competence to handle it, or at least intends to. But even the lawyer who is genuinely a "quick study" would need days —ideally, weeks—of full-time study in order to develop a working knowledge of death penalty law and procedure, and that much time is rarely available. And this is to speak only of the competence that comes from "book learning." In addition, the process is complex and intricate. Walking through a case or two alongside an experienced lawyer would be desirable, but the urgency of the case and the paucity of experienced and available lawyers mean that any lawyer able to learn the ropes will be thrown into the ropes right away.

The capital collateral lawyer who is truly competent knows the substantive law, with its often slight, yet sometimes significant, differences from state to federal circuit to Supreme Court. The competent collateral lawyer is at home in both trial and appellate litigation, because collateral work involves knowledgeable scrutiny of trial transcripts, then hearings in state and federal trial courts on issues arising out of the original trial and a multitude of others since then, as well as appellate review of all of that. But few lawyers are competent in both trial and appellate work. Indeed, the ordinary lawyer's practice involves little of either, let alone a lot of both. For many older lawyers, moot court in law school may have been the extent of appellate experience; for many younger lawyers, moot court in law school may be the extent of trial experience.

Moreover, the competent collateral lawyer will bridge not only the horizontal divide between trial and appellate experience, but the vertical divide between federal and state law and courts. Few lawyers are equally at home on all sides of these divides.

The differences between appellate and trial work are far more than a mood of formality rather than informality, of communication by correspondence rather than conversation, of matters handled by pleadings and oral argument rather than the give-and-take of negotiation or the rough-and-tumble of trial. Among many other differences, the client is distant, opposing counsel is distant, even the courthouses are distant, rather than relatively close at hand and more or less familiar, as in ordinary legal practice. Few lawyers roam far from their own county, its courthouse, its bench and bar.

One other difference is significant, and ominously so: the collateral stage of capital punishment is unforgiving. In most stages of law, there is a many-layered system of potentially protective decisions between the lawyer and his or her client's fate: police, prosecutor, grand jury, petit jury, judge, reviewing court—at any level of which the decision-maker, on its own motion, so to speak, may intervene beneficially. This expectation gives rise to the Private Slovik syndrome: the notion that someone, somewhere, sometime, down the line of the process will make a "saving" decision. But in Slovik's case, that someone/somewhere/sometime did *not* make such a decision, and Slovik was executed (Huie, 1954). So it is in capital cases. And thus so very much more depends on the advocate!

An Exception for Emergency?

The Rules of Professional Conduct recognize an exception to the rule calling for competence; but the exception itself makes for more difficulty. The Comment states:

In an emergency a lawyer may give advice or assistance in a matter in which the lawyer does not have the skill ordinarily required where referral to or consultation or association with another lawyer would be impractical. Even in an emergency, however, assistance should be limited to that reasonably necessary in the circumstances, for ill-considered action under emergency considerations can jeopardize the client's interest. (West, 1987:601)

But the reality is this: the capital collateral case is an emergency from inception to conclusion, and typically the lawyer who volunteers will enjoy little of the luxury of associating with a more experienced or competent lawyer or developing, as the Comment allows, the "requisite level of competence . . . by reasonable preparation" (West, 1987:601). There is simply too little time and too little help. (It should be noted that my client and I were unusually fortunate in having associated with us, early in the case, one of the very best full-time, veteran capital collateral lawyers in the country. But there are too few of these to go around, and the volunteer cannot count on receiving help from one.)

When these requirements are taken into account, the Rules of Professional Conduct would seem very nearly to bar the ordinary volunteer from capital collateral work, as the Comment suggests:

In determining whether a lawyer employs the requisite knowledge and skill in a particular matter, relevant factors include the relative complexity and specialized nature of the matter, the lawyer's general experience, the lawyer's training and experience in the field in question, the preparation and study the lawyer is able to give the matter, and whether it is feasible to refer the matter to, or associate or consult with, a lawyer of established competence in the field in question. (West, 1987: 601)

Yet here, it must be said, the principle comes face to face with reality: there is an inmate, now not merely on death row but ceremoniously shifted to "death watch," living but a few feet from the execution chamber, who has a date with the executioner less than thirty days away. What should a lawyer of admittedly limited competence do in those circumstances?

Conflicting Interests?

Canon 5, on "independent professional judgment on behalf of a client," entails yet another ethical problem—that of conflicting interests. Ethical consideration EC 5-2 states: "A lawyer should not accept proffered employment if his personal interests or desires will, or there is a reasonable probability that they will, affect adversely the advice to be given or services to be rendered the prospective client" (West, 1981:454). If the lawyer is a death penalty retentionist or is merely indifferent, is there a problem? The Canon addresses standard problems of conflicting interests arising from ownership of property, publication rights, gifts, positions, financial interests, and so forth. These direct and evident benefits make for conflicts in which the clarity itself tends to ensure that the conflict will have little or no effect on professional judgment. Much more difficult are the conflicts stemming from sentiments about the death penalty that may affect zeal or even judgment in a given case.

This issue is partially resolved by Canon 7 (on zealous representation) in its ethical consideration EC 7-17: "The obligation of loyalty to his client applies only to a lawyer in the discharge of his professional duties and implies no obligation to adopt a personal viewpoint favorable to the interests or desires of his client" (West, 1981:462). The subtler issue, however, is whether strongly held views have an influence that is difficult for the lawyer to resist, as when the lawyer's belief in the appropriateness of capital punishment challenges the cause for which he or she might volunteer. By way of analogy, can a staunch anticommunist effectively represent a communist client? The Rules of Professional Conduct address this head on in the case of appointment: "A lawyer shall not seek to avoid appointment by a tribunal to represent a person except for good cause, such as . . . [t]he client or the cause is so repugnant to the lawyer as to be likely to impair the client-lawyer relationship or the lawyer's ability to represent the client" (West, 1987:635). In short, will the lawyer have the stomach, let alone the heart, for the case?

The other side of this coin is the potentially judgment-impairing effect of passion *for* the client's cause: does it or can it plunge the advocate into the pitfalls of wishful thinking?

How Far Pro Bono?

Yet another problem is suggested by the following. The Rules of Professional Conduct state: "A lawyer should render public interest legal service. A lawyer may discharge this responsibility by . . . providing professional services at no fee or a reduced fee to persons of limited means" (West, 1987:634). For the most part, death row inmates and their families have no money at all. How far, then, does the *pro bono* obligation go in this mode of "public interest legal service"?

The Rules of Professional Conduct on acceptance of appointment are applicable to this ethical dilemma, even though the issue here is one of volunteering. "A lawyer shall not seek to avoid appointment by a tribunal to represent a person except for good cause, such as [when] [r]epresenting the client is likely to result in an unreasonable financial burden on the lawyer" (West, 1987:634). The death case in its final stages will impose several burdens, including financial ones. The burdens will be physical and emotional as well. If the job is to be done fully, it will entail high levels of stress. The emotional strains include anticipation of a consequence of legal work that few lawyers ever experience: death of the client after everything has failed that the lawyer could conceivably have done. Only physicians, and especially surgeons, experience this sort of thing— and they have the advantage, if it is that, of learning to cope with the experience early in their careers. For the lawyer, however, that experience must come as a shock and a devastation. The lawyer must anticipate asking, "What else could have been done?" And anticipate looking back at every step along the way and seeing things that could have been done, or done differently. One cannot know at the end whether the outcome would have been different. But as one looks back, it is likely to be difficult to avoid the feeling that any little thing, if attempted or perhaps done differently, might have meant the difference between life and death. Even before the lawyer volunteers to take such a case, he or she must contemplate this.

Conducting the Case

If and when the lawyer agrees to take on the case of the inmate on death row—unpopular, guilty, convicted, reviewed—several more problems of an ethical sort may crop up.

The Case: One of a Kind or One of a Whole?

Canon 5 requires: "A lawyer should [the Rules of Professional Conduct, in Rule 4-2.1, say "shall"] exercise independent professional judgment" (West, 1981:454; West, 1987:622). But the lawyer representing a death row inmate finds that his or her case is one of hundreds that together constitute a very large and dynamically emerging mosaic of constitutional law, the whole or much of which may be altered significantly by the independent movement of an individual piece. This is a problem particularly for lawyers and organizations representing several inmates with a statewide or a multistate responsibility to see this mosaic as a whole. From their perspective some cases present certain issues prematurely or more weakly than others. Such issues, from the broader perspective, should be presented (perhaps later, perhaps in another circuit, perhaps by a better attorney) when and where they will be most effective in their general consequences. But what is the obligation of the volunteer, who will in all likelihood have become highly dependent on and deferential to such lawyers, but whose perspective is fastened on one case in particular, who has "a shot" at some such issue in that case, even if a long shot, if success creates a weak precedent and thereby jeopardizes the success others might have had later if the issue had come up when it was more timely and circumstances were more ripe?

With a Little Help from One's Friends?

Relating to another aspect of the context, what does the volunteer lawyer do about assistance—and assistants—in the huge task and the short time? The Rules of Professional Conduct provide for "nonlawyer assistants." The relevant rule (4-5.3[b]) provides: "A lawyer having direct supervisory authority over the nonlawyer shall make reasonable efforts to ensure that the person's conduct is compatible with the professional obligations of the lawyer" (West, 1987: 633). The Comment provides: "A lawyer should give such assistants appropriate instruction and supervision concerning the ethical aspects of their employment. . . . The measures employed in supervising nonlawyers should take account of the fact that they do not have legal training and are not subject to professional discipline" (West, 1987:633). But the reality is that the lawyer entering a capital collateral case is involved with and thoroughly dependent upon others, and he or she takes help where and as it is offered. Fortunately, the assistance can be very good. Laypersons will materialize, probably veterans of many such campaigns, who are highly skilled at a variety of tasks necessary to collateral work. Those on whom the volunteer lawyer comes to depend will know their roles and their responsibilities very well, and can be depended upon. The lawyer in such a position is hardly able to provide, let alone insist upon, what the Comment calls for.

Advocacy

Canon 7's obligation, "A lawyer should represent a client zealously within the bounds of the law," poses further problems. Ethical consideration EC 7-2 acknowledges that "the bounds of the law in a given case are often difficult to ascertain" (West, 1981:460). This is especially so in death penalty law. The problem is posed sharply by EC 7-4:

> The advocate may urge any permissible construction of the law favorable to his client, without regard to his professional opinion as to the likelihood that the construction will ultimately prevail. His conduct is within the bounds of the law, and therefore permissible, if the position taken is supported by the law or is supportable by a good faith argument for an extension, modification, or reversal of the law. However, a lawyer is not justified in asserting a position in litigation that is frivolous. (West, 1981:460)

In a field as fast-moving as death penalty law, it is sometimes difficult to distinguish today's "good faith argument" from tomorrow's "frivolous" argument, and vice versa. What today seems absurd may persuade a judge tomorrow or another judge down the corridor today.

The Rules of Professional Conduct provide a good deal of latitude for making claims: "A lawyer shall not bring or defend a proceeding, or assert or controvert an issue therein, unless there is a basis for doing so that is not frivolous, which includes a good faith argument for an extension, modification, or reversal of existing law" (West, 1987:623). It continues, however, with what may be a limitation *or* an expansion. "A lawyer for the defendant in a criminal proceeding . . . may nevertheless so defend the proceeding as to require that every element of the case be established" (West, 1987: 625). Are the elements of the death row inmate's case those of definition, which *have* been established; or do the elements include every jot and tittle of procedural nicety?

Is the Capital Collateral Phase Sui Generis?

In any event, as ethical consideration EC 7-11 puts it, "The responsibilities of a lawyer may vary according to . . . the nature of a particular proceeding" (West, 1981:461). Ethical consideration EC 7-11 mentions administrative and legislative bodies, which suggests that judicial proceedings are all of one kind. But collateral litigation, though within the framework of judicial proceedings, is really a particular proceeding, "the nature" of which differs dramatically from the usual run of litigation, so much so that the court in such cases is truly a special sort of judicial body. Is there a more indulgent—or a more exacting—ethical standard in death cases?

The Media: Another Forum?

The lawyer's obligation to the client has the courtroom as its focus, but surrounding that focus is an environment of influences, some of which may convey information, meanings, even arguments, to a jury (or even to a judge). Thus, publicity has become a part of litigation; cases are tried in the media before and while they are tried in the courtroom. EC 7-33 is aimed at discouraging this: "The attainment of this goal ["that each party shall have his case . . . adjudicated by an impartial tribunal"] may be defeated by dissemination of news or comments which tend to influence judge or jury" (West, 1981: 464). Thus, "[t]he release by a lawyer of out-of-court statements regarding an anticipated or pending trial may improperly affect the impartiality of the tribunal" (West, 1981:464). By implication such releases may affect litigation of an appellate or collateral sort as well. How may—or may not—the capital collateral lawyer "speak" to the judge through the media?

It is unlikely that judges, given their training, experience, and sensibilities, will be influenced much if at all by publicity. But when time is limited and attention is focused on a judge or panel of judges, one does not know. In subtle matters like death penalty law, much influence may not be necessary; a little influence may be sufficient.

If all that is so, and the lawyer is therefore constrained not to make such initiations, what if the media come to the lawyer and the prospects for a favorable, potentially influential story are good? Should the lawyer accommodate the press or not? And if so, how generously? And, a special case, what of the client (who may soon die) who wishes to speak to the press—or, through the press, to the world? "[I]f the lawyer knows or reasonably should know that it will have a substantial likelihood of materially prejudicing an adjudicative proceeding . . . ," the Rules of Professional Conduct say, "[a] lawyer shall not counsel or assist another person to make such a statement" (West, 1987:628). Should the lawyer stand between a dying man and his final declaration?

Time: The Essence of Collateral Practice

Time is of the essence in many matters of law and legal procedure. The Rules of Professional Conduct provide: "A lawyer shall make reasonable efforts to expedite litigation consistent with the interests of the client" (West, 1987:625).

Procrastination is an all-too-human weakness, and perhaps the besetting sin of lawyers. The Rules' Comment acknowledges this: "It is not a justification that similar conduct [delay] is often tolerated by the bench and bar" (West, 1987:625). But the interest of the client in a capital case is often not in acceleration but in *delay*. The interest of the death row inmate may conflict with what the Comment states: "Dilatory practices bring the administration of justice into disrepute. Delay should not be indulged merely for the convenience of the advocates or for the purpose of frustrating an opposing party's attempt to obtain rightful redress or repose" (West, 1987:625).

The ABA Standards for the Defense Function enjoin the same thing. Standard 4-1.2 states: "Defense counsel should avoid unnecessary delay in the disposition of cases" (Morgan and Rotunda, 1983: 334). Standard 4-3.6 goes on to state: "Many important rights of the accused can be protected and preserved only by prompt legal action" (Morgan and Rotunda, 1983:338). The irony, in capital collateral cases, is that the most important right, the right to life, can be protected and preserved only by legal action which prolongs it, unless that right has been forfeited, but that of course is the crux of the case itself.

The recurring problem of delays in capital collateral cases—

more precisely, stays of execution—suggests that lawyers may be neglecting their work until time has all but run out. But that is not the case, at least for the overwhelming majority of delays or stays of execution. The volunteer lawyer enters the case when time is already fast running out, leaving little enough time even for the best of the lawyers in this field of law.

Thus, the courts in this field of litigation are commonly confronted with pleadings—of the most desperate and important sort —with too little time even to read them, let alone digest them and respond fully and fairly within the time available before action must be taken—before, that is, the execution date arrives. The unavoidable step in nearly all instances is a delay in the form of a stay of execution, sometimes for a few hours or days, but more commonly for an indefinite period of time. Such last-minute litigation, though unavoidable, pays off for the inmate in extension of time.

The ethical dilemma would occur when that outcome, predictable in most circumstances, is contemplated as a tactic. There is no instance known to this writer of such exploitation of that circumstance, but its potential surely exists. Thus, a lawyer might withhold the filing of pleadings until such a time that the court can do nothing other than delay the process by means of a stay of execution. Would such action ever be justifiable, given the high stakes and the likelihood that substantially more advocacy of higher quality would be accomplished if more time were available? In death cases, at their very end, *any* amount of time, even an hour, might yield a gain: information or witnesses may come forth, a decision may be rendered by another court, a political change may occur in the system (such as appointment of a new judge). Any one of these changes may happen within hours or days or weeks of the inception of such a period of extension, thereby fundamentally altering substantive or procedural advantages.

When the Client Quits

But what if the client himself wants to bring matters, and his time on earth, to an end? "A lawyer shall abide by a client's decisions concerning the objectives of representation" (Rule 4-1.2[a], West, 1987:601). What does the capital collateral lawyer do when his client announces that he is ready to throw in the towel? Does the lawyer dutifully convey that intention to the court and opposing counsel?

Does he or she advise or urge the client to go on? Does he or she treat such a client as suicidal? Or does the advocate continue to press ahead, as if with deaf ears?

Special Problems of the Writ of Habeas Corpus

In struggling to do everything possible within the limits of the law to keep the client from execution, the volunteer lawyer will use the writ of habeas corpus, the same writ that Anglo-American lawyers have used for centuries. No lawyer would knowingly abuse the Great Writ. But at what point is a successor petition seeking a second writ, a third writ, or more simply one too many? When, in other words, is the writ abused?

There are many authorities, some on the Supreme Court, who perceive this phenomenon of multiple successor petitions as abuse of the writ. No lawyer will feel comfortable with another filing, knowing that it will almost surely be greeted by the state with condemnation as abusive and that many judges will agree—and say so very clearly.

Much of this has to do with questions of whether claims are genuinely new, previously unresolved on the merits, and so forth. The problem is deepened by uncertainty as to what the law does or should call for, but that, too, is not an ethical question. The lawyer will not contemplate filing a successor petition unless the claims legitimately fall within the categories for which successor petitions are appropriate. But sooner or later, as the case becomes more and more desperate, the temptation may arise to file a successor petition simply to gain some additional time—and life—for the client. The ethical rules militate against this, of course. But those rules were not formulated in the context of capital litigation, in which time means life, and loss of time—time running out—may mean death. Does this make a difference?

One claim has become relatively standard in collateral proceedings: ineffectiveness of counsel. Though not the same as incompetence (a competent lawyer can be ineffective in a given case), ineffectiveness is a charge most lawyers are reluctant to make. For one thing, the strategies and tactics of the earlier lawyer that will constitute the basis for the claim are often arguable. And everyone knows that hindsight is 20/20. The collateral lawyer will be inclined to think, "There but for the grace of God go I," and shrink from making that claim. The earlier lawyer was only doing his or her job, and not really so badly at that. Moreover, claims of ineffectiveness threaten to bring the bar into disrepute; lawyers, like other professionals, are inclined to the view that such matters should be dealt with discreetly, not in legal pleadings, let alone in open court.

The dilemma of whether or not to "go after" the earlier lawyer deepens profoundly when the process reaches the point where the earlier lawyer becomes at last—and alas!—that selfsame volunteer! The issue anticipated above is that when all is said and done, in retrospect it will seem that all was *not* said or done (or not said or done so well as it might have been). The feeling that was vague at the time, that something more could have been done, that something could have been done better, begins to crystallize into an arguable claim of ineffectiveness.

At that point the lawyer may have to scrutinize his or her own work and own up to those points where something could have been done, or done better. Does the lawyer ever dare to hold his or her work up to an exacting standard and say, "I failed," or stand aside and in effect (or explicitly) invite another lawyer to say just that?

Beyond the Call of Duty

In David Paul Brown's "Capital Hints for Capital Cases" (which dates back well over a century), the next-to-the-last hint is this: "The sentence having been passed, the death warrant issues—your application for a pardon having been refused—the drop falls, and then, and not till then, your duties are done" (Association of American Law Schools, 1962:283).

In all of this, up to the end, the lawyer has been the representative of the client, standing for him, speaking for him. But the time may come for a final act that cannot be taken by the lawyer but only by the inmate. At that point the lawyer cannot represent the inmate, but he or she can stand at his side, in a manner of speaking, and witness to the execution. This is not a duty, yet for some lawyers it may be the full realization of responsible representation and bring the ordeal to closure. It will be the final choice the capital collateral lawyer must make.

In all of these final phases, though not in that last act of the lawyer when advocacy is over and friendship alone remains, there may be inspiration or consolation in the last of Brown's "Capital Hints":

> To conclude, the condition of an advocate for a defendant, in a capital cause, may be aptly compared to that of a commander of a ship in a storm; the cordage snaps, the masts go by the board, the bulwarks are carried away, the hull springs a leak —every dependence from time to time fails, and ruin appears to be inevitable; but still amidst the "wreck of matter," sustained by the immortal mind, with a resolved will, the gallant commander stands by his helm to the last, determined either to steer his shattered vessel into port, or to perish gloriously in the faithful discharge of his duty. (Association of American Law Schools, 1962:283)

Note

1. The Code of Professional Responsibility (West, 1981:439–70), to which belong the "Canons" and "Ethical Considerations" mentioned and quoted here, has been superseded by the Rules of Professional Conduct (West, 1987:599–641), to which belong the "Comments." Reference has been made to the former, as well as to other bodies of ethical rules such as that of the American College of Trial Lawyers (Morgan and Rotunda, 1976:430–39), because my purpose here is identification rather than authoritative disposition of ethical issues.

   For legal aspects of the capital collateral setting, the reader should consult Goldstein (1987). For many aspects of the institutional and procedural setting, see Mello (1988).

References

Association of American Law Schools. 1962. *Selected Readings on the Legal Profession*. St. Paul, Minn.: West.

Goldstein, Steven. 1987. "Application of *Res Judicata* Principles to Successive Federal Habeas Corpus Petitions in Capital Cases: The Search for an Equitable Approach." *University of California–Davis Law Review* 21:45–122.

Huie, William Bradford. 1954. *The Execution of Private Slovik*. New York: Dell.

Mello, Michael. 1988. "Facing Death Alone: The Post-Conviction Attorney Crisis on Death Row." *American University Law Review* 37:513–607.

Morgan, Thomas D., and Ronald D. Rotunda. 1976. *Problems and Materials on Professional Responsibility*. Mineola, N.Y.: Foundation Press.

———. 1983. *1983 Selected Standards Supplement*. Mineola, N.Y.: Foundation Press.

West's Desk Copy. 1981. *Florida Rules of Court—State and Federal*. St. Paul, Minn.: West.

———. 1987. *Florida Rules of Court—State*. St. Paul, Minn.: West.

8

Ministering to the Condemned

A Case Study

JOSEPH B. INGLE

I am firmly convinced that if the citizens of the United States fully understood the nature and effects of the death penalty, we would no longer allow the punishment to be imposed. Unfortunately, however, many people have been misinformed or have closed their minds about this issue, and the media coverage of executions, if present at all, is steadily shrinking. Furthermore, the media that still provide coverage have continually failed to describe what the inmate is actually like and what he and his family experience during his final hours. We learn about the final meal, the last statement, and the body's reaction when it is electrocuted, but not about the actual ways in which people experience their own or their loved one's planned death.

For the last 13 years, I have traveled throughout the South ministering to inmates condemned to death. This work led to the establishment of a prison reform organization called the Southern Coalition on Jails and Prisons, with affiliate offices now located in eight states. In the course of this work, I have formed several close relationships with condemned inmates and their families.

In this essay, I would like to describe David Washington, a man I came to love and respect, and the events surrounding his execution in Florida in July 1984 (Magee, 1980:149–61). David's crimes were horrible, and I am no less appalled by them than are the strongest death penalty advocates. I do not believe, however, that the Christian command to forgive is a conditional directive; nor does the commandment "thou shalt not kill" add "except in retribution." David Washington would be happy to know that others, with varying stands on the question of capital punishment, might learn more about death (and life) by hearing a little bit about his final days.

The Person

We called him Pee Wee. It was a nickname coined on the streets of Miami, and one that David Washington brought with him to Florida State Prison's death row. It was an odd nickname, as he was not a small man—he stood six feet tall and was acknowledged to be one of the best basketball players on death row. His smooth, caramel skin and dark eyes were regularly accompanied by a warm smile. As his many friendships in Miami confirmed, Pee Wee radiated a genuine charm.

The events that sent David to the electric chair involved the deaths of three victims. A product of Liberty City, the black ghetto in Miami, David was a street-wise youth, but he never used his social background as an excuse for his crimes. Rather, he readily admitted his full responsibility to the police and to the courts. He turned himself in to the police, fully cooperated with their investigations, and pleaded guilty. Pee Wee threw himself on the mercy of the court, waiving his right to a jury trial. But the court had no mercy, and in 1976 David was sentenced to three consecutive death sentences.

In my visits with David over the years, I found a deeply troubled soul. He was so distressed over his crimes that occasionally he would sit in his cell in a nearly catatonic state, refusing any outside contacts. If my visit coincided with one of these retreats, he would refuse to come out to see me, and would instead remain in the solace of his cell, reflecting over his crimes and the lives of the people he had murdered, seeking an understanding and forgiveness that could only come from within. In a real sense, David carried these victims with him until the hour of his death. They were his burden to bear, and like most other death row prisoners I have known, David felt remorse and pain in living with the responsibility for his crime.

When Pee Wee was sociable, his kindness and concern were second to no one else's in the prison. In every meaningful sense, he was not the same person who committed those horrible crimes on the streets. Indeed, though many will choose not to believe this, I found that David resonated a sweetness of character and true humility. David was not some rabid dog; like the rest of us, he was a unique individual who had both good and bad parts.

David, unlike many people on death row, rarely discussed his legal proceedings with me. He had accepted his guilt on a personal level, and whatever the courts did could not affect these feelings. The guilt and responsibility he experienced were real no matter what any court did to him. Thus, almost all our visits were personal and spiritual in nature. We came to care a great deal for one another, to hate the sin but love the sinner.

In the course of one visit, Pee Wee struggled to explain why he had not come out for my last visit: "Joe, I want you to know that it has nothing to do with you. Sometimes I just get back there thinking about those people I killed and I don't say nothing to nobody. I just sit there for days, waiting for it all to go through me so I can feel right again."

In a sense, it was if all three victims were alive and inhabiting David's soul. Talking with Pee Wee was often like talking with someone who had lost a family member to murder. David never forgot his victims; his struggle was to accept himself and to learn forgiveness for what he had done, and to try to repay a debt he knew he never could. It was a difficult pilgrimage that Pee Wee had undertaken.

It is often stated that when the lives of the saints are examined, their souls become windowpanes through which we can see God. Saints are able to become transparent so that others can experience or see God through their lives. While David was no saint, his suffering served as a reminder to others on death row, and those of us on the outside who came to know him, of the presence of his victims in our lives. He was a living reminder of the value of life. David became a windowpane through which we could see God acting in the world, working for reconciliation, forgiveness, and the preservation of life. Through him I reinforced my view that destruction of life, whether in a random street killing or in the electric chair, must be stopped. Responsibility for these needless deaths must be borne by those involved in them; it is only when we come to see our complicity in murder and our responsibility for it that we can move onto the level of a forgiveness and a reconciliation that transcend the wrongful deed. David taught others this painful and difficult lesson by his example as he lived out his days in his 50-square-foot death row cell.

Pee Wee arrived on death row in November 1976. The first person he befriended upon his arrival, the person who took him under a protective wing, was John Spenkelink, who was executed less than three years later. In Pee Wee's words: "I was ignorant when I came to death row. I didn't know nothing about it. John Spenkelink spent time with me. He explained the way things worked, introduced me to the guys, eased my way. He was a real friend to me and a lot of the guys. He was quiet, calm—a real leader. If we wanted changes made, we came to John. He made sure things were right."

I will leave it to other contributors to this volume to explain the struggles faced by men on death row when their close friends are taken to the electric chair. In this case, with the help of John Spenkelink, David became familiar with the routine of death row: the countless hours locked in a cell, with televisions and radios blaring, the loud conversations, the Florida heat, and, worst of all, the waiting and the uncertainty of dealing with impending death and the pain of watching his family trying to cope. Simply sitting there alone, David was unable to explain to himself or to his God why he had murdered. Sometimes he would cry. Weeping for what he had done, he quietly worked his way through his guilt. As the years passed, the suffering he endured was impossible to escape. He did make his peace with God; he had sought forgiveness and knew that although his community could not grant it, his God could. But he could never forget what he had done, so the suffering remained with him. How can any of us live our own lives, or face our death, when there is no way to rectify the errors we have made, and there is no societal support for the forgiveness we ask? Capital punishment dooms all of its victims to a death with important unfinished business remaining. It is a lonely death.

Meanwhile, David's legal situation steadily deteriorated. His case was chosen by the Supreme Court to determine standards for effective assistance of counsel in death penalty cases, and in 1984 the Court ruled unfavorably (*Strickland v. Washington*, 466 U.S. 668 [1984]). At that time, we were quite sure that David had only a few months to live, and the roller coaster of preparation for death started to accelerate. In mid-June Governor Bob Graham signed David's death warrant, setting the execution date for 12 July. It was David's third death warrant, and thus the third time his possessions were packed and he was moved to a holding cell, under 24-hour personal guard, next to the death chamber.

Life Under a Death Warrant

While there is always uncertainty for those on death row (Radelet et al., 1983), the uncertainty reaches its apex after a death warrant has been issued (roughly a month before the scheduled execution). Condemned inmates on "death watch," as it is called in Florida, are fortunate because opponents of the death penalty have taken great pains to ensure that the death will not be faced alone. Thus, when I arrived at Florida State Prison on 9 July, three days before the scheduled execution, David was not alone. A paralegal, Margaret, and an attorney who has taken hospice training, Susan, had seen him frequently in the preceding weeks.

The legal prognosis was poor, but still somewhat unpredictable. Although we knew that David would probably be put to death, the arbitrariness that characterizes the imposition of the death penalty in Florida (Bowers and Pierce, 1980; Gross and Mauro, 1984; Radelet, 1981; Radelet and Mello, 1986; Radelet and Pierce, 1985) also seems to characterize the odds of winning on appeal (Radelet and Vandiver, 1983) and of getting a stay of execution once a warrant is signed. If his legal papers were seen by the right judge on the right day, a stay might be granted. Thus, there was reason to hope, but we had to guard against the risk that this hope might cloud David's ability to deal with the reality of his impending death.

In this case, the unexpected indeed happened. David obtained a stay of execution from the trial court on 6 July. However, the state immediately appealed this action to the Florida Supreme Court. This court, in turn, using imperative judicial language, urged the trial court to lift its stay. By remanding the case to the trial court, the supreme court's message was clear: it's time to execute David Washington, and let's get on with it. When I left for the prison on the night of 9 July, we were awaiting a response from the trial court judge to this demand.

Before I entered the prison, the trial court had acted—and acted in a way that rebuffed the state supreme court and underscored the mockery of the ping-pong game the appellate courts play with human life. Rather than lift the stay, the trial judge *vacated* all three death sentences. Thus, as I entered the prison, I found a jovial atmosphere.

During the death watch, at a time when the inmate needs so clearly to be near those who love him (and vice versa), the inmate is separated from his family and friends by a glass barrier (cynics might argue that this barrier creates the impression that his loved ones, rather than the state, are the ones trying to put him to death). Pee Wee and I thus greeted each other by placing our palms on opposite sides of the glass window. He was smiling as I asked him to repeat what his lawyer had just told him on the phone. He relayed the conversation, and I leaned back in my chair and expressed, in relief, disbelief that it had really happened.

As the evening progressed, the effects of being free from the sentence of death for the first time in eight years revealed themselves in Pee Wee. He was lighthearted, joyous, laughing, and teasing. The joy and happiness we experienced had rarely been felt in the bowels of the prison. We did not talk seriously about our fear (indeed, our confidence) that the state would appeal this last ruling to the Florida Supreme Court, but David had a very realistic appraisal of the slim odds he would have if such an appeal was launched. He expected the state to prevail upon appeal, but decided to worry about that prospect when and if it developed. This night, for the first time since we had met, David was unburdened by a death sentence. Along with the volunteer lawyer and paralegal who had come to visit, we celebrated the persistent efforts of his attorneys and David's freedom from death. As the volunteers and I left the prison two hours later, we radiated David's joy; seldom have I exited a prison so hopeful and joyous. If only for a few hours, we relished David's freedom from the manacles of death.

During the 40-mile drive back to Gainesville, we speculated on prospective events in the courts. We all agreed that despite the outstanding work of David's lawyer, the state supreme court would in all likelihood reinstate the death sentences. But it was as if David's dwelling wholly in the present had communicated itself to us. We would let tomorrow take care of itself; this night was for celebration.

The volunteer paralegal put it best as she described David's attitude toward adverse legal rulings in his case: "David received news about the legal proceedings very gracefully. He was glad there were people who cared about him and who were making the effort for him, but he had no attachment to the results of what happened in court. He had a tremendous serenity, a kind of holy indifference, as to the outcome of any of the legal proceedings. It was not the most important thing going on with him. He never manifested more than a polite indifference about the legal issues. At the same time, he received news of the legal efforts gratefully but in no way could anything that happened in the court disturb what was happening in him."

The next evening provided a delightful interlude, as I visited friends who had nothing to do with the death penalty. Regrettably, however, the telephone interrupted our conversation. David's death sentences had been reinstated by the state supreme court. Although expected, the news that I knew would lead to the taking of my friend's life was piercingly painful.

The Last Visits

The next day, a federal district court judge granted David a 24-hour stay of execution; the execution was rescheduled for 7:00 A.M., 13 July. I sought to maintain a facade of indifference to these complicated legal proceedings, as did David, as I ministered to him and his family. We still had hope, but tried to keep that hope from dominating our time together.

On the evening of 11 July, the volunteer attorney, the paralegal, and I joined 11 members of David's family for a visit with him. There were 36 more hours to live. For three hours we crowded into the noncontact visiting area and talked with him through the glass barrier. Three small children, aged three through five, enlivened the occasion by talking with their uncle through the glass. David teased them, put happy smiles on their faces, and sought to uplift all of our spirits. His stepfather, a quiet and large man, radiated strength for all of us. David's mother relived some of the memories she shared with her son. David spoke intently to his younger brother, who was clearly having an especially difficult time. At one point David asked me to take special care in helping his brother make it through the ordeal. Although all the family members suffered, the pain of David's 12-year-old daughter was perhaps the most visible. She had not seen her dad in years, and she had difficulty expressing her love amid the horror of this occasion. She broke down in tears several times, and it was only David's constant support and encouragement that kept her intact.

At one point during the visit, I joined David's brother at a window overlooking the prison parking lot. He was standing, silently crying, while gazing toward the wing that housed the electric chair. As we stood there passively staring, I spoke quietly with him. After several minutes he stopped crying long enough to tell me that he simply could not take it. I assured him that there was no reason he should; it was an insane situation, and the important thing was to remember David's request that he not do anything stupid or rash. He nodded and again we stood in silence. He did not return to the prison the following night.

We bade David adieu when our visiting time was expended. We knew that there was to be another day for us and for David. We went over the final visiting plans for the next day, David's last full day on earth, and parted for the night.

The next evening all of David's family returned, with the exception of his brother. In contrast to the previous night, when we knew there would be another day, the finality of this night enveloped us all. The three children cried throughout most of the visit, not fully understanding why they and all the adults in the room were so sad. David summoned each of us to the glass to talk privately. In seeking to comfort his loved ones, he poured himself out to each. At one point, he asked Margaret, Susan, and me to come to the glass. As Margaret later recalled: "David said that apart from his family, we had shown him more love than anyone else. He tried to express his gratitude and told us also of his concern for us. He was worried because we were being hit so hard by every execution and personally involved with each one. We immediately let David know how very much he and the other men had given us and that we were doing what we were doing because we wanted to do it. He had given us more than we could ever return to him, and more than the state could ever take away by executing him."

During the course of the conversation, David mentioned how much this assurance meant to him. I echoed the sentiments, and we talked about love being the uniting reality through life and death. It was clear that David was comfortable and spiritually at ease.

At midnight David's mother and daughter, along with Susan and me, were permitted to have a one-hour contact visit with him.

The remainder of the family and Margaret remained on the other side of the glass partition. After each of us hugged him, we sat in chairs around him. As he had done throughout the death warrant, he proceeded to minister to us. He began with his mother: "I ain't believing this! I ain't believin' you're crying! You've always been the strong one—I never expected this. Now come on, we can't have this. You dry those tears and sit up straight."

His mother, forcing a smile through her sobs, looked at David and said, "But you're my baby." David, his voice catching, almost overcome with tears himself, embraced her despite the handcuffs. There were no words to be said as mother and son hugged each other a final time.

David's primary concern was for his daughter. He agonized over her having to endure the horror of his execution. He sat her on his lap, her lanky body draping his. She was crying openly, the tears streaming down her face, and David spoke to her: "I want you to make me proud. I don't want you messin' up like I did. You listen to your grandmother and do what she tells you. I want you to do better than I did. I didn't listen, and you see what happened to me. Now I want you to get your books—to study. School is important and I want you to do well. Don't you be makin' the mistakes I did, thinkin' school wasn't important."

As Pee Wee spoke softly to his daughter, he wiped her tears away. I sat in my chair, stricken by the pathos of the moment. Father was saying goodbye to daughter, imparting advice to help her survive in this world after his death. He was trying to leave a legacy to stand with her through the years. As I looked at his daughter's stricken face, gazed at his mother with her handkerchief crumpled to hide her tears, I heard a soft sobbing. I looked to the window and there, peering through the glass, was the three-year-old niece. Her face was pressed against the glass, a river of tears flowing down her cheeks. As I saw her and felt her tears, I realized that she and I were equally unable to fathom the events at hand. Neither of us, though bearing witness to the final parting, was able to understand it. Why was Pee Wee going to his death? Why was this unnecessary pain deemed necessary by our fellow citizens? The dispenser of so much love and grace, the sufferer of such grief, was going to be taken from those who loved him. Was the only thing our society could do for the families of homicide victims to double the number of innocent families who experience the tragic loss of a loved one?

Soon it was almost one o'clock, and we were saying our final goodbyes. We knew that David would be put to death in six hours. David once again thanked us for our friendship. As we filed out the door, each of us hugged him one last time. The guards handcuffed David's hands behind his back and led him down the hallway. As David was led away, I gazed about me. His daughter was sobbing in Susan's firm embrace, watching her father leave for the last time, shouting, "Please don't kill my daddy." The small children were near hysterics, his mother's shoulders were heaving with sorrow, and his stepfather tried to comfort us all. As David neared the door that would take him from us, I called down the prison corridor, "We love you," and several others echoed these words. David looked back over his shoulder, looking at his family for the last time. His expression was tender and sorrowful. His gaze rendered us speechless, and a gentle smile creased his smooth face. Then he was gone.

We remained transfixed. None of us moved. It was as if by holding the moment, by not moving, we could retain David with us. We stood planted in the middle of the prison corridor like fixtures. Then a prison colonel, the head of the execution team, entered the hall and walked through our midst. The spell was broken, and we stumbled to the parking lot, wailing, grief-stricken, and inconsolable. Society's retribution had produced a family bereaved, a wounded child, and another mourning mother.

The only conclusion I can offer from the above case, and from the many others like it that remain untold, is that capital punishment takes the lives of people who can be quite remarkable despite their appalling crimes, and that its pains touch many more people than the individual inmate himself. It is a punishment done in all our names, and although crimes of the prisoner have caused immense suffering to the innocent, I fail to see how that suffering is alleviated by creating a whole new family of innocent people who mourn the loss of a loved one.

References

Bowers, William J., and Glenn L. Pierce. 1980. "Arbitrariness and Discrimination Under Post-*Furman* Capital Statutes." *Crime and Delinquency* 26:563–635.

Gross, Samuel R., and Robert Mauro. 1984. "Patterns of Death: An Analysis of Racial Disparities in Capital Sentencing and Homicide Victimization." *Stanford Law Review* 37:27–153.

Magee, Doug. 1980. *Slow Coming Dark: Interviews on Death Row.* New York: Pilgrim Press.

Radelet, Michael L. 1981. "Racial Characteristics and the Imposition of the Death Penalty." *American Sociological Review* 46:918–27.

Radelet, Michael L., and Michael Mello. 1986. "Executing Those Who Kill Blacks: An 'Unusual Case' Study." *Mercer Law Review* 37:911–25.

Radelet, Michael L., and Glenn L. Pierce. 1985. "Race and Prosecutorial Discretion in Homicide Cases." *Law and Society Review* 19:587–621.

Radelet, Michael L., and Margaret Vandiver. 1983. "The Florida Supreme Court and Death Penalty Appeals." *Journal of Criminal Law and Criminology* 74:913–26.

Radelet, Michael L.; Margaret Vandiver; and Felix M. Berardo. 1983. "Families, Prisons, and Death Row Inmates: Men with Death Sentences." *Journal of Family Issues* 4:593–612.

Case Cited

Strickland v. Washington, 466 U.S. 668 (1984).

9

Coping with Death

Families of the Terminally Ill, Homicide Victims, and Condemned Prisoners

MARGARET VANDIVER

The experiences of the families of the terminally ill and the institutional supports available to them have been extensively studied. In contrast, the literature on the families of homicide victims is surprisingly sparse, and almost nothing has been written about the families of condemned prisoners. To some extent, this may reflect the number of people involved in each situation. Each year, thousands of Americans die after prolonged illnesses, and some 19,000 are the victims of homicide (U.S. Department of Justice, 1986), whereas between 1977 and the end of 1988 there were just over a hundred executions, and the death row population at the end of 1988 stood at just over two thousand (NAACP Legal Defense and Educational Fund, 1988).

Families of the Terminally Ill

Families of the terminally ill experience a period of anticipatory grief before their relatives' deaths. Anticipatory grief is "grief expressed in advance when the loss is perceived as inevitable" (Aldrich, 1974:4). It begins with the initial symptoms and diagnosis of terminal illness, and at first resembles the grief felt after a death (Sourkes, 1982:67). As time passes and the illness progresses, the family may experience all the typical phases of grief (Fulton and Fulton, 1980:89).

The burdens of a family with a terminally ill member are very great (Heimlich and Kutscher, 1970). "Family members spoke of feeling like prisoners, captives. . . . [they told] of their own increasing and, at times unbearable, emotional fatigue. They described their burden of sorrow coupled with their increased responsibilities" (Martocchio, 1982:136). Families react in different ways to the terminal illness of a relative. Martocchio observed that previously cohesive families tended to be more so after a member was diagnosed as terminally ill, while fragile families often disintegrated still further (Martocchio, 1982:135).

It is generally expected that families will care for their terminally ill relatives, whether they are prepared and willing to do so or not (Martocchio, 1982:137). Care of the patient usually requires the family to perform a large number of unfamiliar tasks, which at best will give temporary comfort to their relative, without hope of healing. A father whose daughter died of cystic fibrosis reported that "the major emotion pressing upon me was the feeling of inadequacy. . . . The most lost of lost causes is the one for which you must continue to apply effort even when you know it is pointless" (Deford, 1986:97). As the disease progresses, the quality of the patient's daily life may diminish to an intolerable level (Koenig, 1980:9). If the illness is prolonged and painful, family members may find themselves wishing their relative would die and then feeling guilty for having such thoughts. The actual death, when it comes, may be felt at first as a relief (Weizman and Kamm, 1985:46).

In addition to the physical demands of patient care, the family must cope with unfamiliar emotional demands. These may be contradictory in nature. Family members mourn the anticipated death while also trying to keep or establish an intimate relationship with their relative (Weizman and Kamm, 1985:102). Relatives are trying to let go of the terminal patient and to draw closer at the same time. It sometimes happens that the family's disengagement becomes or is perceived by the patient as abandonment (Sourkes, 1982:73). This "turning away" can be intensely distressing for the patient (Fulton and Fulton, 1980:93).

The period of anticipatory grief gives families time in which to take care of "unfinished business" with each other, work out problems, resolve conflicts, and express their affection. The pain of the eventual death may be somewhat eased by the mourning that occurred during the illness. Nevertheless, the grief of the family even after a long and difficult illness is still immense. A bereaved father observed that "nobody ever told me quite how easy dying is. . . . No, the trouble is more afterward; it's the missing that's so hard" (Deford, 1986:28). Hogan and Lienhart reported that the people they interviewed felt that their grief after a family member's death "was insurmountable and would never end" (1985:112).

Families of Homicide Victims

Loss is sudden for the families of homicide victims, and they must cope with tremendous shock as well as grief. "There is nothing to compare with the impact and profound shock of a sudden unexpected death" (Weizman and Kamm, 1985:101). Family members have had no opportunity to prepare for death, and no chance to say goodbye to their relative. "Sudden and unexpected deaths are especially cruel to the survivors" (Kalish, 1980:71). Magee recorded a woman's reaction to the news of the murder of her only daughter:

> For the first time, the other detective spoke. "We think we've found her. Yes, we have her body," he blurted. Iras was sitting on the floor and suddenly her whole body was one huge sound: a scream, a cry, a wail. . . . She heard the detective say something like "beaten to death," and everything in the room became blurry. (Magee, 1983:107)

Believing that the death has happened and absorbing the initial shock may take months (Weizman and Kamm, 1985:46). Only after the shock has worn off do relatives begin to experience the normal phases of grief.

In addition to the fact of their relative's death, the homicide victim's family must come to terms with its violent and intentional nature. A psychiatrist's study of 15 individuals bereaved by homicide found that they all "noted the presence of intensive repetitive images of the homicide . . . focus[ing] on the terror and helplessness of the victim" (Rynearson, 1984:1453). A husband said of his wife's murder: "You can face a lot of things, but when somebody's abusing you at their own whim and in their own fashion, that's terror and that's torture and no one should have to experience that in a lifetime, no one should!" (Kinder, 1982:66–67). Families of homicide victims have a very clear focus for their rage. But for the actions of the murderer, their relative would be alive and uninjured. "The shock of the death is complicated by hate for the killer, preoccupation with judgment and retribution" (Raphael, 1983:29). The anger and fear felt by the victim's family may be so great as to obstruct the typical process of grieving (Weizman and Kamm, 1985:103).

Families of homicide victims sometimes fear for their own safety (Barkas, 1978:39). The shock of violence is so great that all sense of normalcy may be lost. The death of an aged person from disease, although sad and painful, can be seen as occurring within the normal order of events. Homicide, on the other hand, profoundly disrupts fundamental assumptions about society, individuals, and purpose in life. "It makes you feel you cannot trust anyone or count on anything" (Weizman and Kamm, 1985:45). In describing the feelings of a woman whose four sons were murdered, Magee wrote:

> What earthly reason was there for her to be walking and breathing when those four boys were dead? . . . Then there were the waves and waves of anger . . . [and a] sense of meaninglessness to her life. She felt suicidal and on the brink of a breakdown. (Magee, 1983:66, 74)

Months and even years after the event, families of homicide victims may continue to suffer. A daughter "still cries every day. She states that she doesn't sleep through a single night and thinks a part of her died too when her parents were killed. She reports she doesn't find much joy in anything" (*Booth v. Maryland,* 107 S.Ct. 2529 [1987]). The prolonged anguish of these families has led one writer to conclude: "Death by homicide seems to be one death a family can *never* accept" (Barkas, 1978:43).

Families of the Condemned

Families of condemned prisoners typically face a decade or more between the time a death sentence is imposed and the time it is carried out. Prolonged anticipation of death creates enormous strains and problems for families. "The families of men sentenced to die are helpless bystanders in a slow dying process that they know can be stopped" (Radelet et al., 1983:600). The process of appellate litigation is tedious and complex; however, it holds out substantial hope for reversal of the death sentence, or even release of the prisoner (Boger, 1986:16). This continued hope makes it difficult for the families to accept the possibility that their relative will eventually be executed. Each adverse decision as the case moves through the courts decreases the chance of relief and vividly reminds the prisoner and the family of their vulnerability. During the years of appeals, the prisoner's family is in a state of continuous anxiety and suspense. Like families of terminal patients, they may find themselves wishing for an end to the period of waiting, and then feel guilty for having such thoughts. But the period of waiting can be used to express affection, work out old conflicts, and reminisce about other times.

Guilt feelings are common to families in all three situations, but for the relatives of prisoners, such feelings come from two sources. Families will ask what in their relative's background and upbringing could have led to the commission of the offense, particularly if the attorneys choose to use the inmate's troubled family history as an argument for mitigation of the sentence. Publicity about the crime and media interest in the family's history and problems increase their sense of guilt and humiliation (Danto, 1982:94). Smykla noted the prevalence of "self-accusation" among the families of death row inmates; in interviews, some relatives said, "It's all my fault" (1987:342–43). The families may also believe that they could have altered the result of the trial and appeals. They may think that a different lawyer or another legal strategy could have resulted in success, and blame themselves for the outcome.

Like the families of dying patients, families of condemned prisoners experience grief and loss in anticipation of eventual death. Because there is very little families can do to cure disease or to obtain favorable decisions from appellate courts, the period of waiting is one of helplessness and frustration. The sister of a condemned man said:

It hurts you can't do anything. There's nothing you can do.
It's like we're a million miles away and there's nothing we can
do. Every day I wish I could do something, but I can't. It's
very frustrating, extremely frustrating that we can't help him
or make life easier for him while he's there. (Smykla, 1987:
343)

An experience common to the families of the condemned and
the families of homicide victims is the loss of a relative by violent
means, although the type of violence is very different in the two
situations. The homicide victim dies by sudden, passionate, individual violence, while the condemned prisoner dies by slow, deliberate, and collective violence. The survivors of both must live with
the knowledge that their relative died from the intentional acts of
others, and that the death was avoidable.[1]

Not only is the death penalty deliberately imposed, but it is
selectively imposed. Disease and homicide may happen to anyone,
but only very rarely are middle- or upper-class people sentenced to
death, and a large body of research documents racial bias in capital
sentencing (Gross and Mauro, 1984). The families are acutely aware
of the unfairness of the judicial system, and their sense of injustice
frequently leads to anger and distrust toward the system and all those
who are a part of it.

Unlike families of homicide victims, who have a clear focus for
their anger in the murderers (Weizman and Kamm, 1985:52–53),
families of condemned prisoners must direct their anger at a much
larger and less specific group. A characteristic of the death penalty
as it is administered in modern America is the wide diffusion of responsibility, so that no one individual can be held accountable for
the ultimate death of the prisoner. The bereaved relative may feel
anger toward the police, prosecutors, co-defendants, court personnel, jurors, press, prison officials, elected authorities, and the general
public. But none of these people is a clearly defined target in the way
that the murderer is for the victim's family. The dispassionate collu-
sion of a large number of people in bringing about a family member's
death causes great pain and alienation for the survivors.

Families of condemned prisoners must also cope with the
knowledge that their relatives' deaths are actively desired. Terminal
illness is nearly universally regretted, and homicide nearly universally condemned, but today in the United States executions have a

high level of public support. This support frequently involves merely a general approval of the abstract idea of capital punishment, but in the days preceding a planned execution, particularly one of a widely known inmate, the desire for the prisoner's death becomes quite specific and vehement. The crowds that have gathered during executions at prisons in several southern states strongly resemble lynch mobs. At an execution in Virginia in 1985:

> [Demonstrators,] men and women, sported signs saying, "Fry Em," "Burn Briley Burn," and "Kill the Negro." Some waved Confederate flags . . . and uttered all manner of racial epithets . . . one white woman carried a sign reading, "How does it feel to be burned in a chair? Burn—damn you—koon!" (Dance, 1987:135–36, 139–40)

These "gloating crowds demanding that the convict's death come quickly" (Kaplan, 1984:185) are unlike anything experienced by families in the other situations, with the exception of recent hysterical outbursts against people infected with AIDS and their families (Shilts, 1987).

Social Supports

Families in the three situations outlined above face multiple problems. Their needs for information, assistance, and emotional support are enormous. Unfortunately, assistance is often limited or unavailable.

Physicians and other medical personnel are immensely important to the families of the terminally ill. The physicians have more information about the relative's condition, prognosis, and life expectancy than anyone else. There may be no one else available to explain to the family what is wrong, what course the disease can be expected to take, and how much time their relative has to live. Good communication with a trusted health care worker can significantly ease the family's distress, even when there is only bad news to be told.

Unfortunately, good relations between doctors and patients' families do not always exist. Wende Bowie described her experiences with the physicians and other medical staff who treated her dying first-born child. Her requests for information were resented by the staff, who perceived her and her husband as "confused" and intrusive. Although the hospital made several serious mistakes in caring for the Bowies' child, the staff were not receptive to the parents' suggestions for better communication and care, and were insensitive to their emotional needs (Bowie, 1980).

Physicians and other medical staff cannot allow themselves to take each patient's death personally. They must maintain a professional distance and composure (Coombs and Powers, 1976:16). For their own sake and for the smooth functioning of the hospital, they maintain a certain detachment from the patient and from the grieving family. For these reasons, Kavanaugh has suggested the use of intermediaries to assist families:

> Until you stand in the halls of a large hospital night after night, a timid and tired stranger, you might not comprehend the need for an ombudsman to help. Unless treated coldly by a doctor, the last link to life for someone you love, or brusquely by nurses who appeared indifferent to one you treasure, you will not fully comprehend how much families need an advocate, especially when death is in the offing. (Kavanaugh, 1972:175)

Hospitals often have chaplains and social workers to help families, and nurses may also assist them. Without such services, families may be treated as "non-persons" (Glaser and Strauss, 1965:171). And even when such help is available, the hospital itself may be a cause of distress. Large, impersonal, cold, and confusing, it may overwhelm the already unhappy and anxious visitor. "Psychologically, [the hospital] assaults with its alien machines, rhythms, language, and routines" (May, 1977:413–14).

Hospices can offer an alternative to hospital care, and a source of help and support for terminal patients and their families. Hospices emphasize the dignity of the dying person, the importance of the patient's family, and comprehensive services to the patient and family (Koff, 1980; Krant, 1978). Home care is appropriate after treatment of the disease is no longer helpful. Rather than continuing to fight against the disease when death is imminent, "[h]ighest priority is given to physical and emotional comfort. . . . It is best pursued in an environment which supports privacy, relationship, intimacy, and continuity" (Little, 1985:7). Perhaps the greatest benefit of hospice care is that it returns as much control over events as possible to the patient and family.

The institutions encountered by the families of homicide victims are principally the police and the courts. Although these institutions formally support the families, they are often insensitive to their needs. Police officers, like doctors, may severely limit their emotional involvement with grieving people in order to protect themselves. Typically they have little or no training in dealing with bereavement. Staff in the medical examiner's office and members of the media frequently become hardened as well. Prosecutors may believe that they support the victim's family, but in general the courts offer little assistance to survivors (Danto, 1982:93–94).

Arrest of the offender and imposition of sentence may assist the victim's family in their healing; and unsolved and unpunished murder "remains a painful and preoccupying riddle" (Rynearson, 1984:1454). Yet the legal process and the attention focused on the case as a result can cause the survivors great pain. "The victims' son notes that he keeps seeing news reports about his parents' murder which show their house and the police removing their bodies. This is a constant reminder to him" (*Booth v. Maryland*, 107 S.Ct. 2529 [1987]). And if the family chooses to attend the trial, the medical examiner's report, testimony about the homicide, and the sight of the accused murderers are an ordeal. The conviction and sentencing of the accused may bring some sense of closure; victims' families need "some counterbalancing justice" (Magee, 1983:xiv) to restore a sense of equilibrium. It is important to note, however, that the expectation that all victims' families will want vengeance, or will favor a particular sentence, denies the range of reactions that such families actually have. Some bereaved families want revenge, some are uncertain, and others definitely do not.

Families of homicide victims often feel isolated from other people, even from those who wish to help them. Surviving relatives have a great need to talk about their loss, but frequently find their friends unwilling to discuss the homicide or the victim. The father of a murder victim told a counselor:

> Something else that we've noticed—they—when people, friends, are discussing family and children, there always seems to be a sort of tension where they stop the conversation. Even

when we meet strangers that friends of ours have already introduced to us, that they never ask about our children. I think
that somebody's warning them all about us. (Shneidman, 1980:
174–75)

The survivors may feel cut off even from their closest friends as a
result. "No one comprehended that really he was ill, that grief had
made him so, that grief had drawn a circle around him he could not
escape from and others could not enter," Truman Capote wrote of
one survivor (1965:203).

In recent years there has been an increasing concern for victims' rights. Legislation providing victim compensation and giving
victims greater access to the courts has been passed in many states
(Magee, 1983:xv). In addition, self-help groups such as Parents of
Murdered Children offer support and understanding for families bereaved by homicide. Existing health and welfare agencies offer little
to these families, but might be able to develop programs to lend
further assistance (Danto, 1982).

Support for the families of condemned inmates is nearly non-
existent. No organizations exist for them. The individual families of
men sentenced to death are unlikely to know each other and are
widely scattered geographically. Thus, "they cannot rely on each
other for information, mutual support, and emotional release" (Radelet et al., 1983:599).

To be condemned is "the most desolating of rejections" (van
den Haag, 1975:212); the stigma of a death sentence is such that it
affects the family as well as the condemned prisoner. This stigma
and strong public support for executions make it difficult for family
members to find support and assistance. The sister of a condemned
man described her experiences at work:

I wanted to tell the world this was my brother they were talking
about. . . . People around me, I knew they were whispering.
I was like a mechanical woman, going to work, clocking in,
doing the best eight hours I knew how. I was suppressing the
feelings of jeers and things said around me. (Smykla, 1987:345)

Some death row families are afraid to let anyone know of their situation for fear of possible hostility and rejection. Friends may abandon
the family out of embarrassment at their inability to help, or shame

at the charges and conviction. Families become "victims of a collective sense of guilt" (Danto, 1982:94). Some families turn to their
churches or synagogues, and find support and help, but many face
the long wait and eventual execution alone (Kane, 1986:35).

Lawyers are as important to the families of the condemned as
doctors are to the families of the terminally ill.[2] The lawyer is often
the only source of information on the relative's case in particular and
on the legal system in general. The lawyer is the only person who
can give the family a reasonable estimate of their relative's chances
of winning on appeal, and of how long the process of appeals may
take.

Relations between the lawyers and their clients' families are
often marked by frustration and mistrust on the part of the families.
Although some lawyers consistently keep families informed, explain
legal issues in simple, understandable language, and assure relatives
of their commitment to the case, others are brusque and indifferent. Phone calls and letters may go unanswered, leaving families
frightened and bewildered by a process that they do not understand,
but that they know can kill their relative. Families may feel compelled to ruin themselves financially in an attempt to secure good
representation. Smykla recorded the reaction of two sisters to the
news that their brother's execution date had been set:

> I was going to the bank. I knew all I had to do was throw down
> those deeds [to her home] . . . take it to the lawyers and say,
> "Save him." Then I called my sister, and she said, "Don't do
> it. They knew we were going to do this. They took all we got,
> almost. . . ." I was crying so hard. We was crying. It was a
> mess. It was the darkest day I ever had in my life. (Smykla,
> 1987:345)

For these families, the prison is the principal institution encountered. There are similarities between prisons and hospitals, but
although hospitals may often seem threatening, hostile, or indifferent
to individuals, prisons are deliberately designed to have such characteristics. Individual correctional officers may be kind and helpful to
families, but the atmosphere of the prison is never welcoming. Death
rows are usually located in rural areas where little public transportation is available; many of the local residents may be employed by the
prison. Visits at the prison, even by the inmate's immediate family

members, are a privilege and not a right, and can be forbidden at
the discretion of the prison administration. Visits are limited to a
few hours per week, and in some states the prisoner is kept behind
a screen or glass partition. Visitors may be required to submit to
humiliating strip searches before they are allowed to see their relative. All these factors increase the isolation of the prisoner and make
sustained close contact with the family very difficult.

Death row families experience many of the same miseries as
families of terminally ill patients. Dying is prolonged, quality of life
may be poor, there are financial hardships, much uncertainty, and
an inability to get on with life (Westbrook and Viney, 1982). Comparisons of degrees of suffering are probably meaningless, but the
many years of appeals, the stigma of the crime and sentence, prison
restrictions on visiting and contact, lack of external support, and the
degrading violence of the eventual death may make the ordeal of the
prisoner's family even greater than that of the patient's. As Albert
Camus wrote:

> [T]he relatives of the condemned man then discover an excess
> of suffering that punishes them beyond all justice. A mother's
> or a father's long months of waiting, the visiting room, the arti-
> ficial conversations filling up the brief moments spent with the
> condemned man, the visions of the executions are all tortures.
> (Camus, 1974:205)

Despite the lack of formal organizational support for these
families, some informal assistance is available to them. In Florida,
the state with the highest number of condemned inmates in the
United States (NAACP Legal Defense and Educational Fund, 1988),
a handful of people concerned about these families has formed the
Family Support Project.[3] The project raises small amounts of money,
mainly through churches and synagogues, for transportation, provides housing for visiting families, helps interpret and explain what
is happening in the courts, and, when requested, contacts local ministers and makes burial and funeral arrangements. Because so few
people are involved in the project and so little money is available,
assistance is usually limited to families of inmates under a death warrant that is expected to lead to an execution within a few weeks.
Almost no assistance is available to the families during the preceding years when their relatives' appeals are being taken through the

courts, and the limited resources usually allow no followup assistance.

In large part, the misery of bereavement is a private experience that must be endured by the survivors, whatever the cause of the death. To the extent that grief is not entirely personal, but is exacerbated by other problems, the difficulties of family members can be reduced and some of their needs met. Better institutional supports and wider understanding of the experience of loss could alleviate much egregious suffering.

Notes

1. The family of the homicide victim and the family of the condemned are the same in the rare cases in which a person goes to death row for a crime against a member of his or her family. Surviving relatives experience all the loss and shock and grief of other families who lose a member to murder, but in addition they face the public humiliation, disgrace, and stress of the families of condemned prisoners.
2. Many condemned inmates are unrepresented for long periods of time. There are few provisions for supplying free legal counsel after an early point in the appellate process, and in states with large death row populations, dozens of condemned prisoners may be without legal counsel at any one time. Prisoners have come within a week of a scheduled execution before lawyers could be found to represent them.
3. Nearly all of those involved in this effort and similar ones in other states are actively committed to abolishing the death penalty. Some abolitionists have raised the concern that ameliorating the fear and pain of individual prisoners and their families may make executions easier for the state to perform, and for the public to accept. The moral question of some degree of cooperation with the agent of death does not confront caregivers in the other situations described. When an execution occurs, the desperate needs of a family facing violent bereavement outweigh abstract qualms about "sanitizing" the process.

References

Aldrich, C. K. 1974. "Some Dynamics of Anticipatory Grief." Pp. 3–9 in *Anticipatory Grief*, edited by Bernard Schoenberg, A. C. Carr, A. H. Kutscher, David Peretz, and I. K. Goldberg. New York: Columbia University Press.

Barkas, J. L. 1978. *Victims*. New York: Charles Scribner's Sons.

Boger, Jack. 1986. "Interview with Jack Boger." *The Defender* 8 (July–Aug.): 15–18.

Bowie, Wende K. 1980. "Story of a First Born." Pp. 45–61 in *Caring Relationships: The Dying and the Bereaved*, edited by R. A. Kalish. Farmingdale, N.Y.: Baywood.

Camus, Albert. 1974. "Reflections on the Guillotine." Pp. 173–234 in *Resistance, Rebellion, and Death*. New York: Vintage.

Capote, Truman. 1965. *In Cold Blood*. New York: Random House.

Coombs, R. H., and P. S. Powers. 1976. "Socialization for Death: The Physician's Role." Pp. 15–36 in *Toward a Sociology of Death and Dying*, edited by Lynn Lofland. Beverly Hills, Calif.: Sage.

Dance, Daryl Cumber. 1987. *Long Gone: The Mecklenburg Six and the Theme of Escape in Black Folklore*. Knoxville: University of Tennessee Press.

Danto, B. L. 1982. "Survivors of Homicide." Pp. 85–97 in *The Human Side of Homicide*, edited by B. L. Danto, John Bruhns, and A. H. Kutscher. New York: Columbia University Press.

Deford, Frank. 1986. *Alex: The Life of a Child*. New York: New American Library.

Fulton, Robert, and Julie Fulton. 1980. "A Psychosocial Aspect of Terminal Care: Anticipatory Grief." Pp. 87–96 in *Caring Relationships: The Dying and the Bereaved*, edited by R. A. Kalish. Farmingdale, N.Y.: Baywood.

Glaser, Barney G., and Anselm L. Strauss. 1965. *Awareness of Dying*. Chicago: Aldine.

Gross, Samuel R., and Robert Mauro. 1984. "Patterns of Death: An Analysis of Racial Disparities in Capital Sentencing and Homicide Victimization." *Stanford Law Review* 37:27–153.

Heimlich, H. J. and A. H. Kutscher. 1970. "The Family's Reaction to Terminal Illness." Pp. 270–79 in *Loss and Grief: Psychological Management in Medical Practice*, edited by Bernard Schoenberg, A. C. Carr, David Peretz, and A. H. Kutscher. New York: Columbia University Press.

Hogan, R. A., and G. A. Lienhart. 1985. "The Preparation of a Crisis Counselor for the Terminally Ill and Their Families." Pp. 108–16 in *Loss, Grief, and Bereavement: A Guide for Counseling*, edited by Otto Margolis, H. C. Raether, A. H. Kutscher, S. C. Klagsbrun, Eric Marcus, V. R. Pine, and D. J. Cherico. New York: Praeger.

Kalish, Richard A. 1980. *Caring Relationships: The Dying and the Bereaved*. Farmingdale, N.Y.: Baywood.

Kane, Karen. 1986. "Forgotten Families of Death Row." *The Defender* 8 (July–Aug.):33–35.

Kaplan, John. 1984. "Administering Capital Punishment." *University of Florida Law Review* 36:177–92.

Kavanaugh, Robert E. 1972. *Facing Death*. New York: Penguin Books.

Kinder, Gary. 1982. *Victim: The Other Side of Murder*. New York: Dell.

Koenig, Ronald. 1980. "Dying vs. Well-Being." Pp. 9–22 in *Caring Relationships: The Dying and the Bereaved*, edited by R. A. Kalish. Farmingdale, N.Y.: Baywood.

Koff, Theodore H. 1980. *Hospice: A Caring Community*. Cambridge, Mass.: Winthrop.

Krant, M. J. 1978. "The Hospice Movement." *New England Journal of Medicine* 299:546–49.

Little, Deborah W. 1985. *Home Care for the Dying: A Reassuring Comprehensive Guide to Physical and Emotional Care*. Garden City, N.Y.: Dial Press.

Magee, Doug. 1983. *What Murder Leaves Behind: The Victim's Family*. New York: Dodd, Mead.

Martocchio, Benita. 1982. *Living While Dying*. Bowie, Md.: Robert J. Brady.

May, W. F. 1977. "Institutions as Symbols of Death." Pp. 407–26 in *Death and Society: A Book of Readings and Sources*, edited by James P. Carse and Arlene B. Dallery. New York: Harcourt Brace Jovanovich.

NAACP Legal Defense and Educational Fund. 1988. "Death Row, U.S.A." Unpublished compilation, available from 99 Hudson St., New York, N.Y. 10013.

Radelet, Michael L.; Margaret Vandiver, and Felix M. Berardo. 1983. "Families, Prisons, and Men with Death Sentences: The Human Impact of Structured Uncertainty." *Journal of Family Issues* 4:593–612.

Raphael, Beverly. 1983. *The Anatomy of Bereavement*. New York: Basic Books.

Rynearson, E. K. 1984. "Bereavement After Homicide: A Descriptive Study." *American Journal of Psychiatry* 141:1452–54.

Shilts, Randy. 1987. *And the Band Played On: Politics, People, and the AIDS Epidemic*. New York: St. Martin's Press.

Shneidman, Edwin S. 1980. *Voices of Death*. New York: Harper and Row.

Smykla, John O. 1987. "The Human Impact of Capital Punishment: Interviews with Families of Persons on Death Row." *Journal of Criminal Justice* 15:331–47.

Sourkes, Barbara M. 1982. *The Deepening Shade: Psychological Aspects of Life-Threatening Illness*. Pittsburgh: University of Pittsburgh Press.

U.S. Department of Justice. 1986. *Crime in the U.S.—1985*. Washington, D.C.: U.S. Government Printing Office.

van den Haag, Ernest. 1975. *Punishing Criminals: Concerning a Very Old and Painful Question*. New York: Basic Books.

Weizman, Savine G., and Phyllis Kamm. 1985. *About Mourning: Support and Guidance for the Bereaved*. New York: Human Sciences Press.

Westbrook, M. T., and L. L. Viney. 1982. "Psychological Reactions to the Onset of Chronic Illness." *Social Science and Medicine* 16:899–905.

Case Cited

Booth v. Maryland, 107 S.Ct. 2529 (1987).

10

Rituals of Death

Capital Punishment and Human Sacrifice

ELIZABETH D. PURDUM AND
J. ANTHONY PAREDES

We were perplexed by the resurgence of enthusiasm for the death penalty in the United States. According to a 1986 *Gallup Report*, support for the death penalty in America has reached a near-record high in 50 years of polling, with 70 percent of Americans favoring execution of convicted murderers (Gallup, 1986). In a 1983 poll conducted in Florida, 72 percent of respondents were found to support the death penalty, compared with 45 percent in 1964 (Cambridge Survey Research, 1985). Still more perplexing is the finding that nearly half of those supporting the death penalty agree that "only the poor and unfortunate are likely to be executed" (Ellsworth and Ross, 1983:153). Equally startling is the revelation that although deterrence is often given as a primary justification for the death

An earlier, abbreviated version of this chapter was presented at the 1985 annual meeting of the American Anthropological Association. We extend our sincere gratitude to Scharlette Holdman, Larry Spalding, and Gail Anderson for their assistance in our research for this paper. Thanks go also to Mary Pohl for directing us to sources on the Aztecs. Michael Radelet was very generous in his comments on an earlier draft and provided us with references to many important sources. Our debts to others notwithstanding, we assume full responsibility for the accuracy of information and the ideas presented here.

penalty, most people would continue to support it even if convinced that it had no greater deterrent effect than that of a life sentence (P. Harris, 1986). In addition, there is little if any evidence that capital punishment reduces the crime rate; there seems, rather, to be some historical evidence for a reverse correlation. Pickpocketing, a crime then punishable by hanging, was rampant among spectators at executions in England circa 1700 (Lofland, 1977). Bowers and Pierce (1980) argue, on the basis of increased murder rates in New York State in the month following executions, that capital punishment has a "brutalizing" effect and leads to more, not less, violence. Why, then, does capital punishment receive such widespread support in modern America?

Capital Punishment—Another "Riddle of Culture"

In theory, capital punishment should be no more a puzzle than any other seemingly bizarre, nonrational custom. Either human cultures are amenable to scientific explanation or they are not. And we anthropologists have not been timid about tackling everything from Arunta penile subincision to Hindu cow love as problems for scientific explication. As a first step in this task, we will compare capital punishment in Florida, the leader in the United States in death sentencing since Florida's 1972 capital punishment statute was affirmed by the U.S. Supreme Court in 1976, with certain forms of human sacrifice as practiced by the Aztecs of Mexico in the sixteenth century. This is not a capricious comparison. John Cooper (1976) pointedly seeks the "socio-religious origins of capital punishment" in ancient rites of, to use his term, "propitiatory death." But his study is narrowly constrained by canons of Western philosophy and history. By making a more exotic comparison, we hope to point the way to more nomothetic principles for understanding state-sanctioned homicide in complex societies. Albert Camus (1959) also perceived elements of religious ritual in French capital punishment, but argued that the practice continued only because hidden from the view of the general public. Anticipating our comparisons here, anthropologist Colin Turnbull concludes in his article "Death by Decree" that the key to understanding capital punishment is to be found in its ritual element (1978). John Lofland (1977) has compared the dramaturgy of state executions circa 1700 in England with those of contemporary America, concluding that modern executions in their impersonal, unemotional, and private aspects appear humane, yet deny the reality of death and strip the condemned of any opportunity to die with dignity or courage.

It was the public media spectacle surrounding recent executions in Florida that triggered the thoughts leading to this paper. Detailed, minute-by-minute accounts of Florida's first post-1976 execution, widely reported press conferences with death row inmates, television images of the ambulance bearing the body of an executed criminal, news photos of mourners and revelers outside the prison on the night before an execution—all these served to transform a closely guarded, hidden expression of the ultimate power of the state into a very public ceremonial event. We were reminded of the pomp and circumstance for the masses accompanying the weird rites of Tenochtitlan that greeted sixteenth-century Spaniards. In such similarities, we thought, might lie the key to a dispassionate, anthropological understanding of capital punishment in modern America.

Before proceeding we must note that the Aztec state itself imposed capital punishment for a variety of crimes, ranging from murder to fornication to violations of the dress code for commoners. The available sources indicate, however, that among the Aztecs capital punishment was swift, rather unceremonious, and even brutish. It is the high drama of Aztec rituals of human sacrifice that shows the closest parallels with the bureaucratically regulated procedures for electrocution of the condemned at Starke, Florida, in the 1980s.

The Victims of Execution and Sacrifice

The death penalty is imposed on only a small percentage of Americans convicted of homicide—5 percent, according to a 1980 Georgia study (Baldus et al., 1983). Today there are 2,182 people on death row in the United States; 296 of these are in Florida (NAACP Legal Defense and Educational Fund, 1988). Since 1976, 18 persons have been executed in Florida. Prior to 1972, when the Supreme Court voided state death penalty statutes, it was clear that the death penalty was disproportionately applied to black men. Fifty-four percent of the 3,859 people executed in the United States between 1930 and 1967 were nonwhite. Among those executed for rape during the same period, 405 of 455 were black (U.S. Department of Justice, 1986). Nakell and Hardy's study of homicide cases in North Carolina from 1977 and 1978 revealed the effects of race of victim and race of defendant throughout the criminal justice process (1987). The relationship between race and execution consistently holds even when one controls for such factors as differential conviction rates and the relationship between the defendant and the victim (Radelet, 1981).

Recent studies (for example, Baldus et al., 1983; Bowers and Pierce, 1980b; Gross and Mauro, 1984; Pasternoster, 1983; and Radelet, 1981) suggest that the defendant's race, since the reinstatement of the death penalty in 1976, is less important than it once was in predicting death sentences. These studies conclude that a more significant factor is the race of the victim: that is, people who kill whites are more likely to receive the death penalty than people who kill blacks.

Statistics aside, people familiar with death row inmates readily acknowledge that they are marginal members of society—economically, socially, and, even, in the case of Florida, geographically. Many come from backgrounds of extreme poverty and abuse. Michael Radelet and his colleagues (1983) report one common denominator among families who have members in prison: low socioeconomic status. Poverty makes it hard, if not impossible, for families to maintain ties with prisoners. Many inmates on death row have few family or social ties. Only about 15 of the 208 men on death row in Florida in 1983 had visitors each week; 60 others had visitors about once a month; and fewer than half received a visitor in any given year (Radelet et al., 1983). Many of Florida's inmates are from out of state. More than a few of Florida's death row inmates are also crazy, retarded, or both. For instance, Arthur Goode, who was convicted of murdering a nine-year-old boy, ate a half-gallon of butter pecan ice cream, his requested "last meal," then gave as his final statement his desire to marry a young boy. In the three weeks before his execution, Goode wrote letters to the governor and other prominent officials complaining of the lack of toilet paper to blow his nose (Radelet and Barnard, 1986). There is an inmate who believes that one of the people helping him with his court appeals is alternately a dead disc jockey or one of his own seven wives. Or, there is James Douglas Hill, a 26-year-old with an IQ of 66 and a serious speech impediment, who, having learned to read and write while in prison, sent to his mother this message:

> Hi mom me hour are you doing to day fine i hope i am doing ok for now But i miss you so varry varry much that i can cry But i am to Big to cry. . . . i miss you i miss you love James all way. By now. (Sherrill, 1984:555)

In 1987 James Douglas Hill was released on bail when substantial doubt about his guilt surfaced.

Detailed statistics on *whom* the Aztecs put to death in their rites of human sacrifice are not available, nor is the exact number of sacrificial victims. Nonetheless, the Aztecs of Central Mexico sacrificed humans on a scale unprecedented in any other society. Putting aside the question of whether the Aztecs were nutritionally motivated toward this human slaughter (Harner, 1977), annual estimates for central Mexico in the first decades of the sixteenth century vary from 20,000 (Cortes, as quoted by Fagan, 1984:230) to 250,000 sacrificed victims (Woodrow Borah, as quoted by Harner, 1977:119).

Most of the sacrificial victims were able-bodied male war captives from neighboring kingdoms, but the Aztecs reportedly also sacrificed large numbers of children—sold to the priests by the poor. The children's tears were believed to be particularly appealing to Tlaloc, the rain god. Women were also sometimes sacrificed, some of them presented as impersonations of certain female deities. Similarly, one of the most frequently recounted, and often highly romanticized, forms of Aztec human sacrifice was that in which a flawless young war captive was pampered and indulged for a year as the embodiment of a god, then killed with great ritual and sadness while the victim dutifully played his role in the deicidal drama. Most Aztec war captives enjoyed no such protracted special treatment. How god-impersonators were selected we do not know. Neither do we know how many war captives' lives were spared, if any, nor how many were doomed to a life of slavery.

Paralleling the numerous means of execution employed in the United States—electrocution, hanging, firing squad, deadly gas, lethal injection—the Aztecs sacrificed their victims with a variety of techniques. These included beheading, burning, and flights of arrows, but the most common method was to spread the victim on a large, elaborately carved stone, cut open his chest with an obsidian knife, then tear out his heart. We present here a brief, composite account of "ordinary" war captive sacrifice using the method of coronary excision.

Announcement of Death

According to Fray Diego Duran's account of the aftermath of a battle between the Aztecs and the Tepeacas, the Tepeacan captives were taken back to the Aztec capital, Tenochtitlan, with collars around their necks and their hands bound behind them. The captives "went along singing sadly, weeping and lamenting their fate," knowing they were to be sacrificed. Once they were in the capital, priests threw incense on them, offered them maize bread, and said:

> We welcome you
> To this city of Mexico Tenochtitlan
>
> . . . .
>
> Do you think that you have come to live;
> You have come to die.
>
> . . . . . .
>
> We salute you and comfort you with these words:
> You have not come because of weakness,
> But because of your manliness.
> You will die here but your fame will live forever.
>   (Duran, 1964:101)

The announcement of a Florida death row inmate's impending death comes with the signing of a death warrant by the state governor, once all routine appeals and bids for clemency have failed. The criteria by which the decision is made to sign a warrant against a particular person at a particular time are not publicly known.

A death warrant is a single-page document in legal language, bordered in black. Each one bears the state seal and is officially witnessed by the secretary of state—not by some seemingly more likely authority such as the attorney general. Each death warrant is publicized by a news release issued shortly after the governor signs. Between 1972 and the end of 1988, Florida's three governors signed over two hundred death warrants. Once the warrant is signed in Tallahassee, the superintendent of Florida State Prison at Starke, 150 miles away, is immediately notified. Prison guards are sent to get the person named in the warrant from his or her cell. They bring the prisoner, who may have no forewarning of what is about to happen, to the assistant superintendent's office. There the superintendent or his designee reads the warrant aloud to the condemned. Following a string of "whereas's" tracing the history of the case, the warrant concludes:

> Now, therefore, I, [names governor], as Governor of the State of Florida and pursuant to the authority and responsibility vested by the Constitution and the Laws of Florida do hereby issue this warrant directing the Superintendent of the Florida State Prison to cause the sentence of death to be executed upon [names person] on some day of the week beginning [for instance] Noon, Tuesday, the 29th day of October, 1989, and ending Noon, Tuesday the 5th day of November, 1989, in accord with the provisions of the laws of the State of Florida.

The warrant is usually dated four weeks before the last day the warrant is in effect. Reportedly, warrants are never issued for executions to take place during the time the state supreme court is not in session or during the Christmas season. After the warrant is read, the prisoner is permitted to telephone a lawyer and a family member, if he or she has any.

Treatment After Announcement of Death

Aztec war captives were served "Divine Wine" (probably pulque) and paraded past images of the Aztec gods and past the emperor, Montezuma. They were given cloaks, loincloths, and sandals —sandals being a mark of nobility. Next, the prisoners were taken to the central marketplace, where they were given flowers and "shields of splendid featherwork" and forced to dance upon a platform. The condemned were also given tobacco to smoke, which, according to Duran, "comforted them greatly" (Duran, 1964:102).

The war captives were dispersed among the several wards of the city, and men were assigned to guard and maintain them with the charge:

Take care that they do not escape
Take care that they do not die!
Behold, they are children of the Sun!
Feed them well; let them be fat and desirable for the sacrifice
    . . . (Duran, 1964:108)

Duran (1964) reports that captives were treated well and honored as if they were gods.

Many days passed during which craftsmen were instructed to carve a stone for the sacrificial altar. A few days later the altar was ready, and temple youths were given instructions about how the sacrifice was to be conducted. Guests were invited from neighboring states, and booths were decorated for spectators.

In Florida, the reading of the death warrant initiates a period officially designated as "death watch," marked by moving the person to a cell in "Q Wing," where he or she will be closer to the electric chair and isolated from other death row inmates. Most of the person's possessions are taken away, including photographs and tennis shoes, the only personally owned item of apparel that inmates are ordinarily allowed; the condemned is allowed to retain only those items listed in the "Execution Guidelines," a 39-page single-spaced document (Florida State Prison, 1983). The only books on the list are "religious tracts as distributed by Institution Chaplain, maximum possession ten (10)." Magazine and newspaper subscriptions may continue, but no new periodicals may be ordered. In a curious specific parallel with Aztec practice, there are no special restrictions on tobacco for prisoners on Q Wing. Three meals a day are fed to all "condemned inmates," and dietary restrictions for "medical reasons" continue to be observed. Indeed, meticulous, detailed instructions are given to prison personnel to ensure that the condemned person is kept in good health and not provided with any item that might be used to harm himself or attempt suicide. Moreover, under current procedures if a prisoner is determined to have become insane on death row, he or she is spared execution until restored to mental health (Radelet and Barnard, 1986).

Once death watch begins, social visits are "noncontact" and held in the "maximum security visiting park" any two days, Monday through Friday, 9 A.M. to 3 P.M. Other death row inmates are permitted "contact" social visits for six hours on Saturdays or Sundays. Legal visits for the condemned may continue to be the "contact" type during the death warrant, but only until one week before execution, when these visits, too, become noncontact. Media visits are scheduled through prison officials on Tuesday, Wednesday, and Thursday until Phase II of death watch begins, five days before the execution is scheduled to occur.

With Phase II of death watch, more property is taken from the prisoner. The condemned is allowed only a few so-called comfort items: "one TV located outside cell, 1 radio, 1 deck of cards, 1 Bible, 1 book, periodical, magazine or newspaper." Very specific day-by-day regulations and procedures now go into effect, beginning with "Execution Day–Minus Five (5)," when the "execution squad" is identified. Likewise, on Execution Day–Minus Four (4), testing of the electrical equipment to be used for execution begins. During Phase II the inmate is subjected to further limitations on visits, but during the 48 hours before the scheduled execution, the condemned may have an interview with a media representative of his or her choice. Execution Day–Minus Four (4) is a particularly busy day: the condemned reinventories his or her property and specifies in writing its disposition; specifies in writing his or her funeral arrangements; and is measured for a suit of clothing—the suit will be cheap—in which the condemned will, if he or she wants, be buried. On Day–Minus Three (3) there are "no activities," and Day–Minus Two (2) is devoted primarily to testing the equipment and "execution squad drill." On Execution Day–Minus One (1) the pace quickens, and it is on this day that the chef takes the person's order for the last meal.

Each time the prisoner is moved during Phase II of death watch, the entire prison is locked down and the condemned undergoes a complete body search upon being returned to his or her cell. A guard sits outside the condemned inmate's cell, as one always does during an active death warrant, but now the guard records every 15 minutes what the prisoner is doing.

Final Preparations for Death

On the day of an Aztec sacrifice, the visiting nobles were seated in their decorated booths and the prisoners were placed in a line before them and made to dance. The victims were smeared with plaster; white feathers were tied to their hair; their eyelids were blackened and their lips painted red. Priests who would perform the actual sacrifice stood in a long row according to their rank. Each priest was disguised as a god and carried a richly decorated sword and shield. The priests sat under a beautifully adorned arbor erected at the summit of a large, truncated pyramid. Chanters came forth and began to dance and sing.

In Florida, sometime around midnight on the night before an execution, the condemned is usually allowed a last one-hour contact visit. The person is permitted to see his own clergyman if he has one, but only the prison chaplain will be permitted to accompany the inmate to the place of execution. At 4:30 A.M. the prisoner is served his or her last meal, to be eaten on a paper plate with a spoon; if the prisoner has requested a steak, the chef has cut the meat into bite-sized pieces beforehand and rearranged them to appear to be an intact steak. No later than 5:30 A.M., the official witnesses to the execution, 12 in number (one of whom may be designated by the condemned), must assemble at the main prison gate. At 5:50 A.M. the media witnesses, also 12 in number, are picked up at the "media onlooker area." Both types of witnesses will later be "escorted to the witness room of the execution chamber." At 6:00 A.M. an administrative assistant, three designated electricians, a physician, and a physician's assistant are assembled in the death chamber. The administrative assistant establishes telephone contact with the state governor's office. Meanwhile, the condemned inmate has his or her head and right calf shaved (to better conduct electricity), takes a shower under the supervision of a high-ranking prison official, and is dressed in his or her new burial clothes, omitting the suit jacket and shoes. Until recently, by informal custom the prison superintendent would then have a drink of whiskey with the condemned in his cell, but public outcry was so great that the practice was discontinued. At 6:50 "conducting gel" is applied to the person's head and leg. The superintendent reads the death warrant to the condemned a final time.

The Moment of Death

Each Aztec victim was taken singly to the sacrificial stone and tethered to it by a rope. In one form of sacrifice, in a mockery of self-defense, the victim was then given a sword edged with feathers rather than obsidian. The high priest rose and descended to the stone, walked around it twice and returned to his seat. Next, an

old man disguised as an ocelot gave the captive four wooden balls
and a drink of "Divine Wine" and instructed him to defend himself.
Many victims tried to defend themselves against a series of ceremo-
nially garbed priest-warriors, but others "unwilling to undergo such
ceremony cast themselves upon the stone seeking a quick death"
(Duran, 1964:112). Death was inevitable: as soon as the captive was
wounded, four priests painted black, with long braided hair and gar-
ments resembling chasubles, spread-eagled the victim on the stone,
each priest holding a limb. The high priest cut open the victim's
chest with an obsidian knife, pulled out the victim's heart and offered
the organ to the sun. The heart was deposited in a jar or placed on a
brazier, and the next victim was brought forward.

The superintendent of Florida State Prison at Starke and two
other prison officials escort the condemned inmate to the death
chamber at 6:56 A.M. The person is strapped into the electric chair.
At 7:00 A.M. the condemned is permitted to make a last statement.
The governor directs the superintendent to proceed with the execution, traditionally concluding with the words "God save us all."
The witnesses have been seated in their peculiarly carved, white
high-backed chairs. The electrician places the sponge and cap on
the inmate's head. The assistant superintendent engages the circuit
breaker. The electrician activates the panel, the superintendent sig-
nals the executioner to throw the switch, and the "automatic cycle
will begin." The actual executioner is an anonymous private citizen
dressed in a black hood and robe who will be paid $150 for his
services. Once the automatic cycle has run its course, the superintendent invites the doctor to conduct the examination. If all has gone
well, the condemned is pronounced dead and the time recorded. A
designated prison official proclaims, "The sentence of —— has been
carried out. Please exit to the rear at this time." By custom, someone
in attendance waves a white cloth just outside the prison to signal the
crowd assembled in a field across from it—reporters, death penalty
opponents and proponents, and any others—that the deed is done.
Official guidelines for the execution of more than one inmate on a
single day exist, but we will dispense with those here.

After Death

Fray Bernardino de Sahagun (1951:24) reports that after each
Aztec captive had been slain, the body was taken gently away and

rolled down the stairs of the sacrificial pyramid. At the bottom, the victim's head was cut off for display on a rack and the remainder of the corpse was taken to one of the special houses, *calpulli*, where "they divided [the bodies] up in order to eat them." Meanwhile, those who had taken part in the sacrifice entered a temple, removed their ritual garb, and were rewarded with fine clothes and a feast. The lords from the provinces who had been brought to observe were "shocked and bewildered."

As soon as a Florida inmate is pronounced dead in the electric chair, ambulance attendants are called into the chamber; they remove the inmate from the chair and take the body to a waiting ambulance, which transports the corpse to the medical examiner's office. There an autopsy is performed. Until recently, portions of the brain were removed for secret study by a University of Florida researcher investigating the relationship between "head trauma and violent behavior." This procedure was followed for 11 of the 13 men executed between 1979 and 1985, but was stopped in response to negative publicity. Once the autopsy is completed, the corpse is released to the funeral home for cremation or burial. If the deceased has made no arrangements for a private funeral, his or her body is interred on the prison grounds. The executioner, meanwhile, is returned to his secret pick-up point and compensated. There is a "debriefing" at the prison of all the other participants in the execution save one.

The Native Explanations

What explanations are given by Aztecs and modern Americans for these decidedly gruesome acts? While we will probably never know what the Aztec man in the street thought of the sacrificial murders committed by his priests and nobles, official theology, if we may trust the sources, held that the gods had to be fed and placated to keep the crops growing, the sun high, and the universe in healthy order. Unfortunately for war captives, one of the gods' favorite foods was human hearts.

The explanations given by Americans for capital punishment generally are clothed in more pragmatic, secular terms. Most commonly, supporters of capital punishment invoke stimulus-response psychology and declare that such punishment will prevent others from committing heinous crimes. For instance, following the exe-

cution of an admitted child-murderer, Florida's governor declared
that "he hoped the execution would be a warning to others who har-
bored the desire to mistreat children" (Sherrill, 1984:553). Other
explanations emphasize the lower cost of execution as compared with
long-term imprisonment, the need to provide families of murder victims with a sense of justice and mental repose, and what might be
called the "social hygiene" approach: "[S]ome people just ought to
be eliminated—we kill rattlesnakes, we don't keep them as pets,"
declared one Florida Supreme Court justice (*Tallahassee Democrat*,
15 Sept. 1985).

Despite the rationalistic cast of the most common public explanations for capital punishment, at least some of the explanations,
or justifications, that surface into public view are unabashedly religious. The author of a letter to the *Tallahassee Democrat* (6 Feb.
1985) cited scripture to argue that earthly governments have the
God-given right and authority "to make and enforce laws, including the right to take human life." He urged his readers to submit
"'to every ordinance of man for the Lord's sake,'" for in so doing
evildoers will be punished, those who do well will be praised, and
"'ye will put to silence the ignorance of foolish men' (I Peter 2:13–
15)." We suspect that beneath more sophisticated explanations for
capital punishment there is, if not an outright appeal to supernatural
authority, the same deep-seated set of nameless fears and anxieties
that motivate humans everywhere to commit ceremonial acts that
reassure and give substance to the Durkheimian view that "religion
is society collectively worshipping itself."

Conclusion

The perceptive reader will have recognized the sometimes
startling points of similarity between the conduct of some forms
of Aztec human sacrifice and capital punishment in Florida. There
are, of course, some profoundly important points of difference as
well. We will not belabor the obvious here, but given the many
commonalities in the organization, procedures, and even physical
appurtenances between Aztec human sacrifice and Florida capital
punishment, it is reasonable to propose that whatever psychosocial
functions human sacrifice might have served in the Aztec empire,
they are matched by similar functions for capital punishment in the

United States. Just as Aztec ripping out of human hearts was couched in mystical terms of maintaining universal order and well-being of the state (putting aside the question of the utility of such practices as terror tactics with which to intimidate neighboring societies), we propose that capital punishment in the United States serves to assure many that society is not out of control after all, that the majesty of the Law reigns, and that God is indeed in his heaven. Precise, emic ("native") corroboration of our interpretation of capital punishment as the ultimate validator of law is provided by an automobile bumper sticker first seen in Tallahassee in 1987, shortly after the Florida legislature passed a controversial statute requiring automobile passengers to wear safety belts:

> I'LL BUCKLE UP—
> WHEN BUNDY DOES
> _____
> IT'S THE LAW

"Bundy" is Theodore Bundy, Florida's most famous prisoner sentenced to be "buckled up" in the electric chair.

Sources as diverse as the populist *National Enquirer* (Mitteager, 1985) and the eminent legal scholar Lawrence Friedman (1973) instruct their readers that the crime rate is actually far lower today than 100 years ago. But through the mass media, the average American is subjected to a daily diet of fanatical terrorists, crazed rapists, revolting child molesters, and ghoulish murderers, to say nothing of dishonest politicians, unruly protestors, welfare and tax cheats, greedy gurus and philandering preachers, marauding street gangs, sexual perverts, and drug fiends, while all the time having to deal with the everyday personal irritations of a society in which, as Marvin Harris (1981) tells us, nothing works, mothers leave home, and gays come out of the closet. In an ironic twist on the anthropological debate (e.g., Isaac, 1983; Ortiz de Montellano, 1982; Price, 1978) over Harner's proposed materialist explanation of Aztec human sacrifice, we hypothesize that the current groundswell of support for capital punishment in the United States springs from the universal, ancient human impulse to do something in times of stress, even if it is only ritual. Bronislaw Malinowski observed that "there are no peoples however primitive without religion and magic" (1954:17); neither are there peoples so civilized that they are devoid of magic.

All peoples turn to magic when knowledge, technology, and experience fail (Malinowski, 1954). In the face of all the evidence that capital punishment does no more to deter crime than the bloody rituals of Tenochtitlan did to keep the sun in the sky, we must seek some broader, noninstrumental function that the death penalty serves. We propose, in short, that modern capital punishment is an institutionalized *magical* response to perceived disorder in American life and in the world at large, an attempted magical solution that has an especial appeal to the beleaguered, white, God-fearing men and women of the working class. And in certain aspiring politicians they find their sacrificial priests.

References

Baldus, David C.; Charles A. Pulaski, Jr.; and George Woodworth. 1983. "Comparative Review of Death Sentences: An Empirical Study of the Georgia Experience." *Journal of Criminal Law and Criminology* 74: 661–753.

Bowers, William J., and Glenn L. Pierce. 1980. "Deterrence or Brutalization: What Is the Effect of Executions?" *Crime and Delinquency* 26: 453–84.

———. 1980. "Arbitrariness and Discrimination Under Post-*Furman* Capital Statutes." *Crime and Delinquency* 26:563–635.

Cambridge Survey Research. 1985. "An Analysis of Attitudes Toward Capital Punishment in Florida." Prepared for Amnesty International.

Camus, Albert. 1959. *Reflections on the Guillotine*. Michigan City, Ind.: Fridtjof-Karla.

Cooper, John W. 1976. "Propitiation as Social Maintenance: A Study of Capital Punishment Through the Sociology of Religion." M.A. thesis, Florida State University.

Duran, Fray Diego. 1964. *The Aztecs*. New York: Orion Press.

Ellsworth, Phoebe C., and Lee Ross. 1983. "Public Opinion and Capital Punishment: A Close Examination of the Views of Abolitionists and Retentionists." *Crime and Delinquency* 29:116–69.

Fagan, Brian M. 1984. *The Aztecs*. New York: W. H. Freeman.

Florida State Prison. 1983. "Execution Guidelines During Active Death Warrant." Starke: Florida State Prison. Reprinted in part at pp. 235–40 of Amnesty International, *United States of America: The Death Penalty*. London: Amnesty International, 1987.

Friedman, Lawrence M. 1973. *A History of American Law*. New York: Simon and Schuster.

Gallup, George. 1986. "The Death Penalty." *Gallup Report* 244–45 (Jan.–Feb.):10–16.

Gross, Samuel R., and Robert Mauro. 1984. "Patterns of Death: An Analysis of Racial Disparities in Capital Sentencing and Homicide Victimization." *Stanford Law Review* 37:27–153.

Harner, Michael. 1977. "The Ecological Basis for Aztec Sacrifice." *American Ethnologist* 4:117–35.

Harris, Marvin. 1981. *America Now: The Anthropology of a Changing Culture*. New York: Simon and Schuster.

Harris, Philip W. 1986. "Over-Simplification and Error in Public Opinion Surveys on Capital Punishment." *Justice Quarterly* 3:429–55.

Isaac, Barry L. 1983. "The Aztec 'Flowery War': A Geopolitical Explanation." *Journal of Anthropological Research* 39:415–32.

Lofland, John. 1977. "The Dramaturgy of State Executions." Pp. 275–325 in *State Executions Viewed Historically and Sociologically*, by Horace Bleackley. Montclair, N.J.: Patterson Smith.

Malinowski, Bronislaw. 1954. *Magic, Science and Religion and Other Essays*. Garden City, N.Y.: Doubleday.

Mitteager, James. 1985. "Think Crime Is Bad Now? It Was Much Worse 100 Years Ago." *National Enquirer*, 25 Nov., p. 25.

NAACP Legal Defense and Educational Fund. 1988. "Death Row, U.S.A." Unpublished compilation, available from 99 Hudson St., New York, N.Y. 10013.

Nakell, Barry, and Kenneth A. Hardy. 1987. *The Arbitrariness of the Death Penalty*. Philadelphia: Temple University Press.

Ortiz de Montellano, Bernard R. 1982. "The Body Dangerous: Physiology and Social Stratification." *Reviews in Anthropology* 9:97–107.

Paternoster, Raymond. 1983. "Race of Victim and Location of Crime: The Decision to Seek the Death Penalty in South Carolina." *Journal of Criminal Law and Criminology* 74:754–85.

Price, Barbara J. 1978. "Demystification, Enriddlement and Aztec Cannibalism: A Materialist Rejoinder to Harner." *American Ethnologist* 5:98–115.

Radelet, Michael L. 1981. "Racial Characteristics and the Imposition of the Death Penalty." *American Sociological Review* 46:918–27.

Radelet, Michael L., and George W. Barnard. 1986. "Ethics and the Psychiatric Determination of Competency to Be Executed." *Bulletin of the American Academy of Psychiatry and the Law* 14:37–53.

Radelet, Michael L.; Margaret Vandiver; and Felix M. Berardo. 1983. "Families, Prisons, and Men with Death Sentences: The Human Impact of Structured Uncertainty." *Journal of Family Issues* 4:593–612.

Sahagun, Fray Bernardino de. 1951. *General History of the Things of New*

    Spain. Santa Fe, N.M.: School of American Research and the University of Utah.
Sherrill, Robert. 1984. "In Florida, Insanity Is No Defense." *The Nation* 239:539, 552–56.
Turnbull, Colin. 1978. "Death by Decree." *Natural History* 87 (May):51–66.
U.S. Department of Justice. 1986. *Capital Punishment, 1984*. Washington, D.C.: U.S. Government Printing Office.

11

The Death Penalty and Anthropology

COLIN M. TURNBULL

To many it may still seem strange that sociocultural anthropology should be concerned with an indigenous institution such as the death penalty. Even among those anthropologists who might support such an interest, there would probably be a sharp divergence as to the approach, both methodological and theoretical.

The divergence I can accept, for such differentiation is most often healthy and constructive. But I cannot and will not accept that antiquated view that anthropologists should not concern themselves with their own society, least of all with issues of deep concern and emotional impact in that society. If we have anything at all to offer to society, it is precisely in such critical areas that we should apply whatever skills we have. And it is because we are then involved, physically, intellectually, and emotionally, that we should also be involved academically. For the same reason, that academic involvement should be as subjective as it is objective.

Just as there are dangers to objectivity, so there are to subjectivity. The blending of the two techniques to some extent mitigates these dangers, but by no means completely so. A study of the death penalty in our own American society brings this issue to the fore, with all the problems *and* the potentials starkly outlined. This may be seen by an account of my own involvement with the institution—not because the results were of any anthropological significance, but because they were *not*, and because of the actual process that unfolded in the natural course of an inquiry made without any special theoretical or practical preparation.

In the seventies, when the death penalty in the United States was still in temporary abeyance, the editor of *Natural History* asked me to write an article on the subject from an anthropological perspective. The result was "Death by Decree" (1978). The article was based only on a survey, but one that had shown (to me, at least) the special advantages of an anthropological approach. I had hoped that the challenge would be taken up by other anthropologists, on the one hand, and that I would be able to continue with a more intensive and prolonged study myself. I was disappointed on both counts. While the article evoked an enormous and wide response from many segments of the general public, it evoked virtually none from anthropologists, and my own efforts to get a major research program off the ground were stymied, more by academe than by the penal system. In fact, the Virginia Department of Corrections worked with me and finally accepted a major research proposal that fell through only because of lack of academic support; and despite my known personal bias against the death penalty, I received more help than hindrance from other correctional systems as well.

That in itself is significant, but the point here is to outline the process and to illustrate some of the strengths and weaknesses of such an approach in order to see just what anthropology *can* add to our understanding of such a crucial issue. In attempting to write such an article as "Death By Decree," I could of course have made a comparative study of capital punishment around the world from literary sources, but since I had been teaching anthropology at the Spring Street maximum-security penitentiary in Richmond, Virginia, and had in my classes a number of inmates who had been on death row when the law was overturned in 1972 and their sentences were commuted to life, that seemed a sensible place to start. I still had in mind a relatively simple comparative study; but that start, because it was "in the field," took me in a very different direction.

While not believing that either sociology or anthropology holds exclusive rights to any particular technique, method, or concept, there are certain approaches that are of particular importance to anthropology and of special significance here. Four come to mind at once, and it is these four I wish to explore briefly in what follows. They are the methodological techniques of field work and comparison, and the conceptual stances of holism and cultural relativity.

Field Work

Within the discipline any divergence of approach to a study of an issue such as the death penalty would be likely to center around that knotty question of involvement, of a subjectivity thought by many to be incompatible with objectivity rather than complementary to it. It is not merely the old argument that we are too involved with our own society to be able to stand apart and regard it critically and dispassionately; I think most anthropologists with any field experience would admit that while there might be some initial difficulties of this kind, they would not prove to be a lasting hindrance. The problem is more deep-seated and reflects on the much-touted anthropological field research technique most often called "participant observation." In point of fact, as practiced (and preached) by many anthropologists, this is really nothing but a technique for stereoscopic observation, with little or no real participation. The so-called participation is merely a device that affords the field worker one or more different perspectives from which to observe. In fact, insofar as such "participation" is limited to playing out some chosen or allotted role in a foreign culture, without the full emotional involvement that seems to be eschewed by most field workers, I would say that it is nothing more than a sham, a pretense, and a self-delusion if not an open, calculated deceit.

This is in no way intended to denigrate good, thorough, objective observation. That is an absolutely essential tool of our trade. But let us not fool ourselves into thinking that we are adding anything of any worth to objective observation by putting on (or taking off) a certain kind of clothing and by engaging in a temporary and limited imitation of the outward appearance of some form of activity that we imagine makes us in some way less conspicuous and gives us an "inside" view. It often does the opposite of both of these things.

Give me the good old-fashioned ethnographer, complete with pith helmet, who never for a moment considered even attempting to become like "the natives," let alone "going native." He kept himself firmly on the outside, with all his bearers and servants and his plethora of imported accoutrements. From that comfortable and overtly outside stance, he was able to observe objectively, and frequently did so in remarkable detail and with an even more remarkable lack of bias, theoretical or otherwise. From such descriptive data, in spite of its obvious limitations, anthropology has derived enormous benefit, precisely because those limitations are so evident. To me, with all its weaknesses, such a study is infinitely more trustworthy than the attempts of some pseudo-scientific anthropologist who thinks that by behaving in some, for him, totally abnormal way, he gains direct access to the minds and hearts of those among whom he is living. It is often such anthropologists who venture into the realm of religion, assuming that the "insider" status conveyed by such superficial imitation somehow enables them to share in a religion that is not theirs. Their pretense at objectivity and relativity is demonstrated, to their own satisfaction at least, by their unctuous acceptance of even the most bizarre behavior in terms of some functional or structural argument. They carefully report on all they see and hear, in quantifiable terms, and convert a people's religion into a system of observable categories of behavior, physical and verbal. They talk glibly of ritual performance and religious belief, and yet, however accurate they may be in this respect (and again, their results, so far as they go, are by no means always bad), they have not touched on the real essence of religion, which has more than a little to do with the less readily observable and quantifiable elements of thought and faith and emotion.

Something is missing from such studies. The attempt at participation demonstrates our awareness of that void, but our confusion of scientific method with an unattainable, total objectivity and detachment and with quantifiability of data places us at an even greater distance from the social (and human) reality than the method of the most ethnocentric of colonial anthropologists. The missing ingredient can at least in part be supplied by the acceptance that a thoroughgoing, rigorous subjectivity is, far from being antithetical to objectivity and detachment, an absolute and complementary prerequisite.

It is this special weakness of the way in which much anthropological research deals with the phenomenon of religion that is relevant here, for the deliberate, consciously planned putting to death of a human being by the state is nothing if not a religious (or sacrilegious) act, and demands closer scrutiny than given by conventional objective methods. In my limited experience of research on death row, the importance of subjective experience during field work was manifest chiefly in two ways: (1) in what it revealed about the inner workings of the institution (one might call this a positive, practical importance); and (2) in the intensity of some of the human relationships created in the course of the research. These were of immense personal and academic importance, but in some cases led to the necessity for choosing between continued academic research and the continuation of that personal relationship.

In the first category, I had in one case the enormous advantage of a number of excellent informants, all of whom had at one time or another occupied the same death row, and some of whom had been there at the same time, spanning a period of ten years. In cross-checking their various accounts, I found remarkably little conflict, none of any significance. In the minutest details there was often total agreement. So even before visiting that death row, I had a clear visual image of what it was like, how the cells were disposed in relation to each other and to the death chamber, onto which some of the cells backed directly. I had a clear idea of the lighting, the lack of color, the way in which sound carried, and the way in which odors similarly traveled, not only between cells, but between the death chamber and death row during and long after an execution. Through these intensive interviews, all my senses had been alerted and informed, and little was left to allow my imagination any rein except in the matter of what it felt like to be either one of those condemned to die or one of those condemned to put others to death.

When I visited that dank basement death row for the first time, the Virginia death penalty was still in abeyance, so the cells were empty, except for one in which an inmate was isolated for his own safety. The walls had been freshly painted, largely to take away, I was told, the smell of burned hair and flesh. But the smell of paint itself somehow assumed a special significance in that tiny, cramped space, as did the pitch and tone and volume of the voice in which the information was given. The lighting was as dismal as everything else, and the normally unremarkable fact that it was electric somehow made it sinister as well as dismal. The slightest sound assumed a special importance, forcing itself on one's attention and demanding explanation and interpretation.

From behind the bars of any one cell, vision was restricted so that not all the other cells could be seen, but because this antiquated death row was small and had been designed with cells facing each other, instead of back to back, visual communication with at least some of the other cells was possible. From two of the cells one was able to look into one or other of the corridors that at each end led around into the death chamber; the occupant of one of those cells was the first to see a new inmate being led in; the occupant of the other was the last to see him as he was led out to die. All of a sudden the placement of the cells assumed a different significance, and I quickly felt a distinct preference as to where I would have preferred to be placed: in the middle and facing away from either corridor, so that I would not have been tortured with either the sight of a new-comer coming into what was to be his last conscious resting place or the sight of a person being led to his death. But placing myself in that cell, I was suddenly acutely aware of a prickling in my back, for of all the cells I had chosen the one that was in closest proximity to the electric chair, just a few feet behind me. So, I imagined, I would have been the one who was closest to a death that was ultimately to be my own—the one for whom the vibrations and the sounds would have been the most intense. And looking out from behind the bars, I would have been able to see, not the incoming or outgoing con-demned man, but the faces of my fellow inmates as *they* reacted to such sights. I tried each of the cells in turn, and was acutely aware of the different sensations to be experienced in each, and of how my feelings toward the other condemned inmates, and toward the guard who used to sit near the entrance, would vary according to the cell in which I was located. The importance of the geography became accentuated when I paused to remember what was above me, both in the block housing other inmates and, for me even more impor-tant, in the yard through which I had walked and from which I had descended to enter death row.

Sitting at the table where the guard used to sit gave me a dif-ferent set of perceptions and feelings, and forced me to imagine how I would handle that situation, seeing men come in and, later, per-haps years later, leave to be put to death. One of my students had had his head shaved in readiness for execution no fewer than three times. If I had been the guard sitting at that table, and over the years had come to know Bernard, even better perhaps than I had come to know him as a student, how would I have handled *that* situation? What would I have *had* to feel about him to justify my position? What would I have felt about the prison administration that placed me in that position? What would my relation have been with other

inmates outside death row, with other officers? And what would I
have talked about with my family when I went home at night, or in
the morning? What would my friends and acquaintances have talked
to me about when they met me the day after an execution, or perhaps that very same day? What would I have felt in their handshake,
or in its withholding?

All these feelings were of course exclusively mine, and were
generated by my own imagination on the basis of a limited number of
factual realities, none of which enabled me to do more than approach
the ultimate reality of being either a condemned man or one of those
whose job it is to oversee the business of death. But such imagination
was in itself a powerful experience with its own reality, and with its
own logic and structure. From that experience a whole new set of
significant research objectives immediately became evident, many
of them of prime importance in the problem-ridden task of prison
management. Factors otherwise easily overlooked suddenly became
of major interest, and in very practical relationship to such issues
as security, stress, and rehabilitation. "Rehabilitation" may seem an
irrelevant factor, but it came to mind nonetheless, and would not
be put aside, for two very good reasons. First, the prison officials
involved in the practical realities of putting others to death were
going to be in need of rehabilitation themselves if their lives in the
outside world (and their own inner mental and spiritual lives) were
to be truly normal. The other reason was that already, in coming
to know as many condemned men as I had, I was beginning to get
the distinct feeling that the experience of being so close to death
had in some way had a positive effect on most of them. This feeling
was augmented as I visited more and more death rows and came to
know more and more condemned men. (I came to know only one
condemned woman, yet from the little I saw, the gender difference
could be crucial in much of this.) For one thing, working inside prisons I had to consider my own security, both physical and mental, and
much to my surprise, I quickly came to find myself feeling both safer
and more comfortable, even happier in a strange way, when among
those who had been condemned to death, including those awaiting
execution. This obviously leads to yet another unexpected avenue of
research, and during tentative exploration with various prison wardens and others, I found it indeed to be of the greatest significance;
for yet another strange irony was that even prison administrators
were able to say that it was among those condemned to death that
they would be likely to find those closest to effective rehabilitation.

As I left that small, cramped, dingy little death row, and went down the corridor leading past the General Electric generator and control booth, into the death chamber, with the witness box directly ahead of me, the "sandbag room" (where the contorted corpses are straightened) to my left, and the chair to my right, a whole new set of sensations arose, both from the point of view of a condemned man and from that of the guards who would have been walking with me. And from the point of view of the witnesses, and of the warden standing by the switch that would tell the executioner to do his work. Even the executioner's quarters and the highly restricted view he had into the death chamber assumed unexpected significance, particularly with respect to just how much or how little society demands from (or offers to) such a person.

Then all of this subjective experience was enriched, reinforced, or modified by allowing myself to have similar feelings, by giving my imagination similarly free rein, in other prisons, on other death rows, in other death chambers, and among other condemned men.

The major *disadvantage* of such involvement, such total participation, is primarily academic. This is not because it detracts from objectivity, for, as can be seen, it ultimately augments observation and brings us closer to an objective view of reality than could ever be otherwise possible. It can only be disadvantageous academically because the emotional involvement becomes so intense that it enters into competition with intellectual, academic involvement, and a choice has to be made. The outcome of that choice cannot be predicted at the outset. In my experience there are times when it is relatively easy to make a choice—a choice is dictated by circumstance rather than personal decision. But there are other times when the choice has to be made, if for no other reason than that of sheer exhaustion. It then becomes a moral choice, and the depth of one's involvement may in fact leave no choice at all. It has little or nothing to do with guilt or innocence; even less to do with the merits of the academic research. It has everything to do with the value of a simple human relationship. And where that relationship, through a total participation, has become full and reciprocal, the potential for academic research, however rich, at a certain point has to be sacrificed if the other is to be preserved. But this is a far cry from the objection that such involvement and subjectivity destroy one's objectivity, for that very involvement has already brought its own crop of rewards. All that is being sacrificed, then, is some unknown future research potential.

Comparison

This is where comparison became productive: both comparison between different prisons with different architecture, with different placement of cells on death row, with different placement of death row in relation to the death chamber, and so on, and comparison between our own way of putting humans to death and the way in which it is done in other cultures. For instance, I had been present at a public execution in another culture, and try as I might, I could not avoid the hard fact that the stark reality of that putting to death of two men, in a rather inefficient way that prolonged their agony much more than had been intended, was *much* more acceptable to me than the mere imagination of what went on here. Try I did, but my feelings were always the same, and they were so strong that they demanded understanding, and that in turn compelled me to consider unexpected factors. Could it be significant whether an execution took place indoors or out of doors? In a brightly lit, potentially sunny death chamber such as the one at the Florida State Prison at Starke ("potentially" because the shades are closed during an execution), or in the windowless basement room in Richmond? In both of these death chambers, the witness box is glassed in, and witnesses have a frontal view of the condemned man as he enters and during the execution. But entering the witness room at San Quentin was to me rather like entering the viewing room in a major aquarium, for jutting into the middle were the angled back and sides of the gas chamber with its two seats, all clearly visible through the large glass panels. You could see the victims being led in, being turned around and sat down on those chairs with perforated seats, under which were the buckets for the acid into which the pellets would be dropped. But at that point you would see only the backs of the victims, and perhaps their arms and hands as they grasped the arms of the chairs while straining not to breathe in that last fatal gasp of gaseous air. The view from the other side was quite different, and so were my feelings.

In all of this it was always perfectly clear that my feelings, during observation/participation *and* while making intellectual comparisons, were my own and might have no resemblance to the feelings of the real actors in the real life drama, and it was equally clear that those personal feelings would almost certainly be different, in intensity if nothing else, were I playing one of those many roles in reality, as I did on that one occasion of the public execution. But that was unimportant, for the feelings, however invalid as evidence or as representative of the feelings of others, led invariably and certainly to new avenues of inquiry and suggested new explanations, new factors to be considered. And they did this almost instantaneously. While I believe that some of the results might have been arrived at in a purely objective manner, it would have taken much longer and the process would have been far less direct; whereas other results might never have been discovered by any objective method. And it was only by this subjective approach that ultimate objectivity was possible, and with it the detached perspective, free of value judgments, so sought after by most anthropologists.

Above all, the subjective experience was directly and unmistakably comparable to a religious experience, and this called for still further investigation and comparison with the ritual factors consciously practiced in different prisons, and between such ritual and religious practice in our own culture and in other cultures. A comparison of the values invoked and involved was found to correspond to a major concern (both intellectual and religious) among death row inmates, focusing primarily on the difference between an essentially retributive system, such as our own, and one that is essentially restitutive, as found in many small-scale societies. This concern often focused, among those who admitted to the murder of which they were accused, on the subtle distinction between pardon and forgiveness, expiation and atonement. Yet while such distinctions were of major importance to them, and in other jural systems known to anthropologists, they are given little or no consideration by our own system.

Such comparisons throw much needed light on the often cited question as to precisely what constitutes "cruel and unusual" punishment. For in making such comparisons, using our own terminology and values, we find that practices elsewhere that might at first sight seem utterly barbaric (largely in terms of the technology involved) are in fact neither cruel nor unusual within that culture. This is where the stance of cultural relativity is helpful.

Relativity

There is a world of difference between making an intellectual connection between either an individual act or a social institution and the cultural context in which that act or institution can be found and the subjective experience of the rightness or inescapable reality of that connection. For one thing, the intellectual judgment is always open to rational doubt, and indeed *should* be questioned, whereas the subjective experience is undeniable, carrying with it a sense of absolute certainty. Although it might shift as a result of external or internal influences, it is not directly assailable and is often impervious to reason. It is the basis for that all-powerful religious phenomenon of faith.

The intellectual stance of cultural relativity is an essential step, and often a first step, toward proper, unbiased, objective judgment, but without the kind of total subjective immersion that I consider to be the only kind of participation deserving the term. It is necessarily partial. It may lack detail and depth, and it will certainly lack in intensity. Thus, although we—be we the general public, the jury, the prosecution, the defense, or the judge—may be in agreement as to what is meant by such words as "guilt" and "innocence," "good" and "bad," "social" versus "individual" rights and liberties, under closer inspection our understanding of such terms is likely to vary according to our position in society. Nonetheless, the level of general agreement that *can* be reached by us we unquestioningly expect to be accepted by the accused. Yet any sensitive participation through the trial process, including jury selection, the prosecution and the defense, the conviction, the sentencing, incarceration, up to the signing of the death warrant and the final days before execution, shows not a confusion about such terms on the part of the condemned man, but a logical and systematic change of perception and understanding in relation to his changing condition and changing proximity to death. The confusion and lack of logic lie in others' expectation that the same words will have even approximately the same meanings in these different contexts. Thus, even the trial process involves mutual misunderstanding, for to some extent we are not speaking the same language.

Participation in the process, from several different viewpoints, can help reveal such problems and suggest solutions, so that we might even reach common agreement on the meaning of the concept of justice, which all too often is taken for granted. Whereas from outside it is easy and relatively accurate to characterize our system as primarily legalistic in comparison with the more moralistic jural systems of small-scale societies, from within, although the differentiation remains approximately the same, there is a shift in values, again in relation to one's position. This is one reason, perhaps, why so many death row inmates become such good candidates for reha-bilitation. The conflict between those supporting the rights of the families of murder victims and those supporting the rights of the con-demned murderers, even when the question of guilt or innocence is not at issue, is as inevitable as it is destructive until we take a relativ-istic stance. I have actually sat in court, throughout a murder trial, with the mother of the savagely murdered boy on my right, and the mother of the admitted murderer (and this was not his first) on my left. It was like living in two different worlds, each with its own sub-jective reality and certainty, and in such terms each opposed to the other. But that participant experience enabled me to bring the two worlds together, to some extent, by acting in a sense as a translator.

The exercise of such cultural relativism is both a moral and an intellectual necessity if we are ever to achieve an end to such conflict, with all its potential for an injustice and inhumanity that taints and harms us all. We then come to a realization that the issue of cruelty (like that of brutality) should not be thought of with respect only to the condemned men and women, and their guards, but with respect to the judges and prison administrators, the attorneys for prosecu-tion and defense, the families of both the accused and the accusers, all others involved, and even, ultimately, the general public, try as it might to shield itself from the grim realities.

And here the holistic approach shows how vital it is to widen our concern from a narrow focus on the death penalty to a much wider area of inquiry.

Holism

Holism, as understood by anthropology, involves the realiza-tion that every aspect of the social fabric is interrelated with every other aspect. Sometimes the interrelationship is so close that the slightest change in the one will directly affect the other, and experi-ence has shown us that a change induced because of its obviously beneficial potential in one area may bring about highly detrimental effects in another area. An economic change that might be undeni-ably advantageous, say, to the economy of the state might result in unforeseen and disastrous results at another level, that of the com-munity, the family, or the individual. It is more than a mere conflict of interests, though that is real enough. The danger lies more deeply hidden in the fact that we simply do not take the time and trouble even to try to predict all the consequences of any given action, even when we know that to some extent every facet of society *will* be affected in some way. So when we focus on the rightness or wrongness of the death penalty and restrict our vision to the fate of the accused or the welfare and rights of the victims and their families, we willfully exclude from consideration the possible effects on all the other individuals involved, *their* families, and through them, in ever widening circles, the general public.

The death penalty is not a private issue, and although we try to make it so, neither is an execution. In a sense it is as public as the one I witnessed in Africa, the major difference being that there the experience was direct and unquestionable, while here it is for most of us indirect and deliberately shrouded in mystery and ignorance. The argument is not for or against public executions, or even for or against the death penalty, but rather for a removal of this ignorance by a depth of understanding of the total institution and its effect on the whole society. It is not merely a jural matter; it touches our domestic life, our concept of family, our respect for community; it has widely unrecognized economic consequences; it is of both political and religious significance.

Holism alone cannot provide us with this depth and breadth of understanding; but by employing it together with the other anthropological tools of cultural relativism, structural comparison, and an intensive field study that is both subjective and objective, and in cooperation with research done by other disciplines with other specialties and techniques and methods, we might at least begin to give the issue the depth of concern that it so urgently needs, on practical as well as moral grounds.

Until then we are unwitting participants in multiple murders: the murder of innocent victims on our streets and in our homes, and the legalized killing, called execution by some and murder by others, of those condemned men and women victimized by an uncomprehending and perhaps uncaring society.

Reference

Turnbull, Colin. 1978. "Death by Decree." *Natural History* 87 (May): 51–66.

12

Working the Dead

JONATHAN R. SORENSEN AND
JAMES W. MARQUART

Death Row is deeded to the notion that these men, of all the criminals in the penitentiary, are special. They are the ones society has said are not capable or deserving of redemption or reform. . . . To give them schooling, training, or therapy would create an ambiguity the system is not ready to manage and which it has no desire to have become overt: it would acknowledge that residence on the Row is still tentative. In order to deal with the Row and what it means, the prison system adopts the posture of the inmate who says, "We're here for one thing: we're here to die." (Jackson and Christian, 1980:27)

The previous excerpt exemplifies the relative nonstatus of death row prisoners. They are segregated from the general inmate population and simply "warehoused for death" (Johnson, 1981). Death row inhabitants are in limbo, and time spent on death row is a period of waiting. Forgotten by society, these persons are left to die a slow death before being legally executed by the state.

Little attention is paid to death row prisoners, with the exception of occasional news flashes about appeals, stays, or executions. Pretending that these prisoners do not exist ignores the reality that death rows across America are holding more people now than ever before, and confining them for much longer periods of time. Also obscured is the fact that executions have become a rarity, and reversals the norm. Since *Furman v. Georgia* (408 U.S. 239 [1972]), and its companion case, *Branch v. Texas*, the new Texas capital statute, implemented in 1973 (affirmed by *Jurek v. Texas*, 428 U.S. 262 [1976]), has resulted in 389 death sentences. Yet as of 1 March 1988, only 27 persons have been executed; 266 remain on death row; and of the remaining 96, several have died of natural causes or suicide and the rest have had their cases reversed or sentences commuted. For the executed prisoners, time spent on death row ranged from 2.10 years to 11.23 years, and the average was 6.31 years.

Behavior of Death Row Inmates

Death row inmates have always been heavily guarded in the belief that they represent a danger to others. Just how much of a threat has rarely been examined. One way researchers contend with this problem is by studying the amount of violent behavior exhibited by inmates who committed capital offenses but did not receive a death sentence. After reviewing the rate of violent acts committed by such inmates, Thorsten Sellin concluded that "[P]rison homicides are not usually committed by prisoners serving sentences for capital murder and that such persons, whether in prison or on parole, pose no special threat to the safety of their fellowmen" (1980:120).

Some argue that even if death row inmates were no more violent than other first-degree murderers in prison, confinement on death row has distorted their personalities to such an extent as to make them dangerous. That is, the rigors of death row itself create violent men. A statement made by two psychiatrists studying death row inhabitants prior to the *Furman* decision best expresses this point of view. Gallemore and Panton claimed that "The [death row] occupants over time become progressively less suitable for reentry into the general prison population or the general public" (1972:171). They warned of the danger death row inhabitants would present to prisoners, keepers, and the general public if the death penalty was not reinstated.

The psychological pressures of death row confinement are multitudinous, although it is not the purpose of this paper to discuss them (see Jackson and Christian, 1980, for an excellent ethnography of death row in Texas and Brasfield and Elliot, 1983, for a first-hand account of life there). The amazing finding of studies on the psychology of death row is that the inmates show an enormous amount of "human resilience and adaptability" (Johnson, 1980:561) and cope with their environment without becoming violent (Bluestone and McGahee, 1962).

The ultimate test of how these individuals behave when they are not under the strict security of death row occurs when they are released into the general prison population or into society. The results of one such natural experiment were documented by Tom Murton (1969) when he became warden of an Arkansas penitentiary and released death row prisoners from the confines of their cells to interact with the general prison population. Giving the death row inmates more and more privileges, Murton observed that they became model inmates, dining with the other prisoners, forming and playing in a prison band that went on excursions outside the prison compound, and participating in dances with members of the general prison population, staff, inmates of the women's prison, and outside girlfriends and wives.

Another natural experiment occurs when death row inmates' sentences are commuted. The handful of available studies illustrate that such inmates do not present a significant threat to society when paroled, having recidivism rates as low as or lower than those of other offenders (Giardini and Farrow, 1952; Stanton, 1969). Two recent studies have followed the *Furman*-released inmates and found Gallemore's and Panton's worries to be unwarranted (Marquart and Sorensen, 1988; Vito and Wilson, 1986).

In the rest of this chapter, we examine a different type of natural experiment, one that involves Texas death row prisoners working in 50-man groups in a prison industry. It shows that many death row prisoners can work with one another, under supervision, without altercations or violence, a picture that goes against much of the conventional wisdom.

The Texas Death House

Texas' death row is located at the Ellis I Unit of the Texas Department of Corrections (TDC), a large maximum-security institution located 13 miles north of Huntsville. The ever increasing death row population occupies five prison wings, each containing three tiers of cells. These wings, together housing 266 inmates, are totally self-contained, including steam tables for food, recreation yards, and dayrooms. Traditionally, as in other states, a premium has been placed on security, keeping inmates locked in their cells 23 hours or more each day. As in other states, too, the prison system has been under court order to reform. Death row has not been exempt.

Ruiz v. Estelle (503 F.Supp. 1265 [1980]) is the largest and most complex prisoners' rights case in American correctional history (see Crouch and Marquart, forthcoming). As part of this ongoing litigation, the TDC signed a consent decree agreeing to classify death row prisoners into two classes, "death row work-capable" and "death row segregation," as stipulated in the 1985 "Death Row Activity Plan." Classification of incoming death row inmates usually takes about ninety days. If the inmate wishes to be considered for work-capable status, the Unit Classification Committee determines eligibility based on psychological evaluations and the following court-ordered considerations: evidence of stability or instability, history of assaultive behavior, escapes, possession of contraband or weapons, destruction of state property, work and school performance, gang affiliation or involvement, medical or psychiatric problems, presence within unit of personal enemies, and the facts of the current commitment offense. The decision is automatically reviewed every six months. The order also specifically outlines the privileges of each group.

Death Row Segregation

Procedures have not changed substantially from the pre-Ruiz era in the treatment of the inmates under death row segregation. They are allowed a few more amenities, especially the right to recreation outside their cells at least three hours a day, five days a week. Even inmates who are considered dangerous (threats to institutional security) are allowed recreation, but in individual "recreation cages." Security, however, is still paramount when dealing with the 152 death row segregated prisoners. Rolling plastic shields and cells girded with thick wire mesh protect guards and inmates from being stabbed, spat upon, or doused with scalding water when walking down the "runs."

All of the daily activities within these cellblocks reflect the predominance of security. Inmates are fed in their cells; guards slip trays of food through steel-covered slots in the cell doors. Whenever the inmates are taken from their cells, whether for showers, recreation, visits, or psychiatric or medical care, strict custody procedures are followed. The following excerpt from the correctional officers' rulebook describes the procedure for recreating death row segregated inmates:

> Prior to placing any inmates in the recreation area, the dayroom and the recreation yard will be shaken down. Placing an inmate into the recreation area will be done by two officers approaching the inmate while he is confined in his cell, and give [sic] him the opportunity to recreate. If the inmate wants to recreate, the inmate must submit to a thorough strip search. The officers will shake down all clothing, shoes etc. All clothing will be retained by the officers except for his underwear, shower shoes or tennis shoes. Once the inmate puts his underwear and shoes on, the officer will order the inmate to back up to the cell door to be handcuffed. The inmate's back of hands will be facing each other with thumbs out. The restraints will be placed on the inmate, and the wing officer will tell the picket officer to open the designated cell. The inmate will be escorted down the run with one officer in front and one officer behind the inmate, both using a hand held shield if no rolling shield is present.
>
> Once the inmate is in the recreation area, the restraints will be removed. Note: At no time shall no [sic] more than one inmate be escorted to the recreation area. While inmates are recreating, officers assigned to the wings will shake down the inmate's cell for contraband. Inmates can bring the following items to the recreation area: 1.) rolled cigarettes 2.) a little coffee and cup. Inmates cannot bring the following items to the recreation areas: 1.) cans of tobacco, 2.) cans of coffee, 3.) large amounts of legal work, books, or anything that contraband could be concealed in, radios, fans, etc.

A similar procedure is utilized in transporting these inmates to and from the single, caged-in showers. The main prison corridor must be cleared when death row segregated prisoners, escorted by two officers at all times, are taken out of their wings for visits or medical/psychiatric care. All general population prisoners step aside when they hear the guards shout, "Dead man comin' through."

Despite the court ruling, the quality of life for these prisoners has not substantially improved. Although the administration ordered in 1988 that all inmates be allowed "piddling" privileges (arts and crafts work in their cells) absent a showing of abuse by individual inmates, the overall atmosphere of death row segregation remains relatively unchanged. As one inmate stated: "There's a lot of hollering, cussing each other out. . . . Someone down on one-row will holler at somebody on three-row. . . . The noise sometimes drives me crazy" (Jackson and Christian, 1980:121).

Death Row Work-Capable

Work-capable prisoners are allowed many more privileges than the segregated inmates, and security is somewhat de-emphasized. Their cells lack the wire mesh. As a rule they are not handcuffed, even when outside their prison wing, nor are they strip-searched. They are fed from the steam tables buffet style and are allowed to eat either in their cells or in dayrooms. They take showers in the general prison population's bathhouse. These prisoners are also permitted to be out of their cells for 14 hours a day on weekdays and 10 hours a day on weekends; 4 of those hours every day may be spent outdoors. Overall, they are treated like the general inmate population.

As of 1 March 1988, work-capable prisoners account for 114 of the 266 death row residents. Some of these inmates are assigned as orderlies or janitors to take care of the cellblock, but 100 (according to the consent agreement) work in a garment factory that was built squarely behind the two work-capable wings of death row. It began operating in July 1986. The factory utilizes 50 death row inmates for each of two four-hour shifts. Inmates trained to work various machines make sheets, aprons, towels, uniforms, and other products. Overall, the garment factory is a model of efficiency, producing more goods per inmate than the other TDC garment factories. Sales of its products to other state agencies totaled over $1.25 million in 1987. The Texas garment factory is considered a model project, being the most extensive program of its kind, and has received visits from numerous state correctional officials.

Although staff and administrators were skeptical about the program at the outset, there was a determination to make it work. As Warden J. R. Petersen stated in an institutional memorandum: "It is the policy of the Ellis I Unit Administration that the Deathrow Work-Capable Program will be secure, safe, fair, and efficient. This program is unique in the area of corrections and it *will* be a successful program" (20 January 1986).

Once the program became operative, views changed. In interviews, guards and inmates reported favorably on the program. Some inmates, however, expressed suspicion that the program was organized to extract as much work as possible from them before their demise. For example, one inmate stated: "Hell, this is slave labor. You know they're working us to get what they can for themselves. It's just like at Auschwitz. They'll get what they can from us before they kill us" (interview with authors, March 1988).

Others complained of the lack of pay and the absence of positive influence on the outcome of their appeals. All of the inmates interviewed, however, conceded that the program had distinct advantages. Even the most skeptical admitted that they would rather be in the work program than segregated.

What would prompt a "dead man" to labor, for free, in a prison industry? The majority of inmates mentioned greater privileges as their reason for participating in the program. Others referred to the short-term psychological advantages of the work-capable program: "The work program gives me a reason to get up in the morning. If I were in segregation, I would probably sleep all day just trying to forget. It gives me a sense of dignity, doing something to completion." Other inmates discussed the long-term advantages, beyond death row: "If I get commuted, working here may show them [the parole board] that I can make it on the outside. It will show them that we aren't a continuing threat to society." Similarly, one inmate commented that learning a skill could, if he were released someday, help him in the free world.

As mentioned earlier, these inmates are very productive. The garment factory and the work-capable wings are clean and quiet, especially when one compares the noise levels of the segregation wings. Overall, the prisoners seem to have much better attitudes, and the quality of life is higher in the work-capable wings. There is less stress. Since the inception of the program, no serious violent incidents have occurred in the living and work areas. The garment factory supervisor stated that disciplinary infractions are rare—less than one a month—and he recalled only one fistfight (interview with authors, March 1988). This is a testimony to the good behavior of these inmates, since the inmate-to-staff ratio in the factory is ten to one: 2 guards and 3 outside staff members supervise 50 inmates each shift. Perhaps this is so because these inmates, as opposed to those in segregation, do have something to lose.

The Irony of Death Row

The inhabitants of death row are typically perceived and treated as fiends, individuals who cannot be allowed any privileges or responsibilities without endangering others. Security measures are paramount to any considerations of rehabilitation or preservation of human dignity on most death rows. The irony is that most of these people who are handcuffed and strip-searched every time they leave their cells will in fact be released through commutations and reversals to the general prison population and eventually to society. At the current rate, Texas death row inmates are four times as likely to have their sentences reversed or commuted as they are to be executed.

There are two major reasons for allowing death row inmates in Texas to work besides the court order. Already mentioned is the likelihood that these inmates may at some future time be released to society. Giving them privileges and responsibilities will no doubt make them more suited for re-entry into society. Reducing inmate idleness may also prevent the austerity of death row from having debilitating psychological effects on its inhabitants that could prevent successful reintegration.

The second reason to allow death row inmates to work is for the sake of humane management. Given the current situation in Texas, a state preoccupied with capital punishment and experiencing an increase in the death row population of four per month, it has become impossible to merely warehouse death row inmates. Forcing people to sit idle for years awaiting their executions, making them die psychologically before finally putting them to death physically, certainly edges toward being excessive punishment. The *Ruiz* directive in Texas and the implementation of similar programs in other states show a growing awareness among judges and correctional administrators of the necessity of humanely managing these prisoners.

References

Bluestone, Harvey, and Carl L. McGahee. 1962. "Reaction to Extreme Stress: Impending Death by Execution." *American Journal of Psychiatry* 119:393–96.

Brasfield, Phillip, and James M. Elliot. 1983. *Deathman Pass Me By: Two Years on Death Row*. San Bernardino, Calif.: Borgo.

Crouch, Ben and James W. Marquart. Forthcoming. *An Appeal to Justice: Litigative Reform of Texas Prisons*. Austin: University of Texas Press.

Gallemore, Johnnie L., Jr., and James H. Panton. 1972. "Inmate Responses to Lengthy Death Row Confinement." *American Journal of Psychiatry* 129:167–72.

Giardini, G. I., and R. G. Farrow. 1952. "The Paroling of Capital Offenders." *Annals of the American Academy of Political and Social Science* 284:85–94.

Jackson, Bruce, and Diane Christian. 1980. *Death Row*. Boston: Beacon.

Johnson, Robert. 1980. "Warehousing for Death: Observations on the Human Environment of Death Row." *Crime and Delinquency* 26:545–62.

Marquart, James W., and Jonathan R. Sorenson. 1988. "Institutional and Post-Release Behavior of *Furman*-Commuted Inmates in Texas" *Criminology* 26:677–93.

Murton, Tom. 1969. "Treatment of Condemned Prisoners." *Crime and Delinquency* 15:94–111.

Sellin, Thorsten. 1980. *The Penalty of Death*. Beverly Hills, Calif.: Sage.

Stanton, John M. 1969. "Murderers on Parole." *Crime and Delinquency* 15:149–55.

Vito, Gennaro, and Deborah Wilson. 1986. "Back from the Dead: Tracking the Progress of Kentucky's *Furman*-Commuted Death Row Population." Kentucky Criminal Justice Statistical Analysis Center, Research Report Series no. 10.

Cases Cited

Branch v. Texas, 408 U.S. 239 (1972).
Furman v. Georgia, 408 U.S. 239 (1972).
Jurek v. Texas, 428 U.S. 262 (1976).
Ruiz v. Estelle, 503 F.Supp. 1265 (1980).

13

How to Argue About the Death Penalty

HUGO ADAM BEDAU

I

Argument over the death penalty—especially in the United States during the past generation—has been concentrated in large part on trying to answer various disputed *questions of fact*. Among them two have been salient: Is the death penalty a better deterrent to crime (especially murder) than the alternative of imprisonment? Is the death penalty administered in a discriminatory way, and, in particular, are black or other nonwhite offenders (or offenders whose victims are white) more likely to be tried, convicted, sentenced to death, and executed than whites (or offenders whose victims are non-white)? Other questions of fact have also been explored, including these two: What is the risk that an innocent person could actually be executed for a crime he did not commit? What is the risk that a person convicted of a capital felony but not executed will commit another capital felony?

Earlier versions of this paper were read to audiences at Hampshire College and Dartmouth College in 1987, and the Jerusalem Conference on Justice and Punishment in 1988. I am grateful for the stimulus these audiences provided. Comments by Jay L. Garfield prompted a major revision in section IV, and written criticisms by Walter Sinnott-Armstrong led to many improvements. Constance Putnam has my gratitude for helping me to improve clarity of expression in many places.

178

Varying degrees of effort have been expended in trying to answer these questions. Although I think the current answers are capable of further refinement, I also think anyone who studies the evidence today must conclude that the best current answers to these four questions are as follows. (1) There is little or no evidence that the death penalty is a better deterrent to murder than is imprisonment; on the contrary, most evidence shows that these two punishments are about equally (in)effective as deterrents to murder. Furthermore, as long as the death penalty continues to be used relatively rarely, there is no prospect of gaining more decisive evidence on the question (Klein et al., 1978). (2) There is evidence that the death penalty has been and continues to be administered, whether intentionally or not, in a manner that produces arbitrary and racially discriminatory results in death sentencing. At the very least, this is true in those jurisdictions where the question has been investigated in recent years (Baldus et al., 1986). (3) It is impossible to calculate the risk that an innocent person will be executed, but the risk is not zero, as the record of convicted, sentenced, and executed innocents shows (Bedau and Radelet, 1987). (4) Recidivism data show that some murderers have killed after a conviction and prison sentence for murder; so there is a risk that others will do so as well (Bedau, 1982:173–80).

Let us assume that my summary of the results of research on these four questions is correct, and that further research will not significantly change these answers. The first thing to notice is that even if everyone agreed on these answers, this would not by itself settle the dispute over whether to keep, expand, reduce, or abolish the death penalty. Knowing these empirical truths about the administration and effects of the death penalty in our society does not entail knowing whether one should support its retention or abolition. This would still be true even if we knew with finality the answers to *all* the factual questions that can be asked about it.

There are two reasons for this. The facts as they currently stand and as seen from the abolitionist perspective do not point strongly and overwhelmingly to the futility of the death penalty or to the harm it does, at least as long as it continues to be used only in the limited and restricted form of the past decade: confined to the crime of murder, with trial courts empowered to exercise "guided discretion" in sentencing, with defense counsel able to introduce anything as mitigating evidence, and with automatic review of both conviction and sentence by some appellate court (*Gregg v. Georgia*, 428 U.S.

153 [1976]; *Proffitt v. Florida*, 428 U.S. 242 [1976]; *Jurek v. Texas*, 428 U.S. 262 [1976]). Nor do the facts show that the alternative of life imprisonment is on balance a noticeably superior punishment. For example, the evidence of racial discrimination in the administration of the death penalty, while incontestable, may be no worse than the racial discrimination that occurs where lesser crimes and punishments are concerned. No one who has studied the data thinks that the administration of justice for murder approaches the level of racial discrimination reached a generation ago in the South by the administration of justice for rape (Wolfgang and Riedel, 1976). Besides, it is always possible to argue that such discrimination is diminishing, or will diminish over time, and that, in any case, since the fault does not lie in the capital statutes themselves—they are color-blind on their face—the remedy does not lie in repealing them.

But the marginal impact of the empirical evidence is not the major factor in explaining why settling disputes over matters of fact does not and cannot settle the larger controversy over the death penalty itself. As a matter of sheer logic, it is not possible to deduce a policy conclusion (such as the desirability of abolishing the death penalty) from any set of factual premises, however general and well supported. Any argument intended to recommend continuing or reforming current policy on the death penalty must include among its premises one or more normative propositions. Unless disputants over the death penalty can agree about these normative propositions, their agreement on the general facts will never suffice to resolve their dispute.

II

Accordingly, the course of wisdom for those interested in arguing about the death penalty is to focus attention on the normative propositions crucial to the dispute, in the hope that some headway may be made in narrowing disagreement over their number, content, and weight.

If this is to be done effectively, the context of these norms in general political ideology needs to be fixed. Suffice it to say here that I proceed from within the context of liberal pluralistic constitutional democracy and the conception of punishment appropriate therein (see Hart, 1968; Rawls, 1971).

Logically prior to the idea of punishment is the idea of a crime. What counts as a criminal harm depends in part on our conception of persons as bearers of rights deserving respect and protection. In this setting, liability to punishment and its actual infliction serve the complex function of reinforcing compliance with a set of laws deemed necessary to protect the fundamental equal rights of all members of society. The normative propositions relevant to the death penalty controversy are interwoven with the basic purposes and principles of liberal society, including the recognition and protection of individual rights to life and liberty, and to security of person and property.

These norms can be divided into two groups: those that express relevant and desirable *social goals* or *purposes*, and those that express relevant and respectable *moral principles*. Punishment is thus a practice or institution defined through various policies—such as the death penalty for murder—and intended to be the means or instrument whereby certain social goals are achieved within the constraints imposed by acknowledged moral principles (cf. Dworkin, 1977:22–23, 169–71).

Reduction of crime, or at least prevention of an increase in crime, is an example of such a goal. This goal influences the choice of punishments because of their impact (hypothesized or verified) on the crime rate. No one, except for purists of a retributive stripe, would dissent from the view that this goal is relevant to the death penalty controversy. Because of its relevance, there is continuing interest in the outcome of research on the differential deterrent efficacy of death versus imprisonment. The only questions normally in dispute are what that research shows (I have summarized it above) and how important this goal is (some regard it as decisive).

Similarly, that no one should be convicted and sentenced to death without a fair trial (i.e., in violation of "due process of law") is a principle of law and morality generally respected. Its general acceptance explains the considerable reformation in the laws governing the death penalty in the United States that have been introduced since 1972 by the Supreme Court (*Furman v. Georgia*, 408 U.S. 238 [1972]). The Court argued that capital trials and death sentencing were in practice unfair (in constitutional jargon, they were in violation of the Eighth and Fourteenth Amendments, which bar "cruel and unusual punishments" and require "equal protection of the laws," respectively). State legislatures and thoughtful observers agreed. Here again the only questions concern how important it is to com-

ply with this principle (some regard it as decisive) and the extent to
which the death penalty currently violates it (I have remarked on
this point above, too).

The chief use of a moral principle in the present setting is to
constrain the methods used in pursuit of policy (as when respect for
"due process" rules out curbstone justice as a tactic in crime fighting). However, identifying the relevant goals, acknowledging the
force of the relevant principles, and agreeing on the relevant general
facts will still not suffice to resolve the dispute. The relative importance of achieving a given goal and the relative weight of a given
principle remain to be settled, and disagreement over these matters
is likely to show up in disagreement over the justification of the death
penalty itself.

If this is a correct sketch of the structural character of debate
and disagreement over the death penalty, then (as I noted earlier) the
best hope for progress may lie in looking more carefully at the non-
factual normative ingredients so far isolated in the dispute. Ideally,
we would identify and evaluate the policy goals relevant to punishment generally, as well as the moral principles that constrain the
structure and content of the penalty schedule. We would also settle
the proper relative weights to attach to these goals and constraints,
if not in general, then at least for their application in the present
context. Then, with whatever relevant general facts are at our dis-
posal, we would be in a position to draw the appropriate inferences
and resolve the entire dispute, confident that we have examined and
duly weighed everything that reason and morality can bring to bear
on the problem.

As an abstract matter, therefore, the question is whether the
set of relevant policies and principles, taken in conjunction with
the relevant facts, favors reduction (even complete abolition) of the
death penalty, or whether it favors retention (or even extension) of
the death penalty. Lurking in the background, of course, is the trou-
bling possibility that the relevant norms and facts underdetermine
the resolution of the dispute. But let us not worry about sharks on
dry land, not yet.

III

Where choice of punishments is concerned, the relevant social
goals, I suggest, are few. Two in particular generally commend themselves:

(G 1) Punishment should contribute to the reduction of crime; accordingly, the punishment for a crime should not be so idle a threat or so slight a deprivation that it has no deterrent or incapacitative effects; and it certainly should not contribute to an increase in crime.

(G 2) Punishments should be "economical"—they should not waste valuable social resources in futile or unnecessarily costly endeavors.

The instrumental character of these purposes and goals is evident. They reflect the fact that society does not institute and maintain the practice of punishment for its own sake, as though it were a good in itself. Rather, punishment is and is seen to be a means to an end or ends. The justification of a society's punitive policies and practices must therefore involve two steps: first, it must be shown that these ends are desirable; second, it must be shown that the practice of punishment is the best means to these ends. What is true of the justification of punishment generally is true a fortiori of justifying the death penalty.

Endorsement of these two policy goals tends to encourage support for the death penalty. Opponents of capital punishment need not reject these goals, however, and its defenders cannot argue that accepting these goals vindicates their preferred policy. Traditionally, it is true, the death penalty has often been supported on the ground that it provides the best social defense and is extremely cheap to administer. But since the time of Beccaria and Bentham, these empirical claims have been challenged (see Bedau, 1983), and rightly so. If support for the death penalty today in a country such as the United States rests on the high priority placed on these goals, then there is much (some would say compelling) evidence to undermine this support. The most that can be said solely by reference to these goals is that recognition of their importance can always be counted on to kindle interest in capital punishment, and to that extent put its opponents on the defensive.

Whether punishment is intended to serve only the two goals so far identified is disputable. An argument can be made that there are two or three further goals:

(G 3) Punishment should rectify the harm and injustice caused by crime.

(G 4) Punishment should serve as a recognized channel for

the release of public indignation and anger at the offender.

(G 5) Punishment should make convicted offenders into better persons rather than leave them as they are or make
them worse.

Obviously, anyone who accepts the fifth goal must reject the
death penalty. I shall not try here to argue the merits of this goal,
either in itself or relative to the other goals of punishment. Whatever
its merits, this goal is less widely sought than the others, and for that
reason alone is less useful in trying to develop rational agreement
over the death penalty. Its persuasive power for those not already
persuaded against the death penalty on other grounds is likely to
be slight to zero. Although I am unwilling to strike it from the list
of goals that punishment in general is and should be practiced to
achieve, it would be unreasonable to stress its pre-eminence in the
present context.

The proposed third goal is open to the objection that rectification of injustice is not really a goal of punishment, even if it is a
desirable goal in other settings. (Indeed, it is widely believed that
rectification is not a goal of punishment but of noncriminal tort judgments.) But even if it is a goal of punishment generally, it seems
irrelevant to the death penalty controversy, because neither death
nor imprisonment (as practiced in the United States) rectifies anything. Nonetheless, this goal may be indirectly important for the
death penalty controversy. To the extent that one believes punishments ought to serve this goal, and that there is no possible way to
rectify the crime of murder, one may come to believe that the fourth
goal is of even greater importance than would otherwise be the case.
Indeed, striving to achieve this fourth goal and embracing the death
penalty as a consequence is quite parallel to striving to achieve the
fifth goal and consequently embracing its abolition.

Does this fourth goal have a greater claim on our support than
I have allowed is true of the fifth goal, so obviously incompatible
with it? Many would say that it does. Some would even argue that
it is this goal, not any of the others, that is the paramount purpose
of punishment under law (Berns, 1979). Whatever else punishment
does, its threat and infliction are to be seen as the expression of
social indignation at deliberate harm to the innocent. Preserving a
socially acceptable vehicle for the expression of anger at offenders is
absolutely crucial to the health of a just society.

There are in principle three ways to respond to this claim insofar as it is part of an argument for capital punishment. One is to reject it out of hand as a false proposition from start to finish. A second is to concede that the goal of providing a visible and acceptable channel for the emotion of anger is legitimate, but to argue that this goal could at best justify the death penalty only in a very small number of cases (the occasional Adolf Eichmann, for example), since otherwise its importance would be vastly exaggerated. A third response is to concede both the legitimacy and the relative importance of this goal, but to point out that its pursuit, like that of all other goals, is nonetheless constrained by moral principles (yet to be examined), and that once these principles are properly employed, the death penalty ceases to be a permissible method of achieving this goal. I think both the second and third objections are sound, and a few further words here about each are appropriate.

First of all, anger is not the same as resentment or indignation, since the latter feeling or emotion can be aroused only through the perceived violation of some moral principle, whereas the former does not have this constraint. But whether the feeling aroused by a horrible murder is really only anger rather than indignation is just the question whether the principles of morality have been violated or not. Knowing that the accused offender has no legal excuse or justification for his criminal conduct is not enough to warrant the inference that he and his conduct are appropriate objects of our unqualified moral hostility. More about the context of the offense and its causation must be supplied; it may well be that in ordinary criminal cases one rarely or never knows enough to reach such a condemnatory judgment with confidence. Even were this not so, one has no reason to suppose that justified anger at offenders is of overriding importance, and that all countervailing considerations must yield to its pre-eminence. For one thing, the righteous anger needed for that role is simply not available in a pluralistic secular society. Even if it were, we have been assured from biblical times that it passes all too easily into self-righteous and hypocritical repression by some sinners of others.

Quite apart from such objections, there is a certain anomaly, even irony, in the defense of the death penalty by appeal to this goal. On the one hand, we are told of the importance of a publicly recognized ritual for extermination of convicted murderers as a necessary vent for otherwise unchanneled disruptive public emotions. On the other hand, our society scrupulously rejects time-honored methods of execution that truly do express hatred and anger at offenders: beheading, crucifixion, dismemberment, and even hanging and the electric chair are disappearing. Execution by lethal injection, increasingly the popular option, hardly seems appropriate as the outlet of choice for such allegedly volatile energies! And is it not ironic that this technique, invented to facilitate life-saving surgery, now turns out to be the preferred channel for the expression of moral indignation?

IV

If the purposes or goals of punishment lend a utilitarian quality to the practice of punishment, the moral principles relevant to the death penalty operate as deontological constraints on their pursuit. Stating all and only the principles relevant to the death penalty controversy is not easy, and the list that follows is no more than the latest approximation to the task (for my previous attempts, see Bedau, 1980:159–60, 1987:24). With some overlap here and there, these principles are six:

(P 1) No one should deliberately and intentionally take another's life where there is a feasible alternative.

(P 2) The more severe a penalty is, the more important it is that it be imposed only on those who truly deserve it.

(P 3) The more severe a penalty is, the weightier the justification required to warrant its imposition on anyone.

(P 4) Whatever the criminal offense, the accused and convicted offender does not forfeit all his rights and dignity as a person. Accordingly, there is an upper limit to the severity—cruelty, destructiveness, finality—of permissible punishments, regardless of the offense.

(P 5) Fairness requires that punishments should be graded in their severity according to the gravity of the offense.

(P 6) If human lives are to be risked, the risk should fall more heavily on wrong-doers (the guilty) than on others (the innocent).

I cannot argue here for all these principles, but they really need no argument from me. Each is recognized implicitly or explicitly in our practice; each can be seen to constrain our conduct as individuals and as officers in democratic institutions. Outright repudiation or cynical disregard of any of these principles would disqualify one from engaging in serious discourse and debate over punishment in a liberal society. All can be seen as corollaries or theorems of the general proposition that life, limb, and security of person—of *all* persons—are of paramount value. Thus, only minimal interference (in the jargon of the law, "the least restrictive means") is warranted with anyone's life, limb, and security in order to protect the rights of others.

How do these principles direct or advise us in regard to the permissibility or desirability of the death penalty? The first thing to note is that evidently none directly rules it out. I know of no moral principle that is both sufficiently rigid and sufficiently well established for us to point to it and say: "The practice of capital punishment is flatly contradictory to the requirements of this moral principle." (Of course, we could invent a principle that would have this consequence, but that is hardly to the point.) This should not be surprising; few if any of the critics or the defenders of the death penalty have supposed otherwise. Second, several of these principles do reflect the heavy burden that properly falls on anyone who advocates that certain human beings be deliberately killed by others, when those to be killed are not at the time a danger to anyone. For example, whereas the first principle may permit lethal force in self-defense, it directly counsels against the death penalty in *all* cases without exception. The second and third principles emphasize the importance of "due process" and "equal protection" as the finality and incompensability of punishments increase. The fourth principle draws attention to the nature and value of persons, even those convicted of terrible crimes. It reminds us that even if crimes know no upper limit in their wantonness, cruelty, destructiveness, and horror, punishments under law in a civilized society cannot imitate crimes in this regard. Punishment does operate under limits, and these limits are not arbitrary.

The final two principles, however, seem to be exceptions to the generalization that the principles as a group tend to favor punishments other than death. The fifth principle seems to entail that if murder is the gravest crime, then it should receive the severest punishment. This does not, of course, *require* a society to invoke the death penalty for murder—unless one accepts *lex talionis* ("a life for a life, an eye for an eye") in a singularly literal-minded manner. Since *lex talionis* is not a sound principle on which to construct the penalty schedule generally, appealing to this interpretation of the fifth principle here simply begs the question. Nevertheless, the principle that punishments should be graded to fit the crime does encourage consideration of the death penalty, especially if it seems that there is no other way to punish murder with the utmost permissible severity.

Of rather more interest is the sixth principle. Some make it the cornerstone of their defense of the death penalty (van den Haag, 1986:1665). They argue that it is better to execute all convicted murderers, lest on a future occasion any of them murder again, than it is to execute none of them, thereby averting the risk of executing any who may be innocent. A policy of complete abolition—at least in the United States today—would result in thousands of convicted killers (only a few of whom are innocent) being held behind bars for life. This cohort would constitute a permanent risk to the safety of many millions of innocent citizens. The sole gain to counterbalance this risk is the guarantee that no lives (innocent or guilty) will be lost through legal executions. The practice of executions thus protects far more innocent citizens than the same practice puts in jeopardy.

This argument is far less conclusive than it may at first seem. Even if we grant it full weight, it is simply unreasonable to use it (or any other argument) as a way of dismissing the relevance of principles that counsel a different result, or as a tactic to imply the subordinate importance of those other principles. If used in this manner, the sixth principle would be thoroughly transformed. It has become a disguised version of the first policy goal (viz., Reduce crime!) and in effect would elevate that goal to pre-eminence over every competing and constraining consideration. The argument also fosters the illusion that we can in fact reasonably estimate, if not actually calculate, the number of lives risked by a policy of abolition as opposed to a policy of capital punishment. This is false; we do not and cannot reasonably hope to know what the risk is of convicting the innocent (see Bedau and Radelet, 1987:78–81, 83–85), even if we could estimate the risk of recidivist murder. We therefore cannot really compare the two risks with any precision. Finally, the argument gains whatever strength it appears to have by tacitly ignoring the following dilemma. If the policy of killing the convicted in order to reduce risk to the innocent is to achieve maximum effect, then death must be the *mandatory* penalty for everyone convicted of murder (never mind other crimes). But such a policy cannot really be carried out.

It flies in the face of two centuries of political reality, which demonstrates the impossibility of enforcing truly mandatory death penalties for murder and other crimes against the person. The only realistic policy alternative is some version of a *discretionary* death penalty. However, every version of this policy actually tried has proved vulnerable to criticism on grounds of inequity in its administration, as critic after critic has shown (e.g., Amsterdam, 1987; Baldus et al., 1986; Bedau, 1987:164–84; Gradess, 1987; Tabak, 1986; Weisberg, 1984). Meanwhile, history tells us that our society is unable to avoid all risk of recidivist murder.

The upshot is that we today run both the risk of executing the innocent and the risk of recidivist murder, even though it is necessary to run only one of these risks.

V

What has our examination of the relevant goals and principles shown about the possibility of resolving the death penalty controversy on rational grounds? First, the death penalty is primarily a means to one or more ends or goals, but it is not the only (and arguably not the best) means to them. Second, several principles of relevance to sound punitive policy in general favor (although they do not demand) abolition of the death penalty. Third, there is no goal or principle that constitutes a conclusive reason favoring either side in the dispute. Unless, of course, some one goal or principle is interpreted or weighted in such a manner (cf. the fifth goal, or the fifth principle). But in that case, one side or the other will refuse to accept it. Finally, the several goals and principles of punishment that have been identified have no obvious rank order or relative weighting. As they stand, these goals and principles do indeed underdetermine the policy dispute over capital punishment. Perhaps such a ranking could be provided by some comprehensive socioethical theory. But the failure of every known such theory to secure general acceptance so far does not bode well for prompt and rational resolution of the controversy along these lines.

Despite the absence of any conclusive reasons or decisive ranking of principles, we may take refuge in the thought (as I have done elsewhere; see Bedau, 1987:44–45, 238–47) that a preponderance of reasons does favor one side rather than the other. Such a preponderance emerges, however, only when the relevant goals and principles of punishment are seen in a certain light, or from a particular angle of vision. Perhaps this amounts to one rather than another weighting of goals and principles but without conscious reliance upon any manifest theory. In any case, I shall mention three such considerations that are important in my assessment of the moral objections to the death penalty.

The first and by far the most important concerns the role and function of *power* in the hands of government. It is in general preferable, *ceteris paribus*, that such power over individuals should shrink rather than expand. Where such power must be used, then let it be devoted to constructive rather than destructive purposes, thus enhancing the autonomy and liberty of those directly affected. But the death penalty contradicts this concern; it is government power used in a dramatically destructive manner upon individuals in the absence of any compelling social necessity. No wonder it is the ultimate symbol of such power.

Another consideration that shapes my interpretation of the goals and principles of evaluation is an orientation to the *future* rather than to the past. We cannot do anything for the dead victims of crime. (How many of those who oppose the death penalty would continue to do so if, *mirabile dictu*, executing the murderer brought the victim back to life?) But we can—or at least we can try to—do something for the living: we can protect the innocent, prevent illegitimate violence, and help those in despair over their own victimization. None of these constructive tasks involves punishing anyone for expressive, vindictive, or retributive reasons. The more we stress these factors in our choice of punishments, the more we orient our punitive policies toward the past—toward trying to use government power over the lives of a few as a socially approved instrument of moral bookkeeping.

Finally, the death penalty projects a false and misleading picture of man and society. Its professed message for those who support it is this: justice requires killing the convicted murderer. So we focus on the death that all murderers supposedly deserve and overlook our inability to give a rational account of why so few actually get it. Hence, the lesson taught by the practice of capital punishment is really quite different. Far from being a symbol of justice, it is a symbol of brutality and stupidity. Perhaps if we lived in a world of autonomous Kantian moral agents, where all the criminals freely expressed their rational will in the intention to kill others without their consent or desert, then death for the convicted murderer might be just (as even Karl Marx was inclined to think; see Marx, 1853). But a closer look at the convicts who actually are on our death rows shows that these killers are a far cry from the rational agents of Kant's metaphysical imagination. We fool ourselves if we think a system of ideal retributive justice designed for such persons is the appropriate model for the penal system in our society.

Have I implicitly conceded that argument over the death penalty is irrational? If I am right that the death penalty controversy does not really turn on controversial social goals or controversial moral principles, any more than it does on disputed general facts, but instead turns on how all three are to be balanced or weighed, does it follow that reason alone cannot resolve the controversy, because reason alone cannot determine which weighting or balancing is the correct one? Or can reason resolve this problem, perhaps by appeal to further theory, theory that would deepen our appreciation of what truly underlies a commitment to liberal institutions and a belief in the possibilities for autonomy of all persons (Bedau, 1987: 123–28)? I think it can—but this is the right place to end the present investigation because we have reached the launching platform for another one.

References

Amsterdam, Anthony G. 1987. "The Supreme Court and Capital Punishment." *Human Rights* 14 (Winter): 14–17, 49–60.

Baldus, David C.; Charles A. Pulaski, Jr.; and George Woodworth. 1986. "Arbitrariness and Discrimination in the Administration of the Death Penalty: A Challenge to State Supreme Courts." *Stetson Law Review* 15: 133–261.

Bedau, Hugo Adam. 1980. "Capital Punishment." Pp. 147–82 in *Matters of Life and Death*, edited by Tom Regan. New York: Random House.

———. 1982. *The Death Penalty in America*. 3d ed. New York: Oxford University Press.

———. 1983. "Bentham's Utilitarian Critique of the Death Penalty." *Journal of Criminal Law and Criminology* 74: 1033–66. Reprinted at pp. 64–91 of H. A. Bedau, *Death Is Different: Studies in the Morality, Law, and Politics of Capital Punishment*. Boston: Northeastern University Press, 1987.

————. 1987. *Death Is Different: Studies in the Morality, Law, and Politics of Capital Punishment*. Boston: Northeastern University Press.

Bedau, Hugo Adam, and Michael L. Radelet. 1987. "Miscarriages of Justice in Potentially Capital Cases." *Stanford Law Review* 40:21–179.

Berns, Walter. 1979. *For Capital Punishment: Crime and the Morality of the Death Penalty*. New York: Basic Books.

Dworkin, Ronald. 1977. *Taking Rights Seriously*. Cambridge: Harvard University Press.

Gradess, Jonathan F. 1987. "The Road From Scottsboro." *Criminal Justice* 2 (2): 2–4, 44–47.

Hart, H. L. A. 1968. *Punishment and Responsibility: Essays in the Philosophy of Law*. New York: Oxford University Press.

Klein, Lawrence R.; Brian Forst; and Victor Filatov. 1978. "The Deterrent Effect of Capital Punishment: An Assessment of the Evidence." Pp. 336–60 in *Deterrence and Incapacitation: Estimating the Effects of Criminal Sanctions on Crime Rates*, edited by Alfred Blumstein, Jacqueline Cohen, and Daniel Nagin. Washington, D.C.: National Academy of Sciences.

Marx, Karl. 1853. "Capital Punishment." Pp. 485–86 in *Basic Writings on Politics and Philosophy: Karl Marx and Frederick Engels*, edited by Lewis Feuer. Garden City, N.Y.: Doubleday Anchor, 1959.

Rawls, John. 1971. *A Theory of Justice*. Cambridge: Harvard University Press.

Tabak, Ronald J. 1986. "The Death of Fairness: The Arbitrary and Capricious Imposition of the Death Penalty in the 1980's." *New York University Review of Law and Social Change* 4:797–848.

van den Haag, Ernest. 1986. "The Ultimate Punishment: A Defense." *Harvard Law Review* 99:1662–69.

Weisberg, Robert. 1984. "Deregulating Death." *Supreme Court Review* 8 (1983):305–95.

Wolfgang, Marvin E., and Marc Riedel. 1976. "Rape, Racial Discrimination, and the Death Peanlty." Pp. 99–121 in *Capital Punishment in the United States*, edited by Hugo Adam Bedau and Chester M. Pierce. New York: AMS Press.

Cases Cited

Furman v. Georgia, 408 U.S. 238 (1972).
Gregg v. Georgia, 428 U.S. 153 (1976).
Jurek v. Texas, 428 U.S. 262 (1976).
Proffitt v. Florida, 428 U.S. 242 (1976).

14

The Pains of Life

JOSEPH M. GIARRATANO

Seven years ago I began the process of awaiting my man-made appointment with death. Since being condemned to death, my days have been spent dealing with the guilt of having been convicted of taking the lives of two human beings, confronting the very real possibility of my own violent death, and coping with the anger, resentment, frustration, helplessness, and grief of having five friends taken from my side to be ritualistically exterminated. These have been nine long years of fighting to maintain my sanity, of growing, and of holding onto a sense of humanity in an environment maintained specifically for the purpose of bombarding the senses with hopelessness.

It is almost impossible to maintain a sense of humanity in a system that ignores the fact that you are a living, breathing human being—a system where you are recognized only as a number, a compilation of legal issues open for debate, a 20- to 50-page legal brief before tribunals that will determine your fate without ever knowing you, as something nonhuman—a piece of tainted meat to be disposed of.

These nine years I've lived on *death row*, a unit isolated not only from the outside world, but also from the rest of the prison population. Contact with others not "like" me is very limited: visits with friends or family that take place in an isolated cubical the size of a telephone booth, with thick security glass separating me from those who still recognize my humanness. There are also contact visits with those who work to save my life through the legal channels. These are individuals who continue to acknowledge my humanity and whom I've come to love as family. When I am permitted to visit these friends, I leave my "home" escorted by an elite group of guards; their black uniforms and combat boots distinguish them from the ordinary correctional officers (whose uniform is light blue). But the true essence of life and death is in the unit where my days are spent. Here, 24 hours a day, is where I experience and interact with the basic emotions of life, and face the reality of death.

On the night of 31, July 1986, four guards came to my unit, with handcuffs and waist-chain, to escort me to the telephone. It was a call that I had been dreading, because I would be saying my final goodbye to another friend. Within three hours after that call, Mike Smith, a man whom I shared a life bond with for seven years, would be coldly strapped into an electric killing machine. Then 2,700 volts of raw current would fry the life out of his body.

Even now I feel the anger I felt at his death, and the pain of having a friend coldly taken from me to be ritualistically put to death. As I walked down the hallway, several guards commented on the wrongness of killing my friend, and stated that Mike was a good man. Fighting back the tears was hard because of the helplessness I experienced at not being able to save him. Memories of the times Mike and I had spent together flooded through me. I wanted to understand why Mike was being taken from me, but it was impossible. Each day I have to interact with the same guards who came to the unit and took him from me. These guards were the same guards who were telling me, "Joe, Mike is a good man. *They* shouldn't kill him." Each time I heard a guard say that, I could feel the anger churning within me. What they were saying made no sense to me. I wanted to scream, "NO!" I wanted to tear down the prison walls and make *them* stop. I hated them.

As I lifted the phone to my ear and heard my friend's voice, I didn't know what to say. Other than quick hellos, our conversation consisted of a few scattered questions tied together with long silences. I could feel the tears leaking from my eyes as the hopelessness overwhelmed me. I wanted to tell Mike to fight the guards until the last second—to take some of them down with him—but all I could say was, "I love you, my friend. I'm sorry I can't stop this." Mike's reply still rings in my ear: "I'll be fine, Joe. You know that I'm going home. Please don't do anything that you might regret later. You have to forgive them."

Walking back to my cell, I could barely move—it felt as if every muscle in my body were cramped. I could hear the guards asking me questions, but I knew that if I responded, my hatred would spew out at them. I felt the helplessness and hopelessness in the pit of my stomach—I wanted to pull my friend back. It wasn't until later that I noticed the blood on my wrists where the cuffs bit into my flesh. I tried to pull Mike back, and I couldn't.

Before that day four other friends had been executed: men whom I ate with, talked with, played with, argued with—men whom I came to know as friends and shared a life bond with. Men whom no matter what their crimes, I *could not* see as anything but human beings—whom I could not see as animals or pieces of meat. James and Linwood Briley, Morris Mason, and Frank Coppola are the men whose tears I saw, whose flesh I touched, whose pain I still feel. I still know the hopelessness, I am still with the guards who took them away to be executed, and I am still trying to understand.

I know the pain that I brought to my victims' family. I know their loss, their anger, their frustration, hatred, and despair. I know their feelings of helplessness and hopelessness. I know these emotions as they, the families of my friends who have been executed, and my family and friends do—a twisted cycle of continuing violence, loss, pain, grief, and helplessness. Unlike those whom we invest with authority, I have learned that killing people is wrong.

Hope is such a frail thing when hopelessness constantly bombards the senses. You can hear its empty sound in the clanging of the steel doors, in the rattle of chains, in the body searches, in the lack of privacy, in the night sounds of death row, and you can see it in the eyes of the guards who never really look at you, but are always watching to see that you do not commit suicide. You can feel the hopelessness each time you are asked to state your number, when you are holding the hand of a friend in chains who is being pulled away from you, never to be seen again. You can hear it in the echo of a system where humanity is constantly denied. Eventually I, like all human beings, will die. But for now I am very much alive, and, until death touches me, I will feel the pain, anger, frustration, despair, and grief at the loss of those close to me. I will feel the fear of my own predetermined death. For Mike's family, life must go on, as is true for all who have lost loved ones. The focus shifts back to life, and the death grows more remote as time passes. But here on the row, where life goes on, death is never distant. Here life and death are one. Both are ever present; while there are times when death seems distant, it is only an illusion: at any time an announcer on television or radio may tell you that your death or the death of a friend is one step closer. You may read about your death in the daily newspaper, or a letter from a court clerk, or hear about it when the guards announce "Let's go,———." Here one can never forget about death for long—on the row where hope and hopelessness coexist daily.

All of these emotions are very real to me, and I can see them in the eyes of the human beings around me, condemned and executioner alike. Anyone who stays on a death row, comes to know someone on the row, or visits regularly can feel the passion of these emotions pulsating in the air. One can hear the sound of guards and prisoners laughing together, talking, sharing meals. There are the ministers who come to visit through the bars—some trying to save our souls, all praying and telling us not to give up hope, but none telling us how this can be done. Many share in our helplessness for a time, but they also have their lives to contend with. That condemned and executioners *live* together is a strange paradox.

I have spoken with many of the guards, most of whom avoid the subject of my death, the possible deaths of the men around me, and their own role in this death ritual. There are a few who will avoid my eyes and say: "Joe, it's not my doing. I don't want to see you die. There are others who deserve it more than you." Many find it easy to avoid the subject, since they will not be the ones who actually pull the switch—they will only escort me to the death house and let their co-workers take over. But their eyes tell all that needs to be said. They have very human eyes, just like the other human beings around me and just like those of my dead friends. Yet they will do their jobs. Standing in this house of death among all these human beings—some who come to visit, some who come to stay, and some never to be seen again—life is not cogent.

Each day I yearn to touch, hold, and be with my loved ones, just as they want me with them. The closeness of death makes me more aware of my human feelings, and constantly adds fuel to a passion for life. It makes me more aware of how much time I have wasted in life, how very responsible we all must be, and how precious each day of living must be. Each day I hear Mike Smith's words to me: "You must forgive them. I love you, too." Hearing these words does

not allow me to ignore the humanity around me, not that of the condemned or the executioner(s). On 31 July 1986, I hated them. Each
day here has been an experience in life. Although death will eventually come, it has not overtaken me yet, and until it does, I live.
Where there is life there is hope, as both thrive through the recognition of humanity—both yours and mine. Each day I spend here is
an experience in Life, as well as in Death.

15

The Isolation of Death Row

C. MICHAEL LAMBRIX

It is no secret among American jail and prison inmates that the conditions of confinement in the states' maximum-security institutions are such that coping with one's day-to-day existence requires constant struggle. Yet, having heard these stories, I must admit that their simplifications and exaggerations create an unrealistic picture of what the experience of being placed in solitary confinement while awaiting my date with the executioner is really like. In this essay, I will not attempt to generate sympathy by trying to convince the reader of how rough life on death row can be. Instead, I would simply like to describe, in a biographical fashion, the struggles and challenges that life under a sentence of death presents.

The foremost challenge is dealing with isolation. Part of this stems from physical constraints, while part stems from a symbolic isolation that comes from living with the fact that 12 members of your community have determined that you are a worthless person who should no longer be permitted to exist. Isolation is an odd emotion for a prisoner to experience; in fact, our crowded prisons usually create too little, rather than too much, privacy. But on death row, with the exception of a few hours a week in a small exercise yard, there is no opportunity to see other people without bars blocking the view. Friendships that are formed are based on the coincidence of the physical proximity of the person's cell, not on the basis of respect, interest, or the common understandings that typify most human relationships.

While most people rely on their families for their major source of support, it is not at all uncommon for this resource to be unavailable to death row prisoners. In my own case, I have never experienced the web of mutually supportive social relationships that families usually offer; in fact this deficit led me to leave my home and nine brothers and sisters at age 15. When I was tried on the capital charge in 1984, no family members came to my trial (in fact, my lawyer was forced to subpoena them to testify on my behalf at the sentencing phase). One critical letter from my father has been the only contact since. In short, if one is to understand the isolation of death row, it must be realized that many of the condemned men do not have the family supports that those on the outside might imagine would be available. Further, this deficit means that few death row inmates ever get outside visitors.

A third element of isolation is the feeling that one has when seeing one's closest friends and neighbors being led off to their doom. My first years on death row were spent in a cage next to a death row veteran, who helped me a great deal by teaching me survival tactics and sharing his meager possessions. He, like others I have known, has now been executed. Death row inmates share a common fate and unity based on our hostility toward those who are trying to kill us, but our mistrust of others spreads to encompass each other. Not only can trust in fellow inmates backfire, but the ability to trust is impeded by the knowledge that any trust or closeness will only add to the pain felt when those you may be close to are led off to their deaths.

A fourth element of isolation germinates from struggles with one's own self. Perhaps my greatest struggle is with my inability to control my own impatience. Minor incidents with the prison authorities or fellow inmates can easily aggravate me; on several occasions I have snapped back at them without first giving it thought, only to realize later that my reaction was ridiculous. Even my closest friends can be the target of my wrath if they ask me a simple question at a moment when my self-control is lacking. I feel isolated from myself.

I am impatient because I believe, as strongly as one can believe, that my conviction and condemnation were unjust, and I should be living my life elsewhere. The lack of evidence against me caused my first trial to end in a hung jury, and ever since that second jury convicted me, I have remained confident that appellate courts would intervene to correct the injustice. Why did it take 18 months for the first appeal to be filed? Why are the courts taking so long to rule? My impatience led me to write frequent letters to the courts demanding an immediate decision. Each Thursday, when the court's decisions are reported on the local news, was another occasion for my anticipation of a decision to be thwarted. In short, the waiting was hell.

And when the court did rule, my appeal was rejected. I was devastated. Some friends with whom I had been exchanging letters stopped writing, perhaps fearing my execution or disappointed in the belief that I had misled them in predicting the success of my appeal. The isolation does not diminish over time; it grows stronger.

After that initial appeal was denied, the isolation of this cell has changed. The knowledge that more time will be required for the injustice to be corrected makes the walls move closer together. I see my absence from the outside world as not a temporary hassle, but one that will now have permanent effects as I miss more and more opportunities that cannot be recreated.

The isolation also stems from leading a life of total dependency. I am dependent on the state for everything from a weekly ration of toilet paper to the appointment of an appellate attorney. I am help-less to speed my appeal. Like other dependencies, this helplessness is yet another threat to my individuality, an assault on my social existence that must be absorbed while the attack on my physical existence is being fought.

Inmates adjust to the realities of death row in different ways. I first turned to the religion of my childhood, spending the first few months on death row studying anything I could find that was even remotely related to Christian doctrine. My study was a search for explanation, meaning, strength, and justice, fueled more by hope than by results. I gradually learned that conventional Christianity— the religion that so many citizens profess at the same time that they voice support for executions—must be substantially modified to fit with my needs and perspective. Thus, my religious orientation is in flux. I remain a spiritual person, satisfying myself with a personal faith in which I find strength. The life of a death row inmate is so isolated that it is nearly impossible to even share a religion with those on the outside.

And I remain a changing person in other ways, albeit worried about the direction of change in which these events have thrust me. I am no longer a trusting person, and my ability to change my family relationships has virtually disappeared. While there is (miraculously) still some growth, I fear that death row means a gradual killing of my humanity which is more painful than any execution can ever be. Could it be that being executed is preferable to a life of such isolation?

DEATH WARRANT
STATE OF FLORIDA

WHEREAS, WILLIE JASPER DARDEN, did on the 18th day of September, 1973, murder James C. Turman, and

WHEREAS, WILLIE JASPER DARDEN was found guilty of murder inthe first degree and was sentenced to death on the 23rd day of January, 1974; and

WHEREAS, on the 18th day of February, 1976, the Florida Supreme Court upheld the sentence of death imposed upon WILLIE JASPER DARDEN and Certiorari to the United States Supreme Court was denied on the 19th day of April, 1977; and

WHEREAS, it has been determined that Executive Clemency, as authorized by Article IV, Section 8(a), Florida Constitution, is not appropriate; and

WHEREAS, attached hereto is a copy of the record pursuant to Section 922.09, Florida Statutes;

NOW, THEREFORE, I, BOB MARTINEZ, as Governor of the State of Florida and pursuant to the authority and responsibility vested by the Constitution and Laws of Florida do hereby issue this warrant directing the Superintendent of the Florida State Prison to cause the sentence of death to be executed upon WILLIE JASPER DARDEN on some day of the week beginning 7:00 a.m., Tuesday, the 15th day of March, 1988, and ending 7:00 a.m., Tuesday, the 22nd day of March, 1988, in accord with the provisions of the laws of the State of Florida.

IN TESTIMONY WHEREOF, I have hereunto set my hand and caused the Great Seal of the State of Florida to be affixed at Tallahassee, the Capitol, this 8th day of March, 1988.

GOVERNOR

ATTEST:

SECRETARY OF STATE

16

An Inhumane Way of Death

WILLIE JASPER DARDEN, JR.

Ironically, there is probably more hope on death row than would be found in most other places. Each of us has been convicted of murder. Some are guilty and a few are innocent. But the one thing we all have in common is that we await our demise side by side—the innocent and the guilty alike. We hope because it would be so easy for our fate to be changed. Hope is one thing we have in common with those stricken with a terminal illness.

Every person in our society is capable of murder. Who among us can say that they have never been so angry that they did foolish things, or that they have not wished for the death of one who destroyed their happiness? Isn't it true that those who advocate the use of capital punishment are just as guilty of homicide as the person executed? Isn't it dangerous for society to preach a message that some of its citizens deserve to die? Like those stricken with a terminal illness, I want to understand.

Before the Colosseum "games" of ancient Rome, the condemned gladiators stood before the royal podium and said, "We who are about to die salute you, Caesar." Humans on death row do not have that immediacy of struggle or that intimacy with their impersonal foe on the field of battle. We are humans who face death because of the faulty wording of a legal appeal or the capriciously bad stomach of a judge or juror. If we executed all murderers, we

203

would execute twenty thousand per year; we face execution because we are the scapegoats. Like those stricken with a terminal illness, I feel I was chosen at random. And, while morally it is no worse to execute the innocent than to execute the guilty, I will proclaim until the electric chair's current silences me that I am innocent of the charge that sent me here.

Our society executes as much "for the person" as "for the crime." We execute for heresy—for being different, or for being at the wrong place at the wrong time. We execute for the traits of the person found guilty. If the person is black, uneducated, poor, outspoken, slightly retarded, eccentric, or odd, he stands a much higher chance of being executed than do those convicted of even worse crimes than he. Juries find it hard to convict one of their own, so middle-class whites are rarely in our ranks. Like those stricken with a terminal illness, I feel a tremendous sense of injustice. Unlike others preparing to die, empirical studies have been conducted by the best minds in America that show I am right.

I have been on death row for 14 years and can honestly say that the only description of this place is hell. We send people to prisons to suffer, and prisons have been highly successful in achieving this goal. We live in a society that fosters the belief that inhumanity, revenge, and retribution are legitimate goals of the state. Like those stricken with a terminal illness, I fight my own anger.

Most, if not all, of the humans on death row have souls that can be made clean through love, compassion, and spirituality. However, to acknowledge this threatens our ability to execute, as we must dehumanize before we can kill in such a predetermined fashion. It takes concern and understanding to identify with one of God's own. Didn't Jesus glorify the shepherd who left his whole flock just to rescue one lamb? I believe it is the duty and obligation of all of God's children to save, heal, and repair the spirit, soul, mind, and body of others. When Jesus said, "Love your neighbor," I don't think he was talking about those whom it is easy to love. Like others preparing for death, I need community.

The one thing all humans want and need is to love and be loved. I often sit and just watch the men here. I watch them change. I watch, and I feel great pity for them. I feel shame, too. Shame because many of my Christian brothers and sisters in society allow this to continue in their names.

One of the most profound teachings of Jesus is, "Judge not that ye be not judged." I think that before we can hold up the lamp of understanding to others, we must hold it up to ourselves. That, I believe, is what death is all about.

About the Authors

Hugo Adam Bedau is the Austin Fletcher Professor of Philosophy at Tufts University, Medford, Massachusetts. His most recent book, *Death Is Different: Studies in the Morality, Law, and Politics of Capital Punishment*, was published by Northeastern University Press in 1987.

Russell F. Canan is a partner in the law firm of Milliken, Van Susteren & Canan in Washington, D.C. He is an adjunct professor of law at Georgetown University Law Center and at the Washington College of Law at the American University. Mr. Canan is a former member of the Southern Prisoner's Defense Committee in Atlanta.

Willie Jasper Darden, Jr., was sentenced to death in 1974. On 15 March 1987, despite worldwide protest, widespread belief in his innocence, and allegations of prosecutorial racism (including features on ABC's "20/20" and CBS's "West 57th Street"), Mr. Darden was executed.

Watt Espy, death penalty historian, consultant, writer, and lecturer, is director of the Capital Punishment Research Project, P.O. Drawer 277, Headland, Alabama 36345. He has confirmed, documented and collected data on over 15,780 legal executions that have taken place under civil authority in the United States.

Joseph M. Giarratano is currently under sentence of death in Virginia. During his ten years on death row, he has been active in death penalty litigation/abolition. He is currently client advisor to the Virginia Coalition on Jails and Prisons.

Joseph B. Ingle is an ordained minister in the United Church of Christ and director of the Southern Coalition on Jails and Prisons, an eight-state organization for criminal justice reform and abolition of the death penalty. One of the co-founders of SCJP in 1974, Ingle has spent the last 15 years advocating for changes in the southern criminal justice system. He is a native of North Carolina, a resident of Tennessee, and was a nominee for the 1988 Nobel Peace Prize.

Michael A. Kroll writes extensively on the death penalty. He helped found the District of Columbia Coalition Against the Death Penalty while coordinating the National Moratorium on Prison Construction. Currently he is an editor for the Pacific News Service in San Francisco.

C. Michael Lambrix is currently on death row in Florida and utilizes his time studying and writing in the hope of promoting public support for the abolition of the death penalty.

James W. Marquart is an assistant professor of Criminal Justice at Sam Houston State University. His current research has examined the institutional and postrelease behavior of *Furman*-commuted inmates in Texas.

Michael Mello is an assistant professor at Vermont Law School. His research interests focus on capital punishment. At the time he drafted his contribution to this collection, Mr. Mello was an attorney with the Office of the Capital Collateral Representative in Tallahassee, Florida, where his legal practice consisted solely of representing condemned inmates on Florida's death row.

J. Anthony Paredes is a professor of anthropology and chairman of the Department of Anthropology at Florida State University. His research includes studies on Chippewa Indian urbanization, Alabama Creek Indian social and cultural revitalization, economic marginalization and mental health in northern Minnesota, social aspects of fisheries management, and tourism in a Mexican town.

Elizabeth D. Purdum is a research associate with the Institute of Science and Public Affairs at Florida State University. She is also an adjunct assistant professor of anthropology. Her research interests include dispute settlement, courts in the United States, and complex organizations.

Michael L. Radelet is an associate professor of sociology at the University of Florida. Over the last ten years he has researched several different aspects of the death penalty and worked closely with Florida death row inmates and their families.

Henry Schwarzschild has served as national director of the Capital Punishment Project for the American Civil Liberties Union since 1976. He was a founder and remains a vice-chairman of the

National Coalition to Abolish the Death Penalty. He has been active in the civil rights and civil liberties movements for the last 35 years.

Jonathan R. Sorensen is a doctoral candidate in criminal justice at Sam Houston State University. His current interest is in the imposition of the death penalty and capital offenders.

Victor L. Streib is professor of law at Cleveland State University. He is the author of *Death Penalty for Juveniles* and co-counsel for Wayne Thompson, an Oklahoma inmate whose challenge to the constitutionality of death sentences for juveniles was decided by the Supreme Court in 1988.

Colin M. Turnbull is professor of anthropology at Vassar College. Among his books are *The Forest People* (1961), *The Mountain People* (1972), and *The Human Cycle* (1983).

Margaret Vandiver is a Ph.D. candidate in the School of Criminology at Florida State University. She has worked extensively with death row inmates and their families.

Laurin A. Wollan, Jr., is an associate professor in the School of Criminology at Florida State University. His academic interests include the privatization of criminal justice.

Index

211